# WRITING
# THE
# GOOD FIGHT

**Recent Titles in**
**Contributions to the Study of World Literature**

There Is No Truer Truth: The Musical Aspect of Browning's Poetry
*Nachum Schoffman*

Reworlding: The Literature of the Indian Diaspora
*Emmanuel S. Nelson, editor*

Caliban in Exile: The Outsider in Caribbean Fiction
*Margaret Paul Joseph*

Sitting at the Feet of the Past: Retelling the North American Folktale
for Children
*Gary D. Schmidt and Donald R. Hettinga, editors*

The Anna Book: Searching for Anna in Literary History
*Mickey Pearlman, editor*

Writing and Reality: A Study of Modern British Diary Fiction
*Andrew Hassam*

Shakespeare's Proverbial Themes: A Rhetorical Context for the Sententia
as *Res*
*Marjorie Donker*

Promptings of Desire: Creativity and the Religious Impulse in the
Works of D. H. Lawrence
*Paul Poplawski*

The Second Best Bed: Shakespeare's Will in a New Light
*Joyce E. Rogers*

Literary Selves: Autobiography and Contemporary American Nonfiction
*James N. Stull*

Storied Cities: Literary Imagining of Florence, Venice and Rome
*Michael L. Ross*

Women Writers in Russian Literature
*Toby W. Clyman and Diana Greene, editors*

# WRITING
# THE
# GOOD FIGHT

## Political Commitment in the International Literature of the Spanish Civil War

Peter Monteath

Contributions to the Study of World Literature, Number 52

**GREENWOOD PRESS**
Westport, Connecticut • London

**Library of Congress Cataloging-in-Publication Data**

Monteath, Peter.
　　Writing the good fight  :  political commitment in the international
　literature of the Spanish Civil War / Peter Monteath.
　　　　p.　cm.—(Contributions to the study of world literature,
　ISSN 0738–9345  ; no. 52)
　　Includes bibliographical references and index.
　　ISBN 0–313–28766–X (alk. paper)
　　1. War in literature.　2. Literature, Modern—20th century—
　History and criticism.　3. Spain—History—Civil war, 1936–1939—
　Literature and the war.　I. Title.　II. Series.
　PN56.W3M66 1994
　809′.93358—dc20　　　　93–21130

British Library Cataloguing in Publication Data is available.

Library of Congress Catalog Card Number: 93–21130
ISBN: 0–313–28766–X
ISSN: 0738-9345

First published in 1994

Greenwood Press, 88 Post Road West, Westport, CT 06881
An imprint of Greenwood Publishing Group, Inc.

Printed in the United States of America

The paper used in this book complies with the
Permanent Paper Standard issued by the National
Information Standards Organization (Z39.48–1984).

10 9 8 7 6 5 4 3 2 1

## Copyright Acknowledgments

Carl Einstein, "Die Kolonne Durruti." In Carl Einstein, *Werke. Band 3. 1929–1940*. Ed. Marion Schmid and Liliane Meffre. Vienna, West Berlin: Medusa, 1985, pp. 459–62. © Fannei & Walz, Berlin.

George Barker, "Elegy on Spain." In George Barker, *Collected Poems, 1930–1955*. London: Faber and Faber Ltd, 1957.

W. H. Auden, "Spain 1937." From *The English Auden* by W. H. Auden. Copyright © 1940 and renewed 1968 by W. H. Auden. Reprinted by permission of Random House, Inc. World rights granted by Faber and Faber Ltd.

Stephen Spender, "Ultima Ratio Regum." From *Selected Poems* by Stephen Spender. Copyright © 1942 and renewed 1970 by Stephen Spender. Reprinted by permission of Random House, Inc. World rights granted by Faber and Faber Ltd.

Stephen Spender, "The Coward," "Two Armies," and "Port Bou." From *Collected Poems 1928–1953* by Stephen Spender. Copyright © 1942 and renewed 1970 by Stephen Spender. Reprinted by permission of Random House, Inc. World rights granted by Faber and Faber Ltd.

Franz Borkenau, *The Spanish Cockpit. An Eye-Witness Account of the Political and Social Conflicts of the Spanish Civil War.* Ann Arbor: University of Michigan Press, 1963.

George Orwell, excerpts form *Homage to Catalonia* and "Looking Back on the Spanish War." Harmondsworth: Penguin, 1966. Reprinted by permission of the estate of the late Sonia Brownell Orwell and Martin Secker & Warburg Ltd. For U.S. rights: Excerpts from *Homage to Catalonia* by George Orwell, copyright 1952 and renewed 1980 by Sonia Brownell Orwell, reprinted by permission of Harcourt Brace & Company.

Extracts from Herbert Read, *Poetry and Anarchism*. London: Faber and Faber, 1938. Reprinted by permission of David Higham Associates.

John Cornford, "Poem," or "Heart of the Heartless World." In Stephen Spender and John Lehmann, eds. *Poems for Spain*. London: Hogarth Press, 1939. Reprinted by permission of Lawrence and Wishart Ltd.

Excerpts from Hugh Thomas, *The Spanish Civil War*, 3rd ed. Harmondsworth: Penguin, 1986. Reprinted by permission of Aitken, Stone & Wylie Limited.

Louis MacNeice, "Autumn Journal." From *The Collected Poems of Louis MacNeice*. Ed. E. R. Dodds. Reprinted by permission of Faber and Faber Ltd.

Every reasonable effort has been made to trace the owners of copyright materials in this book, but in some instances this has proven impossible. The author and publisher will be glad to receive information leading to more complete acknowledgments in subsequent printings of the book and in the meantime extend their apologies for any omissions.

*To Amanda*

# Contents

# Preface

In prefacing a work which deals with the literature of not just one but several countries, a few words should be devoted to the topic of language. With the aim of making this book readily accessible to readers, all of the text, including the many quotations from other languages, appears in English. Where a competent English translation has been readily available, I have used this, and have consistently indicated the use of a translation in the footnotes. In cases where no existing translation was available, the translation into English has been made by me. This applies in all cases where the source provided in the footnoting is that of the original language.

The only exceptions to this rule are the quotations from poems. Given the special interdependence of form and content in poetry, it was considered appropriate to provide the reader with the original, followed by a prose translation in English.

Without going into the details of their particular contributions to work on this thesis, I wish finally to express my gratitude to a number of people. At various times Roy Boland, Richard Bosworth, John Gatt-Rutter, Hans-Ulrich Gumbrecht, Sally Harvey, Judith Keene, Alun Kenwood, Helmut Kreuzer, Keith Leopold, Mariana Muñoz, Malcolm McInnes, Elke Nicolai, Werner Schlick and Martin Travers provided valuable assistance. The patience and efficiency of the library staff of Griffith University, the University of Queensland, the University of Siegen, Deakin University, the University of Western Australia and the Faculty of Philology at the Complutense in Madrid similarly deserve my thanks and praise. Any deficiencies in this work can in no way be attributed to them.

# Introduction

## THE SPANISH CIVIL WAR AS A LITERARY PHENOMENON

The Spanish Civil War began because of popular resistance to an attempted military putsch, a *pronunciamiento*, on July 17-18, 1936. The deeper-lying reasons for the war are to be found in a combination of economic, social and political circumstances, which from the early nineteenth century onwards had plunged Spain into a series of crises. The civil war of 1936-39 was the last link in a chain of political upheavals on the Iberian peninsula; certainly it was also one of the most controversial international events in the 1930s.

The political and military consequences of the Spanish war were considerable. The democratically elected republican government was defeated by the combined forces of the Spanish and the international Right; the radical Left, which had gained control over much of republican territory in the early part of the war, was defeated by an even more complex combination of forces and events. The outcome of the war meant that its survivors, who either voluntarily or compulsorily remained in Spain, were to live, or perhaps die, under a military dictatorship which lasted almost four decades.

These ramifications were felt far beyond Spanish borders, even if the entire war was waged on Spanish soil. Many observers interpreted the Spanish Civil War as a prelude to a war on a much larger scale. This interpretation was confirmed as being entirely accurate in September 1939, just a few months after the cessation of hostilities in Spain, when Hitler set World War II in motion. It was during the Spanish Civil War, and indeed partly because of the Spanish Civil War, that the alignment of forces took place which made a general European war inevitable. Germany and Italy strengthened ties, as their leaders exploited the opportunity to test their newest weapons and military tactics. While the governments of Britain, France and the United States observed events in Spain from a critical distance, Hitler and Mussolini made preparations for a war which, regrettably, has tended to condemn Spain to the status of a trial run. Championing the policy of a Popular Front, which in the Spanish context entailed the suppression of the activities of the revolutionary Left, the Soviet Union sought to protect its foreign policy interests by proving itself to be a reliable ally of the Western democracies.

Historical significance, however, cannot be measured purely in military or political terms. It is not the aim of this study to contribute to the evaluation of the Spanish Civil War as a military and political event; rather, it is to examine the significance of the war as an international literary phenomenon. As an event in literary history, it can legitimately be contended that the Spanish Civil War carries immense, indeed epochal, importance. This importance rests on at least six factors.

Firstly, the Spanish Civil War is significant in literary history because it attracted the attention of an international literary intelligentsia. Whether in the form of public statement, artistic works, journalistic activity or participation on the field of battle, a passionate concern for a war being waged on foreign soil was displayed which on that scale had never been seen before and which perhaps only the Vietnam experience since then could come close to emulating. From Samuel Beckett's pithy "¡UPTHEREPUBLIC!" to the lengthy works of Ernest Hemingway, George Bernanos or Gustav Regler, few hesitated to let their position be known.[1] Without question the sympathies of the vast majority of European and American writers rested with the Spanish Republic,[2] but on both sides the war was seen in Manichaean terms, as a universal battle between good and evil, as a "crusade" or even a "holy war." On both sides writers invested the war with symbolic significance, so that "it was not long before the intelligentsia had transformed the Spanish Civil War into an allegory in which the major conflicts of the decade appeared as the principal adversaries."[3]

Secondly, the Spanish Civil War is momentous because it represents a climax in literary and intellectual history. Thomas Mann wrote in 1937: "In a political form the question of humanity itself is being asked us today with a final and perilous seriousness which earlier times did not know."[4] No decade in this century and indeed in any other century has been able to match the 1930s in the level of devotion to political ideologies on an international scale. As Mann acknowledged, the 1930s generation contemplated the world's problems in political terms and moreover believed that the great problems of the age could be solved through political means. Against the background of failing economies and rising fascism, the 1930s were the decade of an awakening and active social conscience, of an unrivalled political commitment and an ideologically based optimism which often bordered on utopianism. Never before had there been such a close alliance of politics and literature; never had it been so fervently believed that aesthetic practice, or more particularly literary practice, was able to influence political practice. As the American scholar Stanley Weintraub puts it: "At perhaps no other time did the makers of art feel so strongly that art could be a weapon."[5] It was during the Spanish Civil War and partly because of the Spanish Civil War that the alliance of politics and literature achieved its apogee. This applies to the international literature of the war rather than merely to any particular national literature; it applies to the works of already known authors but also to the mass of literature produced by authors of little or no literary fame. In this context it is essential to bear in mind that the literature of the Spanish Civil War in its entirety is more than just war literature in any traditional sense. Much of it is also the literature of revolution – it explicitly addresses the question of radical social and political change. It is equally valid to place the literature of the Spanish Civil War in the tradition of the revolutionary literature of 1789 or 1848 as it is to locate it in the tradition of war literature. [6]

Thirdly, the Spanish Civil War is not just a climax but has been identified as a turning point in literary history. The close alliance of politics and literature and the determined commitment to political ideologies were abandoned by many during the war and, in this instance also, partly because of the war. Spain for several reasons caused a disillusionment with and a deep distrust of political ideologies which characterized the attitudes of large numbers of writers and others well into the post-World War II era. As John M. Muste has argued, the Spanish Civil War "had a great deal to do with the destruction of the political dreams of the thirties, a destruction which left many without the props of dogma or ideology when they were almost immediately confronted by a far more widespread and devastating war." [7] For obvious political reasons, many commentators have been eager to locate the political apostasy generated by the war amongst former communists such as Stephen Spender, Arthur Koestler and Gustav Regler. [8] The Spanish scholar Ricardo de la Cierva, for example, claims that the great loser of the war was international comunism, [9] and the American Frederick Benson tells us that largely due to the Spanish Civil War the "Marxist appeal was almost entirely dispelled by 1940." [10] In defence of communism, however, it must be pointed out that not all communists abandoned their faith in the Party, [11] and that apostasy was by no means confined to that particular section of the political spectrum. Political disillusionment can be detected right across the spectrum, even at the far right. [12] What the Spanish experience brought about was not merely a disillusionment with a particular political ideology but with political ideologies in general. As Maurice Merleau-Ponty pondered in 1947: "One cannot be an anti-communist, one cannot be a communist." [13] With the benefit of even greater hindsight Philip Toynbee, who in 1936 had been an undergraduate communist at Oxford, was able to write in 1954:

It is easy to see now that the Spanish Civil War was, from the very beginning, the tragic, drawn-out death agony of a political epoch. Once the Generals had made their revolt, they would eventually win it: once they had won it, a world war would be fought *against* fascist aggression, but not *for* anything we had hoped for in 1936. And even at the time there was some sense that this was the last chance for the politics of Attempting the Good, as opposed to the subsequent politics of Avoiding the Worse. [14]

For people like Toynbee, Spain shattered the conviction that unyielding commitment to the "good fight" would inevitably lead to political progress. It is for this reason that the Italian intellectual Aldo Garosci, himself a veteran of the war, observed that the literature of the Spanish Civil War possesses greater vitality than most of the literature concerning the World War II.[15] Frederick Benson agrees that the effects of the war in Spain "are manifest in the literature of World War II which is so obviously apolitical and in which writers seem to have extended beyond disillusionment to a desperate and consuming nihilism."[16] This loss of vitality, the abandonment of the faith in political ideologies to change the world for the better, is to be regarded as one of the literary consequences of the Spanish Civil War.

Fourthly, and as already hinted, the Spanish Civil War is important in literary history because of its international repercussions. The alliance of politics and literature was a phenomenon evident throughout Europe and America in the 1930s, even if circumstances influencing literary production varied from country to country. The range of languages and nationalities represented in the body of Spanish Civil War literature has to my knowledge never been accurately assessed, but that in itself is a reflection of its enormity. Although the European and American literatures are predictably most strongly represented, other parts of the world could not remain entirely aloof from an event which was reported widely in the world's newspapers and in the relatively new radio medium.

The war distinguishes itself as a literary phenomenon because of the sheer bulk of literature produced in response to it. One scholar has boldly claimed that "more literature is available regarding the Spanish Civil War than any other twentieth-century war."[17] This cannot be conclusively substantiated, and indeed appears unlikely, but it remains undeniable that the quantity of literary production in numerous languages during the war itself and in the decades since the war is nothing less than immense. The enormous range of literary genres and media (from brigade newspapers to books, from poems to film-scripts and to novels) must be kept in mind, as must the astoundingly large number of participants in literary activity. This applies to the non-combatants, but it applies even more especially to the combatants, because, as Stanley Weintraub again suggests, "possibly never before had so large a proportion of a war's participants been motivated to write about a war, from polemics to poetry."[18] In all likelihood a complete bibliography of Spanish Civil War literature will never be produced. The bibliography of Maryse Bertrand de Muñoz, which lists only the novels of the war, includes some 700 titles. An extension of this list to include other genres, whereby the distinction between belles-lettres and other literary forms is often blurred, would bring a total of many thousands. One estimate puts the figure at over twenty thousand, including eye-witness accounts, belles-lettres, histories, memoirs and propaganda publications.[19]

Finally, the Spanish Civil War was important because it brought to an end the literary careers of a number of writers. Christopher St. John Sprigg, better known as Christopher Caudwell, was a British poet and theorist whose reputation was established posthumously. Caudwell had been killed on his first day in battle in February 1937, covering the retreat of his unit.[20] The poet John Cornford, also a communist, was killed on his twenty-first birthday. The novelist and theorist Ralph Fox also died in December 1936. Charles Donnelly, an Irish poet of great promise, had gone into battle on the same day as Caudwell. He managed to survive it, but only for a short time, for he was killed on 27 February. Virginia Woolf's nephew Julian Bell left for Spain in June 1937, as an ambulance driver, only to be killed the following month. The Hungarian novelist Mata Zalka, better known during the war as General Paul Lukács, was fatally wounded by a shell at Huesca in the same month whilst commanding the 12th International Brigade. The Spanish poets Antonio Machado and Miguel Hernández survived the war itself, but not for long. Machado died in a pension in France, an asthmatic complaint having been aggravated by his evacuation from Spain.[21] Hernández died in 1942 in an Alicante gaol.

On the nationalist side, it can be argued that the distinguished Basque philosopher Miguel de Unamuno was a casualty of the war. Unamuno had unambiguously lent his support to the nationalists at the beginning of the war, but by October 1936 his opinion had changed, and one particular event marked that change of opinion. On 12 October Columbus's discovery of America was celebrated as the "Day of the Race" in the great hall of the University of Salamanca, of which Unamuno was rector. The celebration was attended by a number of franquist dignitaries, including the poet José María Pemán and the founder of the Spanish Foreign Legion, General Millán Astray. One of the speakers, Professor Francisco Maldonado, made a violent attack on Basque and Catalan nationalism, during which a man at the back of the hall shouted the Foreign Legion's motto: "*¡Viva la Muerte!*" (Long live death!). All attention focussed on Unamuno, who was known to dislike Millán Astray. In reply to the Foreign Legion's motto, and to the enthusiastic response it had received from Millán Astray and a number of falangists, Unamuno said:

Just now I heard a necrophilistic and senseless cry: "Long live death." And I, who have spent my life shaping paradoxes which have aroused the uncomprehending anger of others, I must tell you, as an expert authority, that this outlandish paradox is repellent to me. General Millán Astray is a cripple. Let it be said without any slighting undertone. He is a war invalid. So was Cervantes. Unfortunately there are all too many cripples in Spain just now. And soon there will be even more of them, if God does not come to our aid. It pains me to think that General Millán Astray should dictate the pattern of mass psychology. A cripple who lacks the spiritual greatness of a Cervantes is wont to seek ominous relief in causing mutilation around him.[22]

To this Millán Astray shouted "*¡Mueran los intelectuales!*" (Death to the intellectuals!). Desperately seeking common ground, Pemán added, "Down with *false* intellectuals!" But Unamuno continued: "This is the temple of the intellect. And I am its high priest. It is you who profane its sacred precincts. You will win, because you have more than enough brute force. But you will not convince. For to convince, you need to persuade. And in order to persuade you would need what you lack: reason and right in the struggle. I consider it futile to exhort you to think of Spain. I have done."[23]

Shortly after this last public address the senate of the University of Salamanca obtained Unamuno's dismissal from the rectorship. Effectively barred from public life, Unamuno died on the last day of 1936.

## THE SPANISH CIVIL WAR AND LITERARY SCHOLARSHIP

There exists already a large body of secondary material on the literature of the Spanish Civil War, and yet there remain significant gaps in research as well as serious, for the most part politically based, shortcomings in the available secondary material. If much of the primary literature is unashamedly partisan, then it is to be lamented that a large proportion of literary scholarship has failed to free itself from the same or similar forms of political bias.

Existing book-length studies of the literature of the Spanish Civil War are in most cases confined to a particular author, national response, genre or political ideology, and in some instances to a combination of these categories.[24] On many of these works restrictions of genre as well as of nationality have been placed, but the list of studies with generic limitations can easily be extended.[25] Finally, a number of studies are subject of ideological restriction.[26]

Naturally there also exists a considerable body of secondary literature in shorter forms (journal articles, chapters in books devoted primarily to other or broader topics), which cannot be surveyed here in its entirety. It can only be noted that this literature too, as its format dictates, is subject to restrictions similar to those of the above-mentioned monographs. Special issues of literary journals and collections of essays, such as those edited by Luis F. Costa (with Richard Critchfield, Richard J. Golsan and Wulf Koepke), Marc Hanrez, Stephen Hart, John Beals Romeiser, Angels Santa and Günther Schmigalle are able to overcome some of these restrictions by covering a broader range of war literature in its international, generic and ideological complexity, but they lack a unifying purpose and methodology.[27]

The intention of this introductory survey of the existing secondary literature on the literature of the Spanish Civil War is not to consider the faults in individual studies but to point to a major deficiency in the body of secondary literature as a whole. The survey indicates that most literary scholarship has not addressed the historical literary phenomenon "Spanish Civil War literature" but has preferred to deal selectively with specific aspects of the phenomenon. The above-mentioned works make no claim to treating the war literature in its entirety; they quite validly single out particular features of a literary event of enormous range and examine them with varying degrees of success.

There do, however, exist a number of works which are of a much more ambitious design and intention. Brief reference has already been made to the earliest of these – the study entitled *Gli intellettuali e la guerra di Spagna* by the already mentioned Italian war-veteran Aldo Garosci.[28] In what must now be regarded as an outdated work (published in 1959), Garosci examines the impact of the war on the European literary intelligentsia, with particular emphasis on the Spanish literature of the war. In doing so he focusses primarily on writers who sympathized with the Left, especially with communism. Three years later a Spanish scholar by the name of Rafael Calvo Serer published a work under the title *La literatura universal sobre la guerra de España.*[29] The blatant political bias, the inaccuracies and the plagiarism contained in this pro-franquist study were revealed a short time later by the Texan scholar Herbert Southworth in *El mito de la cruzada de Franco*.[30] By challenging in great detail the claims of Calvo Serer and of his pro-franquist colleague Vicente Marrero,[31] Southworth produced an extremely valuable publication which may be described as a sort of annotated bibliography of the international literature of the Spanish Civil War. Southworth brilliantly exposes and refutes the franquist tactic of depicting the war as a crusade against communism on behalf not only of Spain and Christian civilization but of the entire West.

The 1967 work of the American scholar Frederick R. Benson, *Writers in Arms. The Literary Impact of the Spanish Civil War*, has long been considered a classic study of the literature of the war.[32] Benson adopts an international approach, but it too is limited in scope, without apparently being fully aware of the nature and extent of its limitations. Just as communist scholars prefer to deal with with a pro-communist literary canon,[33] and Spanish nationalist scholars prefer to promote pro-nationalist literature,[34] Benson stands in a Western liberal tradition which has a canon of its own, albeit a relatively broad one. It can be traced back as far as Stephen Spender, who wrote in 1949:

Almost the whole literature of the Spanish Civil War depicts the energy of a reviving liberalism rather than the Communist orthodoxy which produced an increasingly deadening effect on all discussion of ideas, all witnessing of the complexity of events. The best books of the War – those by Malraux, Hemingway, Koestler and Orwell – describe the Spanish tragedy from the liberal point of view, and they bear witness against the Communists.[35]

Benson confines his study to the prose literature of the war, and in doing so concentrates on those four authors named by his forerunner Spender, and adds Georges Bernanos and Gustav Regler. The criterion Benson claims to have applied in the choice of these six authors is that each of them "expressed the feeling that the *whole* man emerged during the Spanish struggle, and the intensification of each author's social and political commitment was secondary to the appeal to the writer's conscience as a man."[36] This formulation suggests that Benson's selection is based on ethical rather than political premises, but an examination of the texts considered reveals a subtle political bias. Benson makes very little mention of the literature of the Right and, at the other extreme, claims that the anarchists lacked the necessary talent to make a substantial contribution to the literature of the war.[37] His insistence on "reasonably objective detachment" leads to the omission of Spanish authors, of the vast mass of poetry, as well as dramatic works on the war. Most importantly, in separating the author's "social and political commitment" from his "conscience as a man," Benson applies a set of aesthetic criteria which are of limited relevance for the judgement of the body of literature on the Spanish Civil War. Thus he laments, "Few works transcended the clichés of propaganda and found their inspiration in humanistic ideals rather than partisan politics."[38] These are the criteria of a later generation. To evaluate the importance of the war for literary history in terms of the contribution of a select band of authors to the "humanitarian tradition" is a limitation of the scope of the study which is not justified by the proclaimed subject of the study. [39]

## SUBJECT, METHODOLOGY AND AIMS

In all likelihood not even bibliographies can encompass the full body of literature on the Spanish Civil War, but if literary scholarship is to come to terms with the phenomenon "Spanish Civil War literature," then the quantity and the international, generic and ideological scope of that phenomenon must be acknowledged and contemporaneous aesthetic standards taken into account. The existing secondary material on the literature of the war largely fails to achieve this. It either quite legitimately chooses to deal with a limited aspect of the whole, or, in claiming to represent the whole, it (less legitimately) adopts subtle or perhaps even blatant, for the most part politically motivated, strategies of selection. No single work of literary scholarship can deal with *all* of the literature of the war, but in being necessarily selective it can recognize the broadness of scope of Spanish Civil War literature.

The subject of the present study is the historical phenomenon "Spanish Civil War literature" in its international, generic and ideological complexity. Given the impossibility of dealing with the literature in its entirety, a study of this kind clearly demands a concentration on literary paradigms, that is, on authors and texts which can be regarded as representative of particular aspects of the whole, and which, when considered together within the framework of a single study, constitute a reflection of a highly complex literary event.

Consequently, the selection of authors and texts in this study is designed to acknowledge the full international, generic and ideological scope of the subject. A range of national literatures is represented, as is a range of literary genres. Most importantly of all, and in deliberate contrast to previous studies, the selection covers the entire range of the political spectrum, from Nazism through to anarchism. Finally, the selection of texts is designed to acknowledge the significance of the contribution to Spanish Civil War literature of lesser-known and even anonymous authors. Since one of the above-listed factors in judging the historical significance of Spanish Civil War literature is the sheer quantity of it, it would be anomalous to present it as comprising the contributions of the canonized authors, especially as political bias has played a major role in the process of canonization. Eminently praiseworthy in its appreciation of this aspect of the war literature is the approach adopted by the Spanish scholar Serge Salaün, who regards the poetry of the thousands of mostly anonymous Spanish poets during the war as a single, collective work, as an enormous epos. [40] Quite independently the Germanist Helmut Kreuzer has argued for a similar approach: "That Spanish Civil War literature as a whole and the literature of the International Brigades in particular is less concerned to achieve the individual masterpiece for its own sake than to collectively advocate points of view; that the individual work or author is of less historical significance than the group phenomenon, is not to be disputed. "[41]

Two restrictions have been applied to the selection of texts for the purposes of this study. Firstly, as a study of literature and politics *in* the Spanish Civil War, the selection is limited to literature written during or shortly after the war. The focus is on a clearly identifiable event in literary history which corresponds quite precisely with a politico-military event. Secondly, this study deliberately restricts itself to the examination of the literature of the war and leaves aside other forms of cultural response. It does, however, interpret "literature" generously to include both fictional and nonfictional prose forms as well as lyric and dramatic genres. It includes works which defy ready classification according to these broad categories and appear to be located in areas where the distinctions between genres are blurred.

In studying literary history, the focus, however, is not on literary texts alone. Beyond selected texts, attention is directed to the conditions under which literature was produced. This means the formal, institutional framework within which texts were written and published, whether as independent works or as contributions to journals or newspapers. It means a consideration of the historical conditions under which authors produced literature and under which their readers received it. Finally it also means the less formal, intellectual framework of aesthetic discourse. This work directs attention to the key aesthetic debates which were taking place at the time of the Spanish Civil War and assesses their significance for literature. The treatment of an extra-literary context goes so far as to consider such "events" as the 1937 International Writers' Congress in Valencia and Madrid. It is assumed here that even such an event as a Writers' Congress, which of course cannot be classified as a literary text in any strict sense of the term, is nevertheless an important part of literary history.

Precisely because this work proposes to take into consideration such a broad range of literary texts and contexts, it simultaneously abandons any project of detailed and exhaustive textual exegesis. Such an approach is deliberately avoided because it precludes the possibility of coming to terms with the scope of the topic. To concentrate entirely on a few texts would not constitute a literary history of the war, simply because it ignores one of the key features of the war's literature as identified above, namely its sheer quantity. In acknowledging the scope of the topic, this work seeks a balance of textual and contextual analysis. It examines some texts in detail, but it refers to others only with the aim of identifying salient thematic or generic characteristics. Beyond that it draws attention to the political and intellectual circumstances from which those texts arose.

Having defined the subject of this study, namely the phenomenon of the Spanish Civil War in literary history, it remains to identify its aim. Literary scholarship has tended to judge harshly the undeniably close relationship between politics and literature during the war. Most Spanish Civil War literature, it is frequently contended, is blatantly partisan and doctrinaire, and consequently of little aesthetic value; the "good" literature of the war, Western scholarship argues, is not the literature of political commitment or *engagement*. The canonised authors tend to be those who are not readily identifiable with a particular political ideology. It is my contention, however, that the relationship between politics and literature in the Spanish Civil War was an extraordinarily productive one, and that the key to ascertaining the significance of the Spanish Civil War for literary history lies in an appreciation of the complex and dynamic interaction of political and literary activity. Whether blatantly partisan or not, the overwhelming majority of works on the Spanish Civil War produced during the war *are* centrally concerned with the question of the literary expression of political commitment. To assume that aesthetic quality is inversely proportional to political engagement is to apply a standard which is invalid for the time. It can be demonstrated that precisely this question of political commitment dominated literary production and aesthetic discourse during the period 1936-39.

The impact of the unparalleled political commitment of Spanish Civil War writers on their literature is assessed in two areas. Firstly the work considers the impact of political ideologies, that is, systems of *political* beliefs which served to mobilize people for particular actions, on the content of literature. "Literary content" here refers to the emotions and ideas which are communicated in literary texts. A basic assumption being made here is of course that literary texts are capable of performing a communicative function. It is not denied that many literary texts, including some Spanish Civil War texts, allow or even encourage a wide range of interpretations. This does not apply, however, to the vast bulk of Spanish Civil War literature; the reader is thus left little room for maneuver in the construction of meaning. The central contention here is that right across the range of the political spectrum literature was being used very deliberately to communicate political ideas and to encourage commitment to a particular political ideology.

As a second and subsidiary task, this work examines the impact of political ideologies on literary form. "Form" here is understood in the quite narrow sense of the choice of literary genre or sub-genre. The question is posed as to whether the political radicalism which characterized the age converted itself into a corresponding formal radicalism, that is, a widespread willingness to experiment with new literary genres. If literature was to perform the task of communicating ideas and promoting commitment, both writers and literary theorists had to come to terms with the key question of which literary forms or genres were best suited to achieving those tasks.

To perform this assessment of the impact of political commitment on literature, the first priority is to establish the ideological context of the war. The first chapter therefore undertakes to explain in considerable detail the aims and the functions of the political ideologies and their supporters in the Spanish Civil War. Each of the following chapters then deals with a particular segment of the political spectrum and explores its substantive and formal impact on literature. Beginning with the extreme Right, the work deals with the relationship between Nazism and literature; it works through the centre of the spectrum to the extreme Left, where it concludes with a study of anarchist literature.

In examining the impact of political commitment on literature across the entire spectrum, the attempt is made to prove two things. Firstly, this work shows that the impact of commitment on content is so complex as to demand the abandonment of any notion of a war between "two sides." Although it is possible to detect themes which occupy writers at all points of the spectrum, other substantive interests are present which suggest the necessity of a differentiation not only between "Left" and "Right" but also between various points on the Left and the Right. On the Left in particular, an examination of texts, of aesthetic discourse and even of certain events and personalities reveals the presence of sometimes very deep and bitter antagonisms. The image of internal harmony of Left and Right is misleading, although there are specific reasons that the Right was better able to cope with discord than the Left.

Secondly, this work aims to show that the impact of political commitment on form is quite the reverse. Whereas ideological differences do very clearly express themselves substantively, there appears no such corresponding impact on form. Political radicalism does not translate itself into aesthetic radicalism, and, with some notable exceptions, the outstanding formal tendencies in Spanish Civil War literature tend to *transcend* political divisions. Indeed, it can be shown that ideologically motivated attempts to impose formal standards, as revealed in aesthetic discourse, were eminently unsuccessful. In particular the work tackles the fate of the officially proclaimed communist aesthetic doctrine of "socialist realism."

Attention here is focussed on an *historical* event, or, to be more precise, on an event in international literary history which occurred over fifty years ago. But the investigation of an historical phenomenon is of more than purely historical interest. The peculiar confrontation of ideologies in Spain in the late 1930s will never be repeated; nevertheless the constellation of forces at that time in Spain bears a clear resemblance to countless contemporary struggles, for example in Central America. The literature of the Spanish Civil War deals with themes which are still of great relevance today – the problem of violence, the relationship between politics and morality, the experience of idealism and disillusionment, of hostility and solidarity. Although contemporary Western literature as a whole is not so indelibly marked by political commitment as it was in the late 1930s, it too frequently performs political functions. In a century which more than any other is characterised by a struggle for people's minds, it would seem more necessary than ever to promote an awareness of the strategies which literature adopts to win its readers for a cause.

## NOTES

1. For the response of Beckett and other writers see *Authors Take Sides on the Spanish War*. London: Left Review, 1937. It contains the results of a survey of British and Irish intellectual opinion conducted by Nancy Cunard in cooperation with the periodical *Left Review*. A similar survey under the title *Writers Take Sides. Letters About the War in Spain from 418 American Writers*. New York: League of American Writers, 1938, was carried out in the United States.

2. The above-named surveys show this clearly. In the British survey 86 percent of 148 writers expressed support for the Republic; only 3 percent were against it. Of the 418 American writers only one, Gertrude Atherton, favoured the franquist cause.

3. Hugh D. Ford. *A Poets' War: British Poets and the Spanish Civil War*. Philadelphia: University of Pennsylvania Press; London: Oxford University Press, 1965. p. 21.

4. Thomas Mann. "Spanien." In Thomas Mann. *Gesammelte Werke in zwölf Bänden. Band 12. Reden und Aufsätze 4*. Frankfurt a.M.: Fischer, 1960. p. 794.

5. Stanley Weintraub. *The Last Great Cause. The Intellectuals and the Spanish Civil War*. London: W. H. Allen, 1968. p. 2.

6. As indeed Stephen Spender does. See his essay, "Stephen Spender," in *The God That Failed*. Ed. Richard Crossman, 229-73. New York: Harper and Row, 1949. pp. 243, 247.

7. John M. Muste. *Say That We Saw Spain Die: Literary Consequences of the Spanish Civil War*. Seattle, London: University of Washington Press, 1966. p. 11.

8. Spender's brief membership of the Party is discussed in Chapter 4. Regler and Koestler, it seems, were showing signs of disillusionment even before the war broke out in Spain. The process of disillusionment amongst these and other writers is a complex one. Although it is clear that for many the cynicism of Soviet policy in the Spanish war was a factor, it is also apparent that other events played a role. The Moscow Trials took place at the same time as the Spanish war; the signing of the Hitler-Stalin Pact took place just a few months after it. An outstanding document recording this disillusionment is Richard Crossman's collection of essays by Arthur Koestler, Stephen Spender, Richard Wright, Louis Fischer, André Gide and Ignazio Silone (see note 6). Many prominent figures who are said to have become disillusioned with the Party, such as Auden, Dos Passos, Malraux and Orwell, were in fact never members of it.

9. Ricardo de la Cierva y de Hoces. *Cien libros básicos sobre la Guerra de España*. Madrid: Publicaciones Españolas, 1966. p. 161.

10. Frederick Benson. *Writers in Arms. The Literary Impact of the Spanish Civil War*. London: University of London Press, 1968 (1967). p. 278. For an account which similarly stresses the importance of a disillusionment with communism in particular see Jürgen Rühle. Transl. Jean Steinberg. *Literature and Revolution. A Critical Study of the Writer and Communism in the Twentieth Century*. London: Pall Mall Press, 1969 (1960). pp. 430-34.

11. Rafael Alberti, for example, remained enthusiastically faithful: Paul Eluard did not join the Communist Party until 1942; Pablo Neruda enrolled in the Communist Party of Chile in 1943.

12. By the end of World War II, and with the collapse of European fascism, a number of Spanish writers and intellectuals who had been closely associated with fascism, such as Dionisio Ridruejo, Santiago Montero Díaz, Antonio Tovar and Pedro Laín Entralgo, were distancing themselves from the movement.

13. Maurice Merleau-Ponty, *Humanismus und Terror. Band 2*. 2nd. ed. Frankfurt a.M.: Suhrkamp, 1968. Quoted in Reinhold Görling. *"Dinamita cerebral." Politischer Prozeß und ästhetische Praxis im Spanischen Bürgerkrieg (1936-1939)*. Frankfurt a.M.: Vervuert, 1986. p. 418.

14. Philip Toynbee. *Friends Apart: A Memoir of Esmond Romilly and Jasper Ridley in the Thirties*. London: Macgibbon and Kee, 1954. p. 90.

15. Aldo Garosci. *Gli intellettuali e la guerra di Spagna*. Turin: G. Einaudi, 1959. p. 5.

16. Frederick Benson. *op. cit.* p. xxix.

17. Maryse Bertrand de Muñoz. "Literature." In *Historical Dictionary of the Spanish Civil War, 1936-1939*. Ed. James W. Cortada, 300-304. Westport, CT: Greenwood Press, 1982. p. 300. See also Maryse Bertrand de Muñoz. "Introducción." in Maryse Bertrand de Muñoz. *La Guerra Civil Española en la Novela. Tomo III. Los Años de la Democracía*, 1-86. Madrid: Ediciones José Porrua Turanzas, 1987. p. 83; Maryse Bertrand de Muñoz. "La Guerre Civile Espagnole et la Littérature." *Mosaic* (Autumn 1969): p. 64.

18. Weintraub. *op. cit.* p. 10.

19. Walter Haubrich. "Angst vor neuen Wunden. Spanien erinnert sich seines Bürgerkrieges." *Frankfurter Allgemeine Zeitung* (4 August 1986): p. 21.

20. Weintraub. *op. cit.* p. 40.

21. Hugh Thomas. *The Spanish Civil War*. 3rd. ed. Harmondsworth: Penguin, 1986 (1961). p. 879.

22. Quoted *ibid.* p. 501. Thomas recounts the incident and Unamuno's response to it in greater detail than I have here, though he admits that there will never be complete agreement on what was said and how it was said. For another account, see Ronald Fraser. *Blood of Spain. The Experience of Civil War, 1936-1939*. Harmondsworth: Penguin, 1986. pp. 205-9.

23. *Ibid.* p. 503.

24. Günther Schmigalle and Robert S. Thornberry, for example, have produced studies of Malraux. British reactions to the war have been examined by Hugh D. Ford and Katherine Bail Hoskins; both British and American responses by John M. Muste and Stanley Weintraub, and the American response alone by Allen Guttmann. Thomas P. Anderson, Maryse Bertrand de Muñoz, Hilary Footit and Gottfried Pfeffer have written full-length studies of the French response to the war; Gerhard Georg Mack, Elke Bleier-Staudt and a collective of East German authors have done the same for the German response. The significance of the war for Spanish literary and intellectual history has been evaluated by Fernando Diaz-Plaja, Lucienne Gilhodes, Manfred Lentzen, Barbara Pérez-Ramos and José Luis Ponce de León. See Günther Schmigalle. *André Malraux und der spanische Bürgerkrieg. Zur Genese, Funktion und Bedeutung von "L'Espoir" (1937)*. Bonn: Bouvier, 1980; Robert S. Thornberry. *André Malraux et la Guerre d'Espagne*. Geneva: Droz, 1977; Ford. *op. cit.*; Katherine Bail Hoskins. *Today the Struggle: Literature and Politics in England during the Spanish Civil War*. London, Austin: University of Texas Press, 1969; Muste. *op. cit.*; Weintraub. *op. cit.*; Guttmann. *op. cit.*; Thomas P. Anderson. "The French Intelligentsia and the Spanish Civil War." Unpublished doctoral thesis, Loyola University, 1965; Maryse Bertrand de Muñoz. *La guerre civile espagnole et la littérature française*. Paris: Didier, 1972; Hilary Footit. "French Intellectuals and the Spanish Civil War." Unpublished doctoral thesis, Reading University, 1972; Gottfried Pfeffer, "Der Niederschlag des spanischen Bürgerkrieges 1936-1939 in der französischen Literatur." Unpublished doctoral thesis, Tübingen, 1961; Gerhard Georg Mack. "Der spanische Bürgerkrieg und die deutsche Exilliteratur." Unpublished doctoral thesis, University of Southern California, 1972; Elke Bleier-Staudt. *Die deutschsprachige Lyrik des spanischen Bürgerkriegs*. Reutlingen: 1983; Kollektiv für Literaturgeschichte. *Bodo Uhse. Eduard Claudius. Abriß der Spanienliteratur*. East Berlin: Volk und Wissen, 1961; Fernando Díaz-Plaja. *Si mi pluma valiera tu pistola. Los escritores españoles en la guerra civil*. Barcelona: 1979; Lucienne Gilhodes. "Le roman espagnol sur le thème de la guerre civile 1936 à 1939." Mémoire pour le Diplome d'Etudes Supérieures, Université de Paris, 1958; Manfred Lentzen. *Der spanische Bürgerkrieg und die Dichter. Beispiele politischen Engagements in der Literatur*. Heidelberg: Carl Winter, 1985; Barbara Pérez-Ramos. *Intelligenz und Politik im Spanischen Bürgerkrieg 1936-1939*. Bonn: Bouvier Verlag Herbert Grundmann, 1982; José Luis Ponce de León. *La novela española de la guerra civil 1936-1939*. Madrid: Insula, 1971.

25. Maryse Bertrand de Muñoz's already mentioned annotated bibliography of the novels of the war is a good example. Studies by Douglas H. Armstrong, Erika Block, Robert Marrast, Marilyn Rosenthal and Birgitta Vance are subject to similar restrictions. See Douglas H. Armstrong. "The Novels of the Spanish Civil War – A Thematic Appraisal 1936-1960." Unpublished doctoral thesis, University of Michigan, 1967; Erika Block. "Zum Menschenbild in der Internationalen Antifaschistischen Epik über den

Spanienkrieg (1936-1939)." Unpublished doctoral thesis, Jena, 1972; Robert Marrast. *El teatro en Madrid durante la guerra civil*. Buenos Aires: Editorial Eudeba, 1967; Marilyn Rosenthal. *Poetry of the Spanish Civil War*. New York: New York University Press, 1975; Birgitta Vance. *A Harvest Sown by Death: The Novel of the Spanish Civil War*. New York: Peninsula, 1975.

26. For example, ideologically restricted are my own study of the Nazi literature of the war and the study of Spanish fascist literature by Julio Rodríguez Puértolas. On the other side of the spectrum is Reinhold Görling's investigation of the relationship between political practice and aesthetic theory on the Left of the political spectrum. See Peter Monteath and Elke Nicolai. *Zur Spanienkriegsliteratur. Die Literatur des Dritten Reiches zum Spanischen Bürgerkrieg. Mit einer Bibliographie zur internationalen Spanienkriegsliteratur*. Frankfurt a.M.: Peter Lang, 1986; Julio Rodríguez Puértolas. *Literatura fascista española. Vol. 1. Historia*. Madrid: Akal, 1986; Görling. *op. cit.*

27. See special issues of *Camp de l'Arpa* 48-49 (1978); *Cuadernos de Aldeeu* 5, 1 (April 1989); *Cuadernos el Público* 15 (1986); *The Dolphin* 16 (1988); *Imprévue* 2 (1986); *Letras de Deusto* 16, 35 (May-August 1986); *LiLi. Zeitschrift für Literaturwissenschaft und Linguistik* 15, 60 (1985); *República de las Letras* (1986); *Revue belge de philologie et d'histoire* 65, 3 (1987); *Sinn und Form* (1965); *Spanish Studies* 8 (1986); *Weimarer Beiträge* 30, 7 (1986). For collections of essays in book form see Luis F. Costa, Richard Critchfield, Richard J. Golsan and Wulf Koepke (eds.). *German and International Perspectives on the Spanish Civil War. The Aesthetics of Partisanship*. Columbia, SC: Camden House, 1992; Marc Hanrez (ed.). *Les écrivains et la guerre d'Espagne*. Paris: Pantheon Press France, 1975; Stephen M. Hart (ed.). *"¡No pasarán!" Art, Literature and the Spanish Civil War*. London: Támesis, 1988; John Beals Romeiser (ed.). *Red Flags, Black Flags. Critical Essays on the Literature of the Spanish Civil War*. Madrid: Porrúa Turanzas, 1982; Angels Santa (ed.). *Literatura y Guerra Civil. (Influencias de la guerra de España en las letras francesas e hispánicas) Actas del Coloquio Internacional Lérida, 1-3 Diciembre 1986*. Barcelona: Promociones y Publicaciones Universitarias, 1988; Günther Schmigalle (ed.). *Der Spanische Bürgerkrieg. Literatur und Geschichte*. Frankfurt a.M.: Vervuert, 1986.

28. Garosci. *op. cit.* p. 5.

29. Rafael Calvo Serer. *La literatura universal sobre la guerra de España*. Madrid: Ateneo, 1962.

30. Herbert Southworth. *El mito de la cruzada de Franco*. Paris: Ruedo ibérico, 1963. Published in French as *Le mythe de la croisade de Franco*. Paris: Ruedo ibérico, 1964.

31. Vicente Marrero. *La guerra española y el trust de los cerebros*. 2nd. ed. Madrid: Ediciones Punta Europa, 1962 (1961).

32. Frederick R. Benson. *op. cit.*

33. See for example Lidija M. Jur'eva. "Der spanische Freiheitskampf in der sowjetischen und der sozialistischen deutschen Literatur." In *Begegnung und Bündnis. Sowjetische und deutsche Literatur. Historische und theoretische Aspekte ihrer Beziehungen*. Ed. Gerhard Ziegengeist. 336-41. East Berlin: Akademie-Verlag, 1972; Lidija M. Jurjewa. Transl. Astrid Maaß. "Die weltliterarische Bedeutung des Spanienthemas." In *Internationale Literatur des sozialistischen Realismus 1917-1945*. Ed. Georgi Dimow *et al.* 617-43. East Berlin, Weimar: Aufbau, 1978; Edgar Kirsch. "Der spanische Freiheitskampf 1936-1939 im Spiegel der antifaschistischen deutschen Literatur."*Wissenschaftliche Zeitschrift der Martin-Luther-Universität Halle/Wittenberg. Gesellschafts- und sprachwissenschaftliche Reihe* 4, 1 (1954): pp. 99-119.

34. See especially the above-mentioned works of the franquist scholars Rafael Calvo Serer and Vicente Marrero. By the former see also "Die Literatur über den spanischen

Bürgerkrieg von 1936." In *Politische Ordnung und menschliche Existenz. Festgabe für Eric Voegelin zum 60. Geburtstag*. Ed. Alois Dempf *et al.* 71-104. Munich: Beck, 1962.

35. Stephen Spender. *op. cit.* pp. 247-48.

36. Benson. *op. cit.* p. xxviii.

37. *Ibid.* pp. 25, 10.

38. *Ibid.* p. xxiii.

39. *Ibid.* p. 54.

40. Serge Salaün. "L'expression poétique pendant la guerre d'Espagne." In Hanrez (ed.). *op. cit.* 105-13. p. 107.

41. Helmut Kreuzer. "Zum Spanienkrieg. Prosa deutscher Exilautoren." *LiLi* 15, 60 (1985): p. 39.

# WRITING
# THE
# GOOD FIGHT

# 1. War and Political Ideologies in Spain

## FRANQUISM AS FASCISM

The widespread conception of the ideological homogeneity of the forces of the Right in Spanish politics in the 1930s was a product of the Spanish and the international Left's need for a clearly identifiable opponent and of the Right's own need for a sense of unity as a compensation for actual disunity. To a large extent it is a misconception, an intellectual construct arising from political necessity but lacking a solid basis in political reality. If in retrospect the Spanish Right appeared (and continues to appear) a much more unified political force than the Left, it is because its methods of psychological and physical coercion were eminently more successful, if also more brutal.

Closer inspection reveals that the Spanish Right in the 1930s was by no means ideologically united but embraced a range of political beliefs. Whether as a whole the forces which threw their support behind the generals in July 1936 may be classified as "fascist" is of course a question of definition. While Eastern-bloc historians insist on the accuracy of the term, some Western historians have, with good reason, expressed scepticism regarding its suitability.[1] The question of definition cannot and need not be resolved here, but an overview of the historical development of the Spanish Right in the 1930s, in particular of the impact of the war on the ideology of the Right, indicates that some of the political ideals espoused in radical rightist circles were either compromised or sacrificed as Franco and the generals set about realising their dream of a "new Spain."

At the birth of the Spanish Republic in 1931 the forces of the Right were hopelessly disorganized, but the victory of the moderate Left in the first elections provided impetus for the welding together of disparate conservative political interests. In early 1933 a number of small right-wing groups amalgamated to form the Confederación Española de Derechas Autónomas (CEDA) under the leadership of José María Gil Robles. The binding element for the parties of the CEDA was the promotion of Spanish Catholicism and opposition to the firmly anti-clerical sentiments of the republican government. As such it represented a broad range of socio-economic groups, from large-landowners through landholding peasant farmers to Catholic labour unions and cooperatives. In these circumstances a coherent economic policy was hardly feasible; instead the CEDA sought and indeed attained electoral popularity by preaching the traditional principles of "Religion, Fatherland, Family, Order, Work and Property." Gil Robles claimed a political philosophy of accidentalism, that is, the belief that the question of the form of government is subordinate to the question of the protection of the above-named principles. But his faith in the capacity of parliamentary government to protect the interests of the Spanish Church was by no means boundless; he associated with monarchists, and in some of his 1933 speeches "showed sympathy with nazism, as well as with Dr. Dollfuss's catholic state in Austria."[2]

For the time being, however, the CEDA was willing to work within the framework of the parliamentary system set up in 1931 to replace the monarchy, and in November 1933 it achieved sufficient electoral success to lead a right-wing government up until the February 1936 elections. In leftist circles the period from November 1933 to February 1936 became known as the *bienio negro*, the two black years, because the reformist achievements of the first republican government, particularly in the areas of Church-state relations and land reform, were systematically undone.

The 1933 electoral success of the CEDA was attained in cooperation with two militant monarchist parties. The first of these was Renovación Española, the party of the Alfonsine monarchists, which was founded in March 1933 by Antonio Goicoechea. The second and more potent force were the carlists or traditionalists, who similarly campaigned for the restoration of an authoritarian monarchy, but with a different king in mind. The carlists are truly a remarkable twentieth century political phenomenon. Three times in the nineteenth century they had gone to war against Spanish liberalism, and all three times they had lost. By the 1920s carlism was almost a spent force, but the birth of the republic revived it at a popular level. In 1931 carlism "was indisputably the oldest continually existing popular movement of the extreme right in Europe."[3] The carlist stronghold was in the north, in Aragón, the Levante provinces and Catalonia, but especially in Navarre. Essentially a conservative-reactionary political force, carlism was above all a movement of the rural masses who crusaded against the seemingly dominant tendencies of the modern age – liberalism, socialism, industrialism and atheism. Its supporters were willing to apply violent methods to promote their crusade, but in general were loath to adopt a political program which would entail anything more radical than the re-establishment of a traditional order. The *requetés*, the military appendage of the carlists, repeatedly committed acts of violence against the republic, which they regarded as a grave threat to traditional Spanish customs and institutions. Thus carlism "provided a convenient political refuge for something which transcended banditry but stopped well short of social revolution."[4]

The republic also witnessed the development of the first Spanish versions of a not insignificant European ideology – fascism. In February 1931 the first serious attempts were made to establish a Spanish fascist movement in imitation of Italian and German models. Ramiro Ledesma Ramos and Ernesto Giménez Caballero drafted a manifesto under the title *La Conquista del Estado* (The Conquest of the State). A weekly publication and a political movement employing the same title soon followed. In June of the same year a young Catholic lawyer in Valladolid by the name of Onésimo Redondo Ortega formed a fascist group called Junta Castellana de Actuación Hispánica (Castilian Junta for Hispanic Action) and began publishing a weekly organ entitled *Libertad*. The anti-Semitic content of Spanish fascism, small though it was, is mainly attributable to Redondo. The programs of these early fascist movements are summarised by Herbert Southworth as follows:

The employment of violence and direct action, of extreme nationalist propaganda, and of youth to forge a strong national unity in Spain. This unity was to be threefold: territorial (no regional autonomy), political (no political parties, but a single movement), and socio-economic (suppression of the class struggle and of worker-controlled unions). The movement based on this national unity was to conquer the state and set up a totalitarian structure that would then conquer the new empire. [5]

Late in 1931 Ledesma and Redondo combined forces to form the Juntas de Ofensiva Nacional-Sindicalista (JONS). This party has been described as "a protesting young troop, who sought danger, who affirmed violence as the most effective means in the political struggle, who had in mind as their goals political power and a Spanish empire."[6] Like its predecessors it failed miserably to attract popular support. Nevertheless, the radical Right's hopes of escaping the political fringe were raised by the spectacular success of German fascism in early 1933, an event whch persuaded José Antonio Primo de Rivera, son of the dictator of the 1920s, to form a new group. It called itself the Movimiento Español Sindicalista, and received the subtitle Fascismo Español. Persistent failure to gain widespread support obliged José Antonio to launch a new party in October 1933, this time entitled Falange Española, the initials of which, FE, give the Spanish word for faith. The new name worked no miracles, however, nor did the amalgamation in 1934 of the two competing fascist organisations (to form the Falange Española de las JONS). Without doubt it was a simple lack of popular appeal rather then the cumbersome title which obliged the fascists to continue to take a back seat in Spanish politics.

Not even the charisma of José Antonio could rescue Spanish fascism from political obscurity in the period leading up to the elections of February 1936, at which, just as in November 1933, the fascists managed to win not a single seat in the Cortes.[7] At the time of the February elections the fascist party could claim probably no more than 10,000 regular members. Support was limited geographically (its key centres were Madrid and lower Andalusia) but also socio-economically. An astoundingly large proportion of membership, perhaps 60 or 70 percent, were under twenty-one years of age. Gerald Brenan has estimated that more than half of the members were university students and only one in five of the rest from the working classes.[8] The founding fathers of Spanish fascism, who have been described as "a collection of bizarre intellectuals,"[9] saw themselves as "an heroic élite of young men, whose mission was to release Spain from the poison of Marxism, as from what they took to be the second-rate, dull, provincialism of orthodox liberal values."[10] José Antonio himself was a lawyer whose writings "leave the impression of a talented undergraduate who has read, but not digested, an overlong course of political theory."[11] He had befriended many mediocre writers and intellectuals and participated in a large falange literary group. As its leader, José Antonio "was determined to give the Falange a literary and aesthetic appeal."[12]

Fascist fortunes took a turn for the better after the electoral victory of the Popular Front in February 1936. Whereas fascist violence had been almost uniformly regarded with abhorrence by the Right, it now appeared to the latter that the parliamentary system was no longer capable of protecting conservative interests and that violence might indeed provide a viable alternative. Although the party was outlawed in March 1936 and José Antonio imprisoned, the Falange played a central role in the outbreaks of violence which characterized the period of political crisis immediately prior to the war. It was a period in which the falangists compensated for the severe structural weaknesses of their party by distinguishing themselves "principally as rowdies and gunmen, seeking to disequilibrate the Popular Front through sporadic violence."[13]

The Republic was brought down not by the second-rate intellectuals and hitmen of the Falange, but by a group of Spanish generals with widespread support in conservative and carlist circles. It seems that José Antonio gave his consent to falangist support for the rebellion, although he "feared that it would end, as it did, with falangist support of a right-wing military dictatorship, disguised by the demagogic program of the fascist movement, with no real power of decision in fascist hands."[14]

The next stage in the history of Spanish fascism entails the realization of José Antonio's fear. It was the generals rather than the right-wing parties who assumed control of the nationalist state when, contrary to their hopes, their attempted putsch met spontaneous popular resistance and assumed the dimensions of a civil war. As a political force they possessed no common, unifying ideology, except perhaps a vague wish to restore order, unity and hierarchy in Spain along traditional lines. Some of the generals, such as their designated leader José Sanjurjo, were monarchists and one, Juan de Yagüe, openly proclaimed his adherence to falangism. After the death of Sanjurjo at the beginning of the war, it was the accidentalist Francisco Franco who took over the reigns of the nascent nationalist state. In the past Franco had shown considerable reluctance to identify himself with any political ideology; he "cared little for political forms provided they maintained 'order,' which was threatened, in his view, by socialist violence."[15] Franco's political beliefs "were the simple trilogy of the nineteenth-century soldier: the unity of state (he regarded the war as a war against secessionists – Basques, Catalans, and Marxists), order, hierarchy. To these he added an intense Catholicism and even, initially, a vague social radicalism inherited perhaps from Gil Robles."[16]

Confronted with a full-scale civil war and with their own ideological heterogeneity, Franco and the generals required a credible political program which would assure them of mass support. In April of 1937 Franco acted to seize control of the Falange and amalgamated it with the carlists and those right-wing parties in the nationalist zone which were still tolerated. The carlists greeted the unification decree without enthusiasm; some sections of the Falange greeted it with outright opposition. The leader at that time, Manuel Hedilla, proved particularly hostile to the idea, and was in fact condemned to death (though later had his sentence commuted). The new party thus formed received the title Falange Española Tradicionalista.

Rather then conquering the state, which was the original intention of the Spanish fascists, their party organisation had in essence been pressed into the service of the state. Ironically, it was the promotion of the Falange to the status of official state party which sounded the death-knell of a genuine fascist movement in Spain, because through that act the fascists had given away control over their own movement. In effect, the unification decree meant that the falangists were deprived of the two most basic fascist trademarks, namely their own leader and their own ideology. That meant, as Ernst Nolte suggests, "that Spanish fascism had lost its opportunity for autonomous development and was no longer merely allied to the conservative powers but was enslaved to them."[17]

To what extent can franquism be regarded as fascism? The nationalist state formally adopted the falangist program to fill a political void. It also opted for much of the iconography of falangism – the yoke and arrows as emblem of the regime, the blue shirt of the Falange as the proper dress for militants. The new state was structured along totalitarian lines in accordance with falangist principles – it was a genuine *Führerstaat*, with all power emanating from the Führer, or, in this case, from the Caudillo, around whom a personality cult was established. Franquism adopted much of the ultra-nationalistic propaganda for which the Falange was renowned, and like the pre-war Falange it was eager to refute claims that it was a mimetic movement, that is, that it merely copied the models of German and Italian fascism. But this continuation of the falangist propaganda line "was essentially a display of hollow rhetoric designed to conceal the intellectual poverty of the conservatives and the generals."[18] Finally, franquism willingly adopted a falangist style of political violence to ensure the effective suppression of any traces of political opposition in the nationalist zone and, after the war, in the franquist state. Ironically, even some convinced falangists fell victim to the regime's tactics of political suppression.

Political pragmatism persuaded Franco to cultivate the superficialities of falangism and to adopt its characteristically violent political methodology. But the ideological content beneath the surface was not an example of pristine fascism. Herbert Southworth defines fascism as "a modern, highly organised attempt to save the menaced capitalist structure in certain vulnerable countries through the subversion of the revolutionary élan of the workers, channelling this élan away from the class struggle and towards an enterprise of class collaboration, necessarily and inevitably debouching into an adventure of imperialist conquest."[19] Spain had in living memory been deprived of the last of its imperial possessions, and falangism mourned Spain's demise as a great power and looked to a return of imperial glories. Franquism did not dismiss the imperialist program of the Falange from the outset. But whereas Hitler and Mussolini had been able to gain control of their respective states with relatively little bloodshed, Franco required a civil war which dragged on for almost three years. Whereas Hitler and Mussolini were able to unite national energies to pursue their imperialist schemes, Franco had divided the nation and sapped it of the necessary strength to pursue fascist dreams of foreign conquest and empire. In World War II Franco did not provide substantial military assistance to the axis powers, simply because Spain was not capable of doing so. Whereas German and Italian fascism had harnessed national energies to suppress other nations, franquism directed the forces of suppression against Spain itself, or, "as one could say, Castile re-conquered the peninsula, the original Castilian empire."[20] Franquism, in short, engaged in the theory, but not the practice, of fascist imperialism.

Similarly, Franco had no serious intention of implementing the social-revolutionary goals of Spanish fascism. Vague as their aims and methods may have been, falangist rhetoric demanded the correction of blatant and severe social injustices. José Antonio's syndicalism was designed as a genuine alternative to the appeal of left-wing ideologies. This concern for the predicament of Spanish rural and urban workers gave the falangist movement an almost plebeian character which was repugnant to Spanish conservatism. The latter mockingly labelled the falangists "our Reds" or "FAIlangists" (in reference to the anarchist organisation Federación Anarquista Ibérica, or FAI). Franco, however, undertook no earnest attempt to correct social injustices through wide-reaching reform, but instead acted to preserve traditional status and privileges. The war was fought for the existing hierarchy, for the protection of the interests of clerical, military and landowning elites. It was won by "the conservative-reactionary elements that had owned Spain before the war."[21]


## COMMUNISM AND THE MODERATE LEFT

Whereas power struggles within the Spanish Right were for the most part effectively concealed from national and international attention, bitter antagonisms within the Left were frequently aired publicly. Broadly speaking, the Spanish Left of the 1930s may be divided into two categories – a moderate and a revolutionary Left. Ironically it was communism, the political ideology which supporters of the Spanish and the international Right immediately identified as posing the main revolutionary threat to Spain, which proved in the course of the war to be the voice and instrument of moderation. Rather than giving revolution its unreserved approval, as many expected, it was a force which helped to *save* Spain from the radicalism of the anarchists and the revolutionary Left.

For a time at least, the history of the Communist Party in Spain corresponded in several respects to that of the Falange. Both began as militant political groupings with unashamedly revolutionary intent, and both were condemned to political insignificance up until the February 1936 elections. Both experienced an increase in popularity after those elections, which accelerated markedly after the commencement of the war. But there the similarities end. Whereas falangism was destined to become essentially a tool of the franquist state, the communists were to achieve a position of genuine authority in the republican zone.

The Partido Comunista Española (PCE) was founded in 1921 by a combination of dissident groups from within the socialist movement and a faction from the predominantly anarchist Confederación Nacional del Trabajo (CNT). During the dictatorship of Miguel Primo de Rivera the PCE "never had more than a few hundred members and could not even manage to hold a congress."[22] Throughout that period and in the following decade, the party obediently followed to the letter the directives of the Communist International. Up until the mid-1930s this entailed the espousal of revolutionary goals and violent opposition to capitalism, with the ultimate aim of establishing a workers' state along the lines of the soviet model.

But the revolutionary stance of world communism in general and of Spanish communism in particular was abandoned in 1935. In August of that year, at the Seventh World Congress of the Communist International, a proposal for the adoption of a so-called Popular Front policy was accepted. In practice this meant that in the parliamentary democracies communist parties from this point threw their support behind other left-wing political groupings in order to bolster the electoral clout of an anti-fascist bloc. All communist parties, including the PCE, "spoke of the need to preserve 'parliamentary bourgeois democracy' until it could be replaced by 'proletarian democracy.'"[23] The impulse for this de-radicalization of communism came from the Soviet Union, and for quite pragmatic reasons. Fearful of the prospect of potently belligerent Central European fascism, and mindful of the need to protect "socialism in one country," the Soviet Union sought alliances with the Western European democracies. It could only hope to do so by convincing those democracies that communism was not working to destroy bourgeois democracy, but rather was willing to assist it in the struggle against the common enemy, namely fascism.

What little electoral support it did win, the PCE, as agreed, gave to the moderate Left at the February 1936 elections, contributing in a small way to a Popular Front victory. Only sixteen communist deputies (of a total of 473) were elected to the Cortes, compared with seventy-nine from the Republican Left and thirty-four from the Republican Union. The communists were not yet a forcible presence in Spanish politics, boasting a small membership and a solid proletarian following in only a few places – Asturias, Seville, to a lesser extent in Málaga and Cádiz. Bearing this simple numerical weakness in mind, the often-made claim of the Spanish and the international Right that the military putsch was an attempt to preempt a communist revolution is extravagant. The PCE was nowhere near strong enough to lead a revolution in mid-1936, nor did it possess the desire to do so.

The Socialist Party of Spain, the Partido Socialista Obrero Español (PSOE), had a considerably longer tradition than the PCE. It was founded as far back as 1879 as a Marxist party but failed to achieve true mass support before World War I. This applies also to its larger sister organisation, the trade union Unión General de Trabajadores (UGT, General Workers' Union), which was founded in 1888. But in the 1920s both organisations were able to cultivate strong support in Madrid, in the mining districts of Asturias and in the industrial sectors of the

Basque capital Bilbao. As from 1925 the leader of the UGT and the PSOE was Francisco Largo Caballero, who at that time pursued a moderate policy of reform to the point of collaboration with the dictatorship of Primo de Rivera.

The spirit of collaboration for the sake of reform continued into the 1930s. The PSOE numbered some 20,000 members at the birth of the Republic in April 1931, the UGT nearly 300,000.[24] Both Largo Caballero and his great rival within the socialist movement, Indalecio Prieto, served in the first republican cabinet. As minister of labour, Largo Caballero played a central role in the formulation of policies for agrarian reform, with the result that during the 1930s the popular basis of socialist support was broadened to include large sections of the rural proletariat. In this area, the UGT and PSOE even managed to make progress at the expense of the anarchists. By 1932 they were receiving the support of some 450,000 landless workers in addition to massive urban support.[25]

Size alone did not make socialism a dominant political force; if anything, it hindered it. A split began to develop during the *bienio negro*, one which was later to be severely exacerbated by the war. One section of the movement, that led by Largo Caballero, lost faith in the power of reformism. Driven to pessimism by the reactionary policies of the Right during the *bienio negro*, and influenced also by the fate of socialism in Germany and Austria, Largo Caballero and his followers looked to more radical solutions to the growing problems for Spain's rural and urban proletariat. The reformists of the 1920s and early 1930s now affirmed that social revolution was the only hope of for the Spanish masses. Boasting a UGT membership somewhere in the region of 1.5 million, the socialist movement entered the 1936 elections a large but divided entity, with Largo Caballero leading a revolutionary wing and Prieto leading a reformist wing. Spanish voters sent eighty-eight socialists into the new Cortes, but in the months after the elections the fissures within the movement received increasing public exposure.

Political developments in the republican zone after the outbreak of war have been described as "a cantation of the decline of the socialists and the rise of the communists."[26] For several weeks, *all* political parties in the republican zone were effectively deprived of political power, as the apparatus of state was swamped by the revolutionary fervour of large sections of the population. It was not the republican government but the for the most part crudely armed masses, large proportions of them radical socialists and anarchists with no interest in restoring the Republic, who foiled the generals and spontaneously took over the role of government. But as the central government in Madrid and the regional government in Catalonia (the Generalidad) gradually reasserted their authority in the latter part of 1936, it became evident that the communists had profited most of all from the upheaval of the preceding months, at the expense of the bourgeois-democratic parties (who were quickly and almost without protest reduced to the status of political nonentities) and ultimately also of the radical Left. In Catalonia the communists formally joined forces with the socialists to form the Partido Socialista Unifacado de Cataluña (PSUC, United Socialist Party of Catalonia).[27] Aided by such collaboration with moderate socialists, the communists managed to achieve political preeminence in republican Spain well before the first anniversary of the generals' putsch.

This spectacular success of the communists can be attributed to a number of factors. The PCE was placed in a strong bargaining position by virtue of the fact that the Soviet Union was the only country to grant a substantial supply of arms to republican Spain. Moreover, amidst the divisions in the socialist movement and the general disorder of the republican zone, the communists stood out as the best supplied, best organised and most disciplined political-cum-military force. It was the communist-organised International Brigades which played a vital role in the defence of Madrid, the fall of which would almost certainly have meant an early end to the war. The communists were seen to be welding together a military force capable of resisting an enemy which by November of 1936 was camped on Madrid's doorstep.

Above all, communist influence increased in republican territory because of the PCE's ability to enlist the support of the Spanish middle classes. It was the PCE which offered those classes hope of protection against the ravages of the spontaneous social revolution. Both the PCE and the PSUC "took up the cause of the middle classes who were being dragged into the vortex of the collectivisation movement or who were being crippled by the disruption of trade, the lack of financial resources, and by the requisitions carried out by the working-class militia."[28] The communists acted consistently to suppress the proletarian revolution in the republican zone and to defend the interests of both the urban and rural property owners. Emphasizing the threat posed by German and Italian intervention on behalf of Franco, they argued that the first priority must not be to embark on a program of radical social change but to win the war against fascism, and that to do this a strong, centralised state and a modern, disciplined army were an absolute necessity. The PCE "appeared before the distraught middle classes not only as a defender of property, but as a champion of the Republic and of orderly processes of government."[29] Communism became the dominant force in the move to restore a bourgeois republic and in the campaign to reverse the anarchist program of rural and industrial collectivisation. In short, the PCE became the party of the republican middle classes par excellence.

The motives behind communist policies during the war remain a bone of some contention. To begin with, PCE tactics may be seen as a logical extension of the Popular Front policy. By promoting themselves as worthy allies, if not as champions, of the bourgeoisie, the communists hoped to win the confidence of the Western democracies. Secondly, the communists must have realized that the Western democracies would only be willing to lend support to the Spanish Republic if that Republic were perceived to be a bourgeois-democratic republic and not a hotbed of proletarian revolution. Thirdly, it can be argued that in the context of the war the policies of the communists to postpone the revolution and concentrate the organisation of the state and military apparatus on waging war against the nationalists were more pragmatic than those of the radical Left, who insisted on the primacy of the social revolution. Fourthly, the German historian Patrik von zur Mühlen argues that an important reason for the communist suppression of the revolution was that the communists "could not approve a revolution which was not led by them and which had broken out without their participation."[30] Finally, as a second German historian, Rainer Huhle, has pointed out, communist policies had a firm basis in Marxist theory dating well back into the nineteenth century.[31] According to the theory of historical materialism, the proletarian revolution had to be preceded by a bourgeois-democratic revolution. Spain at the time of the war was still (as communists argued and continue to argue) at the stage of the bourgeois-democratic revolution, so to attempt to implement a proletarian revolution would have been tantamount to jumping a stage in historical progress. Huhle contends that the "battle against hurrying ahead, against the jumping of stages, becomes in 1936/37 the main tenor of the policy of the PCE."[32] Communism, in other words, did not comprehend itself as a counterrevolutionary force, but as an agent in the achievement of the bourgeois-democratic revolution which had begun with the birth of the Republic in 1931.

Whichever motive or combination of motives most closely approximates the truth, the ramifications of communist policy are clear enough. Support for a PCE intent on restoring to full power a state apparatus which worked to suppress proletarian revolution and to mount an organised war effort reached proportions which PCE members before the war could only have dreamed of. According to its own figures, within a few months of the outbreak of war the party became the refuge of 76,700 peasant proprietors and tenant farmers and of 15,845 members of the urban middle classes.[33] Membership increased from about 40,000 in July 1936 to nearly a quarter of a million in March 1937.[34] With mass support on this scale, the communists during the war were able to acquire key positions in government and in the military. For the most part the political progress of the communists was achieved within the framework of the political system which they had helped to restore – through ministerial posts and through political and military appointments. But it must be conceded that they at times resorted to methods of more dubious legitimacy, in particular a secret police which acted with notorious brutality to silence political opponents.

The expansion of communist power was not achieved without considerable opposition from the revolutionary Left – from anarchists, revolutionary marxists and radical socialists. Political tensions  culminated in streetfighting in Barcelona in May of 1937, generally known as the "May events," and described from the viewpoint of the revolutionary Left by George Orwell. The hostilities and the continuing instability gave the communists sufficient pretext to force Largo Caballero as head of the Madrid government to establish police and military authority in Catalonia. Shortly afterwards the communists forced the resignation of Largo Caballero and had him replaced by their ally, the moderate socialist Juan Negrín. With that success, communist power had reached its apogee. Negrín, as the communists well knew, "could never be so popular in the Spanish working class as Largo Caballero had been."[35]

The ignominy of final military defeat should not be allowed to obscure the fact that the performance of communist-controlled and communist-organised military forces, and of the International Brigades in particular, was nothing less than heroic. These forces valiantly confronted a better-equipped and often numerically superior enemy. Nevertheless, it must be acknowledged that the role of communism in the Spanish Civil War is fraught with irony. It is enormously ironic that the Spanish and indeed the international Right employed as the linchpin of their propaganda campaign the argument that the generals had acted to save Spain from a communist revolution. In reality it was communism (which in any case was quite incapable of launching any sort of state-shattering activity in July of 1936) which became the most effective force in *suppressing* the revolution. The PCE was the voice and the force of moderation, of bourgeois democracy and economic rationalism; the falangist program in contrast was of a markedly more radical tone.

A perhaps even more bitter irony has been noted by the writer Hans Magnus Enzensberger. In 1873 Friedrich Engels pronounced a stinging condemnation of anarchism: "Thus the ultra-revolutionary cries of the bakuninists resulted, as soon as it came to action, either in conciliation or in uprisings with no prospect of success from the very beginning or in joining a bourgeois party which politically exploited the workers in the most disgraceful manner and then walked all over them."[36] The irony is that the "bourgeois party" of which Engels speaks was, in the context of the Spanish Civil War, none other than the PCE.

## ANARCHISM AND THE REVOLUTIONARY LEFT

For decades before the outbreak of war, the most potent and militant force on the Left of Spanish politics was anarchism. It maintained that position into the war but lost it as a result of the war and of political developments in republican territory during the war. It is impossible to define Spanish anarchism merely as a political ideology. More than that, it was a faith, a way of life. Rather than seizing control of the existing political system, anarchism proposed to do away with it altogether, to abolish any form of hierarchy which would limit individual freedom. Anarchism was not a Spanish invention, but from the beginning it achieved a popular support in Spain which was the envy of all its ideological competitors.

In October 1868 the Italian anarchist Giuseppe Fanelli, an emissary of Mikhail Bakunin, arrived in Spain to spread the anarchist word. He belonged to the "anti-authoritarian," anti-Marxist wing of the First International, and in a mixture of French and Italian he educated Spanish workers in the fundamental principles of anarchism. Fanelli's success was spectacular; his message was received enthusiastically by workers in western and southern Spain. In 1870, at its first congress, the Spanish workers' movement decided in favour of the ideological line set by Bakunin and against that set by Marx; by 1873 there were some 50,000 "bakuninists" in Spain.[37]

The immediate popularity of anarchism was not solely Fanelli's achievement, though historians are divided in their explanations for its spectacular success. Whereas some see it as an emotionally charged reaction against the onset of modernism, a desire to rescue the idyllic features of life in medieval times, revisionists see anarchism as a secular and rational response to distinctly modern circumstances.[38] Whatever the reasons, it is apparent that Fanelli's ideas fell on extremely fertile ground. The rural south proved particularly receptive. Spanish peasants in the south suffered appalling economic hardship because of the landownership of the wealthy. By 1900, 0.1 percent of the Spanish population owned 33 percent of all arable land, and there were 547,548 landless labourers in Andalusia alone earning less than one peseta a day.[39] A large proportion of the landowners did not even live on their *latifundia* but had them managed by tenants. Labourers (*braceros*) were hired to work on average a twelve-hour day during harvest time for a meagre daily rate. Almost all of the *braceros* were unemployed for about half the year, with the result that poverty and under-nourishment were endemic. The hatred sponsored by such blatant inequality created a state of almost permanent small-scale warfare in Andalusian villages. The landowners and privileged associates employed the Guardia civil to protect themselves from unruly labourers. Unwittingly, this rural proletariat had adopted the tactic of violence as recommended by Bakunin. When the ideology of anarchism was transported to the villages of Andalusia, it was eagerly adopted as a theoretical basis for an already existing contempt for the oppression of humans by humans.

Andalusia was the first stronghold of Spanish anarchism; Catalonia was the second. Economically, Catalonia was the precise opposite of the rural provinces of southern and western Spain. Industrial capitalism established itself on a large scale in Catalonia long before other parts of Spain; its capital, Barcelona, became a thriving port, a centre of banking and of a flourishing textile industry. An inevitable social consequence of this rapid economic development was the creation of a large, highly concentrated industrial proletariat, many of whom were not native to Catalonia but had migrated from southern and western provinces to escape unemployment and poverty.

Like the rural proletariat of the south, the industrial proletariat of Catalonia was spontaneously attracted to anarchism, so that by 1918 some 80 percent of workers in Catalonia were anarchist organised. Northern anarchism adopted violent tactics similar to those of its southern counterpart. In the 1890s a theatre, a number of cafés and a Corpus Christi procession in Barcelona were bombed by anarchists; in 1923 the archbishop of Saragossa was assassinated. Yet conditions peculiar to Catalonia as an industrial centre favoured the development of a distinctive form of anarchism. Firstly, the overwhelmingly industrial proletariat of Catalonia was attracted to a form of anarchism known as anarchosyndicalism. The latter strove for the same revolutionary goals as anarchism, but the means employed were somewhat different. Catalonia was ideally suited for the absorption of French syndicalist ideas which proposed the organisation of industrial labour in large unions. Union or syndicalist organisation, it was argued, would not only help to popularize anarchism but would also provide it with an effective revolutionary agent. Secondly, Catalonian anarchism was influenced in its revolutionary content by Catalonian separatism. Whereas separatist movements in other parts of Spain, most noticeably in the Basque territories, were devoid of revolutionary content, Catalonian separatism was a two-edged sword. Waged by the prosperous middle class, the campaign for Catalonian independence was a means to play down the existence of class tensions within Catalonia. But waged by the massive industrial proletariat, Catalonian separatism assumed genuinely revolutionary traits – the demand for self-administration, contempt for the apparatus of a centrally organised state and a corresponding insistence on the radical decentralisation of power.

Spanish anarchism was by no means a homogeneous phenomenon but, rather, covered an "extraordinary ideological range."[40] Southern anarchism differed from northern anarchism, and even within the northern and southern varieties differences of opinion emerged at times to plague the anarchist movement. Nevertheless, Spanish anarchism is identifiable by a number of principles which generally remained undisputed before the war. The anarchists did not understand themselves as a political party. They did not take part in parliamentary elections and frequently requested their supporters to abstain from voting altogether. Rather than participate in the state or seek to win control of the state, they aimed to abolish it altogether. This act of abolition could occur at any time and need not (as in Marxist theory) be preconditioned by a particular set of socioeconomic circumstances. The thought of people being ruled by other people, elected or not, was anathema to anarchists. In their own organisations they avidly sought to avoid the concentration of power in committees. They rejected the notion of reform, of negotiating with those in power for more favourable working conditions. Instead, adopting the favoured tactics of strikes and guerrilla warfare, they proposed a permanent state of war against the ruling classes until the final victory was achieved. At that point a system of loosely federated, self-governing communities would come into existence, a *comunismo libertario* free of repression by an organised state.

The fervour and devotion displayed by Spanish anarchists in pursuing their revolutionary goals has led some historians to interpret anarchism as an essentially religious movement. Gabriel Jackson, for example, suggests: "Psychologically, rural Spanish anarchism was closely akin to primitive Christianity, to the Gnostic and Montanist communities, and to seventeenth-century utopian sects such as the Levellers, Diggers, and Anabaptists."[41] Catholicism had forfeited its traditional appeal in many parts of Spain, most notably in areas of blatant social inequality, because in those areas the Church was seen to side with the privileged. The Church maintained its influence in areas without massive social inequality, for example in Galicia (where everyone was poor) and in the Basque provinces, Navarre, the Levante and rural Catalonia (where peasant land ownership was not uncommon). "Elsewhere, in the Spain of the *latifundia*, the Church was regarded as an instrument of propaganda and the province of the rich, as the defender of property and an iniquitous social order, and as the determined foe of all social betterment, the enemy of the workers."[42] Paradoxically, Spain in the 1930s was both the most Catholic and the most anti-Catholic country in Europe.[43] As respect for the Church in many parts of Spain evaporated, a vacuum was created which was filled in large part by anarchism. Thus began "the gradual transfer of the allegiance of the peasants and workers from the Church to revolutionary ideologies hostile to it."[44]

Certainly anarchism shared with Christianity a millenarianism, according to which one day the traditional order would be destroyed and replaced by an ideal world. This millenarianism bred in Spanish anarchism the distinctively messianic characteristics of fanaticism and self-sacrifice. With religious passion the anarchists of Andalusia advocated "a creed whose day of triumph would mean the physical destruction of that upper class and its friends and servants."[45] Under anarchist instruction peasants learned to read tracts by Bakunin or by the French theorist Pierre-Joseph Proudhon, and to treat them as sacred texts. In southern Spain the so-called Apostle of the Idea would travel from village to village, teaching anarchist doctrine. In each of these villages there lived at least one "conscious worker," who was outstanding for his moral earnestness, who "neither smoked nor gambled, did not drink, declared himself an atheist, was not married to the woman with whom he lived and to whom he was faithful, did not have his children baptized, read a lot and sought to pass on all that he knew."[46]

The thesis that anarchism performed the function of a substitute religion has much to support it, but the enormous popularity of the anarchist movement and its distinctive political content can be attributed to additional factors which relate to its socioeconomic context. In short, apart from filling a religious and spiritual vacuum, anarchism may also be understood as a movement of resistance against expanding capitalism and against the modern centralised state, both of which it set out to destroy. Anarchists hated capitalism "with a hatred of which their comrades in Western Europe were no longer capable."[47] They rejected all forms of capitalist development outright and forcefully opposed the changes which such development brought with it – a materialism bordering on fetishism, the worship of private property, worker alienation resulting from capitalist work practices. Spanish anarchism without question possessed an element of archaism. It looked back to an ideal precapitalist world which it hoped to locate in Spanish history. The anarchist ideal of the "free commune" was similar to medieval Spanish peasant communities. Anarchism, as Gerald Brenan points out, was "dominated by that nostalgia for the past that is so characteristic of Spain."[48] It "contained as an atavistic utopia . . . many elements of 'anti-modernism.'"[49] This is not to suggest that the anarchists were Luddites. When the opportunity came during the war, the anarchists did not destroy factories and machines, but used them to satisfy their needs. Although borrowing from the past intellectually, their physical energies were devoted to the future, to the creation of a society in which not the material standard of living, but the absence of human domination and repression would be the outstanding achievement.

Given its historical and philosophical basis, the reluctance of Spanish anarchism to organize itself politically is not surprising. Anarchism assumed the form of a revolutionary trade union movement rather than a political movement, but not until 1910 was the Confederación Nacional del Trabajo (CNT) formed, a blanket organisation containing a number of unions which often acted quite independently. At the time of the outbreak of the war it constituted the largest syndicalist union in the world.[50] It was, Hans Magnus Enzensberger claims hyperbolically, "the only revolutionary trade union in the world."[51] The CNT functioned without any substantial bureaucracy – even in 1936 the CNT did not have a single paid functionary, despite being able to boast a membership in excess of a million. If in the fascist or franquist state the power was concentrated at the top, the CNT was the exact organisational opposite – power was concentrated in the mass basis.

Later there was established within Spanish anarchism an organisation of a non-union character which resembled a political party, namely the Federación

Anarquista Ibérica (FAI). Founded in Valencia in 1927, the FAI has been described by the French historians Pierre Broué and Emile Témime as being "not merely an active, anonymous group but a typically Spanish state of mind."[52] Its main aim was to guard against reformist tendencies within the CNT, to ensure that Bakunin's revolutionary doctrine was adhered to without compromise. The FAI was a relatively small, clandestine organisation, with a membership of 30,000 at the most, but because of the dedication and daring of its leaders, most notably of the legendary Buenaventura Durruti, the FAI was a crucial driving force in the anarchist movement. It comprised, so to speak, "the hard core of the anarchist trade unions."[53] Because it attempted to gain control of the CNT, the FAI's relations with the CNT were often strained during the 1930s. At the time of the outbreak of the war, however, (and as the poster art of the period eloquently testifies) the CNT and the FAI had set aside differences to form a formidable force. Even so, under the pressures of war latent ideological differences between CNT "reformists" and the "hard core" of the FAI were to reemerge in the course of the war and to threaten anarchist unity.

Anarchism was certainly the dominant but by no means the sole force of the revolutionary Left. The role of the radical wing of the PSOE, led by Largo Caballero and from late 1933 sceptical of the possibility of progress through negotiation and conciliation, has already been mentioned. The third important element of the revolutionary Left was the Partido Obrero de Unificación Marxista (POUM), a Catalonian-based party of radical marxists who hoped to bring about a revolution modelled on the October revolution. Many POUM members were former communists and indeed continued to consider themselves as communists. But although they proclaimed loyalty to Lenin, they abhorred Stalinism, and in particular rejected the policy of a Popular Front. The PCE branded them "Trotskyites" or at times even as "fascists." In fact, Leon Trotsky had not approved the founding of the POUM in 1935 and had sought to disown it. Nevertheless, it is possible to argue for the existence of an ideological affinity between Trotsky and the "poumists." Unlike the Stalinist PCE, the POUM argued that the Popular Front and the parliamentary system in which it existed were a betrayal of the workers' revolution. But unlike the CNT, the POUM believed not in the abolition of the state but in the seizure of the state and the creation of a workers' state.

When the generals attempted their putsch in July 1936, it was the anarchists and other elements of the revolutionary Left who provided the most effective and enthusiastic resistance. Their aim, however, was not to restore the Republic, which they too despised, but to abolish completely the existing capitalist order, to implement the "social revolution." The central government in Madrid and the Catalonian Generalidad continued to exist in name, but de facto political power in many areas which successfully resisted the rebellion rested squarely in the hands of the anarchists, who were not going to let the opportunity slip to usher in a new age. While their sometimes primitively equipped and poorly trained militias threw themselves heroically against the generals' disciplined armies, behind the front the anarchists set about achieving their utopia.

The revolution was spontaneous and conducted without centralised control. It took the form of the collectivisation of the rural economy, of industrial concerns and the service industries, and the establishment of local committees as the organs of administration. Property records were destroyed, owners fled or were killed, their land confiscated and then either collectivised or distributed among the peasants. The geographic centres of the revolution corresponded closely to prewar anarchist strongholds – industrial Catalonia, rural Aragon, parts of Andalusia still in republican hands, New Castile and the Levante. Anarchists themselves evaluated their achievements as "the most significant social experiment of the twentieth century."[54]

The extent to which the anarchists really did achieve their utopia in these first weeks of the war remains controversial. Historians have been plagued by a lack of reliable information on the social revolution, a deficiency which is attributable in part to the communist policy of suppressing information concerning revolutionary activities. Communists then and now label the revolution an economic and psychological failure. On the other hand, the relatively few reports by anarchists or anarchist sympathisers which managed to appear in print tend towards idealisation. More reliable are reports by independent observers such as the Austrian sociologist Franz Borkenau, who acknowledged the successes of the revolution but also bore witness to some of its failures and to the gradual erosion of revolutionary power.[55]

The debate on the achievements of the Spanish revolution, on the degree to which anarchism manifested or compromised itself, need not be entered here in any detail.[56] More important is the dilemma with which the anarchists were soon confronted. Unlike the communists and the moderate Left, the anarchists and the revolutionary Left insisted that the war and the revolution were inseparable. The war, they argued, provided the ideal opportunity to implement the revolution. It became increasingly apparent, however, that although the war had made the revolution possible, it also made its implementation exasperatingly difficult. The exigencies of war quite simply meant that "from the beginning the recourse to hierarchical organisation models and very soon the retreat from anarchist militia concepts became necessary."[57] The anarchist militias, enthusiastic though they may have been, were too poorly disciplined, organised and equipped to fight a prolonged war. The decentralisation and fragmentation of the economic and political system in anarchist-controlled territory was similarly inimical to the war effort. The anarchist dilemma therefore was whether to pursue the implementation of the revolution (at the risk of losing the war against the Generals) or to participate in the reestablishment of a strong, centralised republican state (at the risk of losing the revolution and compromising their ideals). Ultimately the anarchist leaders decided on the latter alternative. They agreeed to join the central republican government as well as the Catalonian *Generalidad*, thus crucially assisting the political resurrection of those two bodies. With good reason this move has been described as "the most remarkable decision in the course of Spanish anarchism."[58] Anarchist acceptance of ministerial posts in Largo Cabellero's cabinet "caused a *crise de conscience* in the leadership itself and was never popular with the militant masses".[59] The mood of dejection amongst the masses when it became clear that the state would be reestablished, that the war would take priority over the revolution, was captured by the Italian anarchist Bertoni, who wrote: "The war in Spain, bereft

of any new faith, of any idea of social change, and of any revolutionary grandeur
. . . remains a terrible question of life or death but is no longer a war in
affirmation of a new regime and a new humanity."[60]

The fate of the other elements of the revolutionary Left was similar to that of
the anarchists. As George Orwell describes in *Homage to Catalonia*, the
communists dared to single out and confront the relatively small and hence
vulnerable POUM on the streets of Barcelona in May 1937. When shortly
afterwards Largo Caballero was forced from office, the fate of the revolutionary
Left was finally sealed – "a revived middle class, once seemingly consigned to
oblivion, used regionalism, communism, and an odd type of anti-fascism to
dismantle the anarchist revolution."[61] The CNT-FAI predictably found itself in
opposition when Juan Negrín formed his new cabinet; revolutionary militants,
whether anarchists, socialists or poumists, died mysterious deaths, whilst others
survived to witness and mourn the final demise of the revolution.

One of the most mysterious deaths of all during the Spanish Civil War was
that of Buenaventura Durruti. Durruti died in Madrid of a gunshot wound, but it
remains uncertain as to whether the bullet was fired by a nationalist soldier, by
one of his own men or (as seems most likely) accidentally by himself when
climbing out of a car.[62] Durruti was the most charismatic and most revered of
the anarchist leaders; he "had been in turn a terrorist, anarcho-Bolshevik,
fugitive and political exile, insurrectionist and, finally, militia general."[63] His
death, on 20 November 1936, "marked the end of the classic age of Spanish
anarchism."[64] As early as Durruti's untimely death it had become clear to the
most perceptive observers that Spanish anarchism was not going to achieve its
revolutionary goals, and possibly the crowd of 200,000 who attended Durruti's
funeral in Barcelona sensed that the death of their great hero had a symbolic
quality. Coincidentally, José Antonio Primo de Rivera, the similarly charismatic
leader of the Spanish fascists, was executed in a republican prison on the very
day of Durruti's death. "The two most typically 'Spanish' leaders of the civil war
died on the same day, an enormous loss to each side, as the legends and cults
that grew up around both men showed. Hereafter the war belonged more to
international politics than to Spain."[65]

## INTERNATIONALISATION

Eager to maintain international peace or not, Europe was in no position to
ignore a conflict raging in its own backyard. The great powers of the day saw
their foreign policy interests vitally at risk in a nation which, ironically, had
exerted no major political influence on the world community in recent times,
except perhaps to mark its own decline.

Contrary to propaganda claims, neither the German nor the Italian
government was intimately involved in the Generals' putsch preparations.
Without doubt the Generals expected a quick and efficient seizure of power in
the tradition of the *pronunciamiento*, lasting just a few days and causing little
bloodshed. Certainly they did not expect a war which dragged on for almost

three years and cost more than half a million lives. When their plans were foiled, not by the republican government but by spontaneous popular resistance, the Generals turned instinctively to the great fascist powers. Although they displayed some initial reluctance, both Italy and Germany soon agreed to supply the rebels with the military aid which first of all saved them from defeat and finally helped them to win the war.[66] Quantitively, Italian aid was greater than than of the Germans, who never had more than some 6,500 men on Spanish soil at any one time, but the Germans proved themselves to be a more effective military force than the Italians. The socialist republican minister Julio Alvarez del Vayo acknowledged this superiority and also recognized the area in which the Germans excelled most of all: "Numerically the Italians were the dominating force, but in  material and personnel the Germans were throughout the war superior to the Italians. Our enemy in the air was Germany."[67]

Portuguese military aid to the nationalists was relatively insignificant, but Prime  Minister Salazar was willing to allow Franco's forces to use Portugal as a refuge, as an avenue of communication between separated nationalist armies in the early part of the war and as a supply route, especially for German equipment. The role of the Moroccans in Franco's African Army technically does not qualify for the category of "foreign intervention," but the irony of the large-scale participation of these African Moslems in Franco's crusade to save European Christianity did not go unnoticed.

Only two states, Mexico and the Soviet Union, supplied arms to the Spanish republic. Soviet aid was by far the greater, but it had to be paid for in Spanish gold and in political concessions to the communists.[68] The Soviets, too, were above all else mindful of guarding their foreign policy interests and displayed initial hesitancy, but as from the end of August 1936 both the Soviet Union and the Comintern prepared for a major military commitment. Soviet armaments, most notably aircraft and tanks, were not accompanied by troops but by field officers, pilots, tank specialists and flying instructors. A much more crucial source of manpower for the republic was the mass of international volunteers, most of whom joined the International Brigades. In theory at least the Brigades were nonpartisan, but in practice they were communist-organised, and most of their members held party cards.[69] Consisting of volunteers from France, Germany, Austria, Poland, Italy, the United States, Britain, Canada, Yugoslavia, Hungary, Czechoslovakia, Sweden and numerous other countries, their total number was in the region of 35,000 altogether, but probably not more than 18,000 at any one time.[70] To add to these are those foreign volunteers who, in most cases for political reasons, preferred to avoid service in the International Brigades and joined Spanish units or militias. Many volunteers opted for work of a nonmilitary nature, whether in communist or noncommunist organisations. All these forms of personal commitment considered, the number of genuine international volunteers on the republican side was without doubt far greater than on the nationalist side, a fact which is strongly reflected in the literature of the war.

The governments of the Western democracies, Britain, France and the United States, chose to remain on the sidelines of the Spanish conflict, but to follow the course of events with avid interest.[71] The impetus for the formation of a Non-

Intervention Committee (to which, hypocritically, Germany, Italy and the Soviet Union belonged) came in fact from France.[72] Léon Blum's natural sympathies with his Spanish Popular Front counterpart were outweighed by domestic pressures, and a steady flow of arms over the French border suddenly dried up when the war was just three weeks old. In both Britain and the United States a firm desire for peace dictated a policy of neutrality with which all major political parties were in agreement. It was merely a question of what kind of neutrality should be observed. Although public opinion and intellectual debate in these countries were inflamed by the knowledge of events in Spain, political debate was more concerned with whether neutrality permitted the establishment of trade relations with the belligerents.

The course of the military internationalisation of the Spanish Civil War has already been plotted by historians and so need not be dealt with here in great detail. Of far greater importance for the literary historian is the intellectual internationalisation of the war which inevitably accompanied the military internationalisation and indeed was far more widespread than the latter. All over the world the war became a topic of often passionate debate, but in becoming an international issue the Spanish Civil War forfeited much of its Spanishness. The peculiarly Spanish origins of the war, the uniquely Spanish circumstances under which the war was fought and the consequences the war would have for Spain were frequently overlooked in the international context, as "what was fundamentally a life-and-death struggle between the revolutionary left and counter-revolutionary right in one Southwest European country was inflated to symbolic and mythical proportions of a conflict between 'fascism' and 'democracy.'"[73] In examining the international literature of the war, it is important to bear in mind the discrepancy between this conveniently familiar intellectual "construction" of a political constellation and the unique realities of Spanish politics which it served to obscure. Although the dominant political ideologies in Spain in 1936 were without exception of European, non-Spanish origin, the Spanish political landscape was vastly different from that of any other European nation, indeed of any nation in the world. As Gerald Brenan puts it: "Everything to be found in Spain is *sui generis*."[74]

## NOTES

1. The British historian Hugh Trevor-Roper, for example, argues that Franco's government "may be described as 'Fascist' or 'anti-Communist,' but in fact it is neither. It is an ancient Bourbon monarchy, with no parallel in the world, and Franco is not really a dictator in the modern sense: he is a regent." Hugh Trevor-Roper. "Franco's Spain Twenty Years Later." *New York Times Magazine* 2 September 1956. Reprinted in *The Spanish Civil War*. Ed. Gabriel Jackson, 196-203. Chicago: Quadrangle, 1972, p. 198. Of the West German historians, Rainer Wohlfeil avoids using the term "fascist" altogether, and Walther L. Bernecker uses the term "fascistoid-democratic." Rainer Wohlfeil "Der Spanische Bürgerkrieg 1936-1939. Zur Deutung und Nachwirkung." *Vierteljahrshefte für Zeitgeschichte* 16, 2 (1968): p. 118; Walther L. Bernecker. "Spanien im Krieg (1936-

1939). Forschungslage und Desiderate." *Militärgeschichtliche Mitteilungen* 33, 1 (1983): p. 138. See also Sheelagh M. Ellwood. "Falange Española, 1933-1939: From Fascism to Francoism." In *Spain in Conflict 1931-1939. Democracy and its Enemies.* Ed. Martin Blinkhorn, 206-23. London: SAGE, 1986.

2. Hugh Thomas. *The Spanish Civil War* 3rd. ed. Harmondsworth: Penguin, 1986. (1961) p. 109.

3. Martin Blinkhorn. *Carlism and Crisis in Spain, 1931-1939.* Cambridge, London, New York, Melbourne: Cambridge University Press, 1975. p. 2.

4. *Ibid.* p. 15.

5. Herbert R. Southworth. "Spanish Fascism." In *Historical Dictionary of the Spanish Civil War, 1936-1939.* Ed. James W. Cortada, 196-201. Westport, CT: Greenwood, 1982. p. 197.

6. Bernd Nellessen. *Die verbotene Revolution. Aufstieg und Niedergang der Falange.* Hamburg: Leibniz, 1963. p. 64.

7. José Antonio had entered the Cortes in 1933, but not on a fascist ticket.

8. Gerald Brenan. *The Spanish Labyrinth. An Account of the Social and Political Background of the Civil War.* 2nd. ed. Cambridge: Cambridge University Press, 1962. (1943) p. 308.

9. Raymond Carr. *Spain 1808-1975.* 2nd. ed. Oxford: Clarendon Press, 1982. (1966) p. 645.

10. Thomas. *op. cit.* p. 115.

11. *Ibid.* pp. 112-13.

12. Stanley G. Payne. *Falange: A History of Spanish Fascism.* Stanford CA: Stanford University Press, 1961. p. 49.

13. Southworth. *op. cit.* p. 199.

14. *Ibid.* p. 199.

15. Carr. *op. cit.* p. 649.

16. *Ibid.* p. 674.

17. Ernst Nolte. *Die faschistischen Bewegungen.* 2nd. ed. Munich: dtv, 1969. p. 141.

18. Payne. *op. cit.* p. 200.

19. Herbert R. Southworth. "The Falange: An Analysis of Spain's Fascist Heritage." In *Spain in Crisis. The Evolution and Decline of the Franco Régime.* Ed. Paul Preston, 1-22. Sussex: Harvester Press, 1976. p. 1.

20. Herbert R. Southworth. "Möglichkeiten und Grenzen der Definition des Franquismus als Faschismus." In *Der Spanische Bürgerkrieg. Literatur und Geschichte* Ed. Günther Schmigalle, 9-24. Frankfurt a.M.: Vervuert, 1986. p. 19.

21. Southworth. "The Falange: An Analysis of Spain's Fascist Heritage." p. 15.

22. Pierre Broué and Emile Témime. Transl. Terry White. *The Revolution and the Civil War in Spain* London: Faber and Faber, 1972. (1961) p. 69.

23. Hugh Thomas. *op. cit.* p. 123.

24. Statistics *ibid.* p. 39.

25. Statistics according to James W. Cortada. "Spanish Socialist Party." In Cortada (ed.), 439-42. *op. cit.* p. 439.

26. *Ibid.* p. 439.

27. According to Hugh Thomas, "Catalan socialists and communists were already almost indistinguishable in the PSUC." Thomas. *op. cit.* p. 522.

28. Burnett Bolloten. *The Grand Camouflage. The Communist Conspiracy in the Spanish Civil War.* London: Hollis and Carter, 1961. p. 82.

29. *Ibid.* p. 87.

30. Patrik von zur Mühlen. "Säuberungen unter deutschen Spanienkämpfern." In *Exilforschung. Ein internationales Jahrbuch. Band 1. 1983. Stalin und die Intellektuellen*

*und andere Themen*. Ed. Thomas Koebner, Wulf Koepke, Joachim Radkau, 165-76. Munich: edition text + kritik, 1983. p. 167.

31. See Rainer Huhle. *Die Geschichtsvollzieher. Theorie und Politik der Kommunistischen Partei Spaniens 1936 bis 1938*. Gießen: focus verlag, 1980. 13-82.

32. *Ibid.* p. 217.

33. Statistics from Bolloten *op. cit.* p. 82.

34. Statistics from Burnett Bolloten and George Esenwein. "Spanish Communist Party." In Cortada (ed.), 133-39. *op. cit.* p. 135.

35.Thomas. *op. cit.* p. 674.

36.Source uncited, in Hans Magnus Enzensberger. *Der kurze Sommer der Anarchie. Buenaventura Durrutis Leben und Tod*. pbk ed. Frankfurt a.M.: Suhrkamp, 1977. p. 236.

37.Statistics according to Thomas. *op. cit.* p. 60.

38. For a discussion of this debate, see Martha Grace Duncan. "Spanish Anarchism Refracted: Theme and Image in the Millenarian and Revisionist Literature." *Journal of Contemporary History* 23 (1988): pp. 323-46.

39. Figures according to Robert W. Kern. "Anarchists." In Cortada (ed.), 23-28. *op. cit.* p. 23.

40. Walther L. Bernecker (ed.). *Kollektivismus und Freiheit. Quellen zur Sozialen Revolution im Spanischen Bürgerkrieg 1936-1939*. Munich: dtv, 1980. p. 23.

41. Gabriel Jackson. *The Spanish Republic and the Civil War 1931-1939*. Princeton NJ: Princeton University Press, 1967. p. 19.

42. Pierre Broué and Emile Témime *op. cit.* pp. 37-38.

43. Nolte. *op. cit.* p. 136.

44. Gerald Brenan. *op. cit.* p. 90.

45.Thomas. *op. cit.* p. 62.

46. Enzensberger. *op. cit.* p. 31.

47. *Ibid.* p. 37.

48. Brenan. *op. cit.* p. 196.

49. Bernecker. *op. cit.* p. 18.

50. Robert W. Kern. *Red Years/Black Years. A Political History of Spanish Anarchism, 1911-1937*. Philadelphia: Institute for the Study of Human Issues, 1978. p. 1.

51. Enzensberger. *op. cit.* p. 32.

52. Broué and Témime. *op. cit.* p. 56.

53. Enzensberger. *op. cit.* p. 34.

54. Augustin Souchy. *Anarcho-Syndikalisten über Bürgerkrieg und Revolution in Spanien. Ein Bericht*. Darmstadt: März Verlag, 1969. p. 94.

55. Franz Borkenau. *The Spanish Cockpit: An Eye-Witness Account of the Political and Social Conflicts of the Spanish Civil War*. Ann Arbor: University of Michigan Press, 1963. (Originally London: Faber and Faber, 1937.) Borkenau's account is treated in detail in Chapter 6.

56. For a presentation of both sides of the argument see especially Walther L. Bernecker and Jörg Hallerbach. *Anarchismus als Alternative? Die Rolle der Anarchisten im Spanischen Bürgerkrieg. Eine Diskussion*. West Berlin: Karin Kramer, 1986. passim.

57. Bernecker. *op. cit.* p. 9.

58.Carr. *op. cit.* p. 665.

59. *Ibid.* p. 665.

60. Quoted by Camillo Berneri. *Guerre de classes en Espagne*. Paris: Imprimerie Ouvrière, 1938. p. 40. Quoted in Broué and Témime. *op. cit.* p. 235.

61. Kern. *Red Years/Black Years*. p. 239.

62. For the various possibilities see especially Joan Llarch. *La muerte de Durruti*. Barcelona: Ediciones Aura, 1973; also Enzensberger. *op. cit.* pp. 261-80.

63. Kern. "Anarchists." p. 23.

64. Thomas. *op. cit.* p. 485.

65. Kern. *Red Years/Black Years.* p. 205.

66. For a detailed account of Italian involvement in the war, see especially John F. Coverdale. *Italian Intervention in the Spanish Civil War.* Princeton NJ, London: Princeton University Press, 1975. On German involvement see Manfred Merkes. *Die deutsche Politik im spanischen Bürgerkrieg.* 2nd. ed. Bonn: Röhrscheid, 1969 (1961); Hans-Henning Abendroth. *Hitler in der spanischen Arena. Die deutsch-spanischen Beziehungen im Spannungsfeld der europäischen Interessenpolitik vom Ausbruch des Bürgerkrieges bis zum Ausbruch des Weltkrieges 1936-1939.* Paderborn: Ferdinand Schöningh, 1973. For an examination of the motives behind German intervention see my article "Hitler and the Spanish Civil War. A Case Study of Nazi Foreign Policy." *The Australian Journal of Politics and History* 32, 3 (1986): pp. 428-42.

67. Julio Alvarez del Vayo. *Freedom's Battle.* New York: Alfred Knopf, 1940. p. 61.

68. For an account of the Soviet response to the Spanish war, see especially David T. Cattell. *Soviet Diplomacy and the Spanish Civil War.* Berkeley: University of California Press, 1957.

69. Thomas. *op. cit.* p. 455, estimates that 60 percent were communists before volunteering, and another 20 percent became communists during their time in Spain.

70. *Ibid.* p. 982.

71. For a study of the British response to the war see K. W. Watkins. *Britain Divided. The Effect of the Spanish Civil War on British Political Opinion.* London: Thomas Nelson and Sons, 1963. The French response to the war, especially in terms of the propaganda generated by the war, is examined in David Wingeate Pike. *Conjecture, Propaganda, and Deceit and the Spanish Civil War.* Stanford CA: Institute of International Studies, 1968. Allen Guttmann has performed a similar task in an American context. Allen Guttmann. *The Wound in the Heart: America and the Spanish Civil War.* New York: The Free Press of Glencoe, 1962. See also Richard Traina. *American Diplomacy and the Spanish Civil War.* Bloomington: Indiana University Press, 1968; F. Jay Taylor. *The United States and the Spanish Civil War.* New York: Bookman Associates, 1956.

72. See especially Viktor Knoll. "Zur Vorgeschichte des Abkommens über Nichteinmischung in Spanien 1936." *Zeitschrift für Geschichtswissenschaft* 37, 1 (1987): pp. 15-27.

73. Stanley G. Payne (ed.). Editor's introduction to Edward E. Malefakis. "Internal Political Problems and Loyalties: The Republican Side in the Spanish Civil War." In *Politics and Society in Twentieth-Century Spain.* New York, London: New Viewpoints, 1976. p. 145.

74. Brenan. *op. cit.* p. xvii.

# 2. Nazi Literature

## LITERATURE AND PSYCHOLOGICAL MOBILISATION

Amidst the mass of international literature on the Spanish Civil War is a body of works which, despite their popularity and influence at the time of the war and in the immediate post-war period, have generally failed to attract interest since 1945.[1] In assessing the impact of events in Spain from 1936 to 1939 on German literature, one is much more likely to mention the names of exiled and pro-republican authors such as Gustav Regler, Ludwig Renn, Alfred Kantorowicz, Erich Weinert or Bertolt Brecht and to neglect the contribution of such (in those days) popular writers as Werner Beumelburg and Edwin Erich Dwinger. It must be remembered that the exiled authors were confronted with enormous problems as far as publication and readership were concerned, whereas Third Reich authors, although having to work within the framework of state and party control of all the publication media, were able to reach a large reading public. The reader might search in vain for works of literary quality on the Spanish Civil War published in Hitler's Germany, but an examination of this literature is nonetheless justified for two reasons.[2] Firstly, the Nazi literature the war, that is, the literature produced in Nazi Germany with government approval, is distinct from the other literature of the war in that it reflects Nazi mentality and provides insights into that mentality. Secondly, and even more importantly, the Nazi literature is important for the manner in which it fulfilled its specific propaganda function, namely the psychological preparation of the German people for a war on a massive scale.

It may be said that 1936 is a key year in the development of Nazi foreign policy. This fact is worth mentioning, as Nazi literature was geared closely to the requirements of government policy, especially foreign policy. It is the year of the military occupation of the Rhineland by German forces, and is also the year of the implementation of a Four-Year-Plan, which had as its goal the economic and military preparation of Germany for war. At the end of July 1936,

shortly after the outbreak of hostilities in Spain, Hitler received a request from
the rebel General Franco in Spanish Morocco for the supply of aircraft to
transport his African Army to Spain. Hitler agreed to the request; the first airlift
in military history was put into effect, thus rescuing the rebels from probable
defeat and ensuring that an attempted putsch became a civil war. For the first
time since the Great War, German forces became active outside Germany, thus
confirming the trend towards a more aggressive foreign policy.

In November 1936 the German government recognized the Spanish
nationalist regime and increased its military commitment to Franco with the
formation of the Condor Legion, which remained on Spanish soil until the
cessation of hostilities. The employment of a rotation system meant that
members of the Condor Legion spent on average just nine months in Spain, and
although the strength of the Legion probably never exceeded 6,500 men at any
one time, altogether some 18,000 took part in the war. In the Nazi literature of
the war these participants are referred to (and refer to themselves) inaccurately
as "volunteers." In fact they were selected for duty in Spain by their superiors
and sent south under the most secretive circumstances. In his memoirs,
published in 1953, the former flying-ace Adolf Galland recalls:

No-one knew about the strength and the form of the operation in any detail at all. It was
only noticed that one or the other comrade suddenly disappeared without one having
learnt of his transfer or his detachment. So after half a year he was back again, with
brown skin and high spirits, bought himself a new car and related to his most intimate
friends under the greatest secrecy remarkable things from Spain, where the later world
conflict was rehearsed on sandpit-scale, so to speak. 3

Hitler had stepped up his preparations for a large-scale European war but in
1936 was not yet ready to risk a major conflict. Officially the Germans were not
involved in the war at all, and hypocritically the German government continued
to be represented on the Non-Intervention Committee until the end of the war.
But for those familiar with military developments in Spain, particularly in the
wake of the brutal bombing of Guernica, German presence was an open secret.
Nevertheless, the Nazi government persistently refused, both in and outside
Germany, to admit a German military presence. Although German anti-fascists
attempted to inform the German public of the true course of events in Spain
through illegal radio broadcasts and through illegally published and distributed
books and pamphlets, the majority of German citizens remained unaware of the
existence of the Condor Legion until 1939.

That the beginning of this more aggressive phase of Nazi foreign policy in its
buildup to a major war of expansion was accompanied by a more aggressive
propaganda campaign is no coincidence. Very early on, leading Nazis and
military figures in Germany, calling on their experiences during World War I,
had recognized the importance of propaganda, which for the Nazis was by no
means a pejorative term.[4] It was widely held that a modern war would be a "total
war," and that in such a war the psychological attitude of the masses would be a
decisive factor. In explaining the function of the Propaganda Ministry, Joseph
Goebbels stated in 1933:

The Ministry has the task of performing a psychological mobilisation [*geistige Mobilmachung*] in Germany. It is thus in the area of the psyche the same as the War Ministry in the field of military protection. Consequently this Ministry also will demand money, and will receive money, because everyone in the government now realises that the psychological mobilisation is just as important as, perhaps even more important than, the material preparation of the people for war. 5

To prepare for war meant not only to prepare militarily and economically, but also to devote maximum attention to propaganda and psychological preparation. Whereas until 1936 Hitler had been portrayed and indeed had portrayed himself as a prophet of peace, Nazi propaganda, in tune with Nazi foreign policy, assumed much more belligerent overtones at this time.6

This aggressive phase of Nazi propaganda, reaching a climax in 1936 and 1937, was directed primarily towards communism and, more specifically, towards the Soviet Union. In this context, it was the war in Spain which "provided Hitler with the peg for the anti-Communist campaign."7 The fact that the German population could learn next to nothing of the activities of the Condor Legion did not mean that it did not know that a war was raging in Spain. On the contrary, the Spanish Civil War was continually offered as concrete evidence of the bellicose intentions of the Soviet Union. Germans were informed that a battle between the forces of good and evil was being waged in Spain; Franco and his supporters, allegedly embarking on a crusade to save Western civilisation, were depicted as the forces of good, who had taken up arms in order to destroy the evil forces of bolshevism and Judaism. It was implied that Franco was the head of the legal Spanish government, which, with the support of the Spanish people, had confronted the communist invaders. The words "rebels" and even "fascists" were avoided in German publications describing the outbreak of war; instead, the term "nationalists" was preferred. 8

Typical of a spate of publications in this vein, and indeed an excellent example of some of the linguistic strategies of Nazi propaganda, is Joseph Goebbels's booklet *Die Wahrheit über Spanien* (The Truth About Spain).9 The propaganda minister held a speech on this topic at the Reichsparteitag in Nuremberg in 1937, which in the same year appeared in extended form in a thirty-six-page publication with the aim of reinforcing the impact of the original speech. The very title indicates that here, as indeed in much of the Nazi literature of the war, the claim to objectivity is emphasised. This claim is underlined in the course of the work by extensive quotations from the Western democratic press, from such newspapers as the *New York American, Daily Mail, Manchester Guardian*, *Echo de Paris* and *Jour*, but also from the Soviet papers *Pravda* and *Izvestia*. Characteristic also is Goebbels's emphasis on the international implications of the war. In Spain, he argues, the choice had to be made between "bolshevism, that is, destruction and anarchy on one side, and authority, that is, order and construction on the other."10 This simplistic, black-and-white dualism permeates the entire work, whereby for the greater part the accent is on the "evil" forces of bolshevism and Judaism. Goebbels strictly refuses to distinguish between the two, repeatedly mentioning them in combination in order to construct a unified image of the enemy: "For the international nature of bolshevism is after all mainly determined by judaism. Indeed, the Jew operates in bolshevism as the incarnation of all evil."[11] At a later point he argues that "Judaism wants this battle, it is preparing it with all means, it requires it for the introduction of bolshevist world domination."[12] In these and countless other examples of such caustic diatribe, the two main themes of Nazi propaganda, anti-bolshevism and anti-Semitism, are reduced illogically to a common denominator, namely their assumed threat to the German people. For Goebbels the Jew is "the enemy of the world, the destroyer of cultures, the parasite amongst the peoples, the son of chaos, the incarnation of evil, the ferment of decomposition, the plastic demon of the decay of mankind."[13]

Superficially, at least, there is a claim to objectivity, but closer inspection reveals that the appeal is to the emotions, in particular to the negative emotions of fear and hatred, rather than to reason. No attempt is made to differentiate between the complex and in reality disjointed combination of forces opposing Franco, as the enemy is converted into an ideological abstract, losing its human dimensions altogether in the process. By providing examples of the alleged amorality of the enemy, its disrespect for women, children, family and church, Goebbels attempts to arouse an intense hatred and fear of this abstracted enemy which, he contends, was poised to launch an attack on the entire civilised world. Although the present confrontation with these satanic forces may be taking place on the distant battlefields of Spain, Goebbels warns that the Jewish-bolshevist-inspired threat of anarchy, atheism, barbarism and terror was acute for Germany and the rest of the so-called *Kulturvölker*.

An interesting linguistic feature of Goebbels's speech is the use of terms and metaphors drawn from the areas of biology and medicine. This practice was not entirely unknown in Germany before 1933, but as the linguist Siegfried Bork points out, "the 'total' penetration of common language with biological conceptions may certainly be viewed as an 'achievement' of national socialism."[14] It was an attempt to legitimate Nazi doctrine by providing it with a pseudo-scientific basis, although in most cases, as indeed in the work under consideration here, the terminology was employed in an almost exclusively pejorative manner. Goebbels for example warns of the "ever-spreading bolshevist infection in Europe" and the "dangerous infection" threatening the world.[15] The apparent unity of bolshevism and western liberal intellectualism is described as "a psychological illness."[16] "It has already driven on its herd of contagion so far that even humans are infected by it."[17] Goebbels labels bolshevism a "deadly illness" and a "creeping plague."[18]

This tirade against "Jewish-bolshevism" is accompanied by national socialist self-praise and by a fine example of the promotion of the Führer-cult. In contrast to the contemptibly naive Western democracies, claims Goebbels, Germany was at least willing to perceive and confront the bolshevist danger. The Nazis were "the most conscious and most uncompromising champions of the anti-bolshevist world front."[19] A second favoured source of Nazi terminology was religion,[20] and this is exploited fully as Hitler is promoted to the status of an idolized hero of world history: "The Führer is arisen to us as saviour. If history is still being written in 500 years then his name will shine amongst the great names of the occident. For he has saved Europe for us from the red flood, at a time of the most frightful paralysis."[21] In Germany the battle against the global enemy had already been won, but the final victory had not yet been attained. "We thank the Führer that he has appointed us to join in this great fight and in doing so gave our life its actual meaning and purpose. He has taught us to recognise the bitter necessity of this historical conflict, and beyond that to carry it through properly and end it victoriously."[22]

On the final page of this call to battle the words *Kampf* (battle, struggle) or *kämpfen* (to battle, to struggle) appear five times. *Kampf*, deriving much of its expressive weight from the social-Darwinist theory of *Kampf ums Dasein* (struggle for existence), to which the Nazis subscribed enthusiastically, was a key word in Nazi doctrine. It is used here by Goebbels to prepare the German people psychologically for the coming, inevitable confrontation with the enemy. The reader is asked to prepare for battle and to be unquestioningly obedient to the Führer, a veritable demigod. Noteworthy is the strict avoidance of the term *Krieg* (war), a word with a much more precise semantic value than *Kampf*, and one which would have had unpleasant connotations for many Germans.

The emphasis on the existence of an immediate danger and of the evil, amoral nature of the communist arch-enemy are the main features of the polemical propaganda writings of the pre-1939 period, and were also important elements in the eye-witness accounts published at this time.[23] Members of the Condor Legion were not yet permitted to report on their experiences in Spain, but others, including some non-German writers, providing they toed the line ideologically and did not mention the Condor Legion, were permitted to publish accounts of their experiences in the form of reportage or diaries. The former consul Felix Schlayer, for example, wrote a book entitled *Diplomat im roten Madrid* (Diplomat in Red Madrid), which deals primarily with republican atrocities in Spain's capital. The well-known war novelist Edwin Erich Dwinger travelled to Spain in September 1936, and in his book *Spanische Silhouetten. Tagebuch einer Frontreise* (Spanish Silhouettes. Diary of a Journey to the Front), published in the following year, he describes his altogether favourable impressions of nationalist Spain. But he too does not neglect to criticise *die Roten* (the Reds, as republican forces are usually labelled in Nazi texts), with whom he himself had no direct contact. Relying on hearsay evidence and probably also on his own imagination, Dwinger depicts a ruthless, fanatical enemy, thus complementing Goebbels's portrayal. Similarly, in the few fictional works of this pre-1939 period,[24] as well as in supposedly factual accounts written by those who observed events in Spain from a safe distance,[25] the image of the satanic bolshevist fiend propagated by the explicit propaganda works is given further reinforcement.

## SECOND PHASE PROPAGANDA

Nazi propaganda underwent a marked change of emphasis, beginning in about October-November 1938. Instead of concentrating solely upon the evils of bolshevism, the propaganda effort was directed more towards the creation of greater confidence amongst the German population in Germany's economy and, more especially, Germany's armed forces. The reasons for this change in emphasis are to be found in the apparent failure of propaganda during the Czechoslovakian crisis. The German population's sentiments against Czechoslovakia were not raised to the point of readiness to go to war. The destruction of the Czechoslovakian state had been presented to the Germans as the only means to solve the Sudetenland problem, but the lack of popular enthusiasm for a military solution persuaded Hitler to resort to diplomatic means. "The perception that the demonisation of the enemy alone could not provoke a war mood led . . . to a change of the conception of psychological mobilisation, which now comprised, apart from engendering hatred of the perceived object of aggression and its allies, the strengthening of the confidence of the German population in its own capabilities and its own military might."[26] The German population's fear of war which surfaced during the propaganda preparation for a confrontation with Czechoslovakia was then itself exploited by Nazi propagandists. Fear was interpreted in such a way as to functionalise it: rather than being seen as a liability, it was presented by the Nazis as a determination to go to war. Germans were instructed that if they wished to preserve peace and to avoid war, they would at least have to be prepared for the latter.

This change of strategy helps to explain how the content of Nazi literature changed as from the latter part of 1938. It must also be taken into account that 1939 was the year of the Hitler-Stalin Pact, and although this pact was not finally signed until August, the German people had to be prepared for it psychologically months in advance. Propaganda directed explicitly at the Soviet Union, as was to be found in Goebbels's 1937 address and in countless other propaganda works of that vintage, was no longer permitted. One could condemn bolshevism in general, but in doing so had to avoid specific reference to the Soviet state.

The Condor Legion arrived back in Germany on 31 May 1939, at a time when propaganda attacks on the Soviet Union had ceased and when the main aim of propaganda was to convince the German people of Germany's economic and military preparedness for war. These things considered, the return of the Condor Legion could hardly have been better timed. The Spanish Civil War, which until then had served primarily as a vehicle of anti-communist, anti-Soviet propaganda, took on new roles. The official admission of German military participation in Spain took place on 19 May 1939, the day of the nationalist victory parade in Madrid, and on 30 May, the day before the Condor Legion's arrival in Germany, the name "Condor Legion" was sanctioned for use in all media.[27] The spectacular parades conducted in Hamburg on 31 May and in Berlin on 6 June to welcome members of the Condor Legion were an integral part of a massive propaganda effort, as were films, books, radio broadcasts and press reports.

The period immediately following the return of the Condor Legion until the outbreak of World War II represents the climax of the production of Nazi literature on the Spanish Civil War. As if to make up for almost three years of enforced silence, a mass of literature appeared which sought to publicise the role of the Condor Legion in Spain and to glorify the Legion as the epitome of German military virtue. This literature can broadly be divided into two categories: firstly the works written by members of the Condor Legion, and secondly works by nonparticipants, who nonetheless place the German war effort in the centre of attention, praising the German war effort endlessly with the aim of boosting German confidence in a war machine which was by now prepared for a much larger test.

Hannes Trautloft's book *Als Jagdflieger in Spanien. Aus dem Tagebuch eines deutschen Legionär* (As a Fighter Pilot in Spain: From the Diary of a German Legionnaire) is in many ways representative of the first category. With good reason, the fame or notoriety of the Condor Legion rests mainly on the achievements of its pilots, and many of the works in this category were written by pilots. It should also be pointed out though that there are also works by a communications officer, two gunners and even a parson,[28] as well as shorter reports by representatives of all branches of the armed forces,[29] reminding the readers that the Condor Legion was not just an air force. But firsthand accounts by pilots such as Trautloft seem to have made a particularly strong impact on the German reading public. These works fulfilled the function of a sort of advertisement for the profession of pilot, which may help to explain the fact that after the outbreak of World War II the Luftwaffe remained the only section of the German armed forces which could draw solely on volunteers.[30] This function is explicitly referred to in Horst Udet's foreword to Trautloft's book. There it is stated that the young should witness the life of a pilot, "then Germany's rising generation of pilots will be well provided for."[31]

Trautloft's book reveals that the author was among the first pilots sent to Spain. Written in the form of a diary, the first entry is dated 28 July 1936 and deals with Trautloft's enthusiastic reception of the news that he would soon be at war in Spain; the last is dated 3 March 1937 and describes the return to Germany. It is characteristic of the works by members of the Condor Legion that they deal with a chronologically and geographically confined section of the war, since they are based closely on personal experiences.

An outstanding feature of the content of this work is the impetuosity with which the narrator confronts the war. In the section describing the departure from Germany, Trautloft expresses the wish "to steam away from Hamburg as quickly as possible so that we would not possibly arrive too late."[32] Similarly, in Spain he expresses annoyance whenever unfavourable weather prohibits action, or when the "reds" fail to appear, because, as he writes, "just to live in readiness for take off, that is too monotonous in the long run. We want to fly, to fight, that is why we came here."[33] Even the order to return to Germany is greeted with a certain amount of bitterness. "'The farewell to war is so difficult for you,' I grumble to myself. How strange! I am supposed to fly homewards, as if the war here would not go on, as if it had ended. The soldier in me rebels, a bitter feeling rises up."[34]

Trautloft treats the war as a sort of adventure. He feels most comfortable when seated in his aeroplane, almost hermetically sealed off from the rest of the world and from the brutality of the war being waged below him, in a realm where questions of morality are never raised. Dieter Kühn has made a study of the mentality of fighter and bomber pilots as expressed in literature. Although not dealing specifically with the literature of the Spanish Civil War, Kühn reaches the conclusion that flying acts as a sort of drug. The pilot forgets his own problems and comes to terms with himself when flying, but in the process he also forgets the conditions under which the civilian population has to suffer during and after the war.[35] Trautloft's book firmly supports Kühn's thesis, as indeed does much of the literature produced by Condor Legion pilots. Trautloft, for example, describes one bombing mission in the following manner: "Undisturbed we reach Madrid. In series the bombs whiz downwards, and this time their effect is tremendous. There where the positions of the reds are situated I see entire blocks of houses collapsing. They say that everything which moves there and was not killed must have fled in a terrified panic."[36] (So much for the claim that civilian targets were never attacked!) Another pilot writes: "Strange, how little one notices of the bloody battles which right at this time are raging down there: we know how fierce the fighting is, but we do not see it and it is as if we are cut off from all earthly happenings in our lonely heights."[37] Max Graf Hoyos even takes great delight in observing from a safe distance the destruction he has caused: "Meanwhile it must have sparked brilliantly at our target too. These 23 bombs have staged a fireworks display as not even an expert could have managed. Fiery fountains climb upwards in ever-changing variations. I would have liked to hear it explode, but against the roar of the motors I was denied this pleasure."[38]

The élitism of the pilots comes across very strongly in the Nazi literature, providing a detached, bird's-eye perspective of the war (as opposed to the *Froschperspektive* in much of the literature by nonpilots), in which sympathy with the fate of the enemy is lacking. It must be remembered that the Spanish Civil War was a different sort of war from World War I. The development of military technology, in particular the increasingly important role accorded the air force, meant that to a far greater extent than in the Great War it was possible to inflict enormous suffering on the enemy and on the civilian population without having to experience it. The brutal bombing of Guernica is an excellent illustration of the point. Pilots like Trautloft remained isolated from the death and destruction they caused; their literature never deals with the misery of war.

This notable lack of sympathy is at least partially attributable also to ideological factors. Trautloft's book may not address ideological issues as explicitly as Goebbels's speech does, but the political opinions expressed are ideologically "correct." In the Nazi literature there is a great depth of ideologically and racially motivated contempt for the enemy. Such a degree of contempt is not to be found in the literature of World War I, but it *is* to be found frequently in the works of pro-republican authors, many of whom denounced the evils of fascism and its supporters. There is, however, a key difference in the content of the literature of the two sides. The pro-republican authors, as will be shown later, treat the war with great seriousness: they recognise it as a necessary evil, as the last available means to confront and conquer the ideological foe. Nazi literature, in contrast, assumes the quality of a celebration of war. Trautloft and his comrades welcome the war as an experience in which atavistic desires can be satisfied. Trautloft writes: "We are allowed to fight, and that is enough, that satisfies us entirely. Here, it seems, primeval instincts have broken through which were blocked up for a long time, the instincts of the hunter. We have found our way back to the beginnings of manliness, a promise that the time of our white race is by no means over yet. How philistine is the hue and cry that we have fallen back into barbarism."[39] The explicit racism cannot be overlooked, though it appears ironic when it is considered that these Germans fought on the same side as Franco's Moroccan Army.

References to other nationalist forces are rare in Trautloft's book, as indeed in most of the Nazi literature. The sense of international solidarity, a prevalent feature of the pro-republican literature of the war, is absent here. The members of the Condor Legion generally preferred to remain amongst themselves; its leaders had serious doubts about the military ability of the Spaniards and the Italians. Nevertheless, and for obvious propaganda purposes, the literature praises the performance and achievements of all the nationalist forces, and the Condor Legion's relationship with its allies is depicted as being entirely harmonious.

The third and final work to be considered here is an example of the group of works released soon after the return of the Condor Legion but written by nonparticipants, namely Werner Beumelburg's *Kampf um Spanien. Die Geschichte der Legion Condor* (Battle for Spain: The History of the Condor Legion). Primarily owing to the success of his trilogy set in World War I, Beumelburg had achieved considerable popular success even before Hitler came to power.[40] In 1933 Beumelburg was appointed general secretary of the *Deutsche Akademie der Dichtung* (German Literature Academy) and thereafter continued to produce popular historical novels. Aware of Beumelburg's ideological reliability, Göring's Air Ministry sent him as an observer to Spain in August 1937 and again in November 1938 to prepare a book on the role of the Condor Legion. The title page of the book bears the words, "Prepared by order of the Reich Air Ministry." Such patronage is symptomatic of the extraordinarily close relationship between politics and literature in the Third Reich. Furthermore, it is apparent that military documents relating to the Condor Legion were made available to the author, which led to the production of a quasi-official record of German involvement in Spain with, as the statistics show, considerable appeal for the German public.[41] Beumelburg also provided the script for the propaganda film *Im Kampf gegen den Weltfeind* (In Battle Against the Global Enemy), which premiered in German cinemas on 15 June 1939, two weeks after the Condor Legion's return.[42]

In contrast to Trautloft, who employs the diary form to guarantee authenticity, Beumelburg does not write in the first person of his own experiences in Spain. Rather, he attempts to create the impression of rigorous objectivity, labelling his work as "History" and preferring to employ the past tense, with the exception of a few sections where, presumably to increase suspense, the present tense is used. Beumelburg makes it clear in his foreword that his aim was not to produce a comprehensive political or military history of the war. On the contrary, his book "confines itself consciously to the portrayal of the activity of our volunteers."[43] The use of the words "our volunteers" immediately reveals that the claim to objectivity rests on shaky foundations. "Political necessities," Beumelburg argues, had made it essential to keep secret the role of German forces until the day of victory.[44] The main point that needed to be stressed was "that German soldiers, no matter where their orders took them, in their achievements and in their conduct were the equal of all those whose names and deeds fill the over-flowing book of German war history."[45] In short, Beumelburg's intention is to raise the reader's confidence in Germany's armed forces and to glorify a military tradition which had been extended by participation in the Spanish conflict. That Germany could look back on such a long and rich history of war is regarded positively.

"The fallen of the Condor Legion belong with the fallen of the World War and with all those who died for the new Germany."[46] With this statement Beumelburg establishes a link not only with the Great War, but also with the political struggle at the time of the Weimar Republic, which for him acquires the quality of a war, in which one must be prepared to "fall." The activity of the Condor Legion is, however, regarded not only as the extension of a tradition but also as a vital impulse to the formation of a new Europe, in particular to the founding of a *Großdeutsches Reich* (Greater German Empire). "In the years in which they doggedly and courageously fulfilled their duty, far from their homeland and under unfamiliar conditions, against a fanatically fighting enemy from almost all countries of the world, the Greater German Empire came into being in central Europe. Every sacrifice in blood which they made down there counted, in a higher sense, towards this goal."[47] As does Goebbels, Beumelburg wishes to lay great emphasis on the international ramifications of the war, in particular on the implications for a threatened but powerful Germany, a Germany which was ready to respond.

In a work of over 300 pages, Beumelburg delivers a detailed account of Germany's military involvement in Spain. Unlike the accounts written by Condor Legion members, he covers the entire length of the war and does not confine his attention to any particular region. He provides information on the political background to the war, accentuating the chaos resulting from the election of a Popular Front government in February 1936. But the main interest is devoted to developments on the field of battle. Beumelburg delivers what is almost a day-by-day account of German military activity in Spain, from the beginning to the very end of hostilities. As far as purely military matters relating to the Condor Legion are concerned, his report not only feigns but also genuinely achieves a degree of objectivity, a feature which is commonly lacking in other Nazi works. For example, the superiority of French and Soviet fighter aircraft in the early part of the war is admitted, and it is conceded that the town of Guernica had indeed been bombed, a fact which the participants in the Guernica-debate would have been well advised to note. Beumelburg does, however, claim that the bulk of the damage was caused by the "reds."[48]

Despite this objectivity, the enthusiasm for war so evident in the works by Condor Legion members such as Trautloft comes across strongly in Beumelburg's book. Describing the reaction of German pilots to the news that they would be allowed to engage in hostilities, he writes: "Never has a command been greeted more joyfully."[49] The Germans "fought on with cheerful valour and recorded achievements which were worthy of their comrades from the World War."[50] Once again the opportunity to refer to Germany's military tradition is exploited.

Placing so much attention on the Condor Legion leaves other aspects of the war untouched. In line with the propaganda guidelines of the time, the criticism of the Soviet Union is suppressed, and even the opponent's alleged atrocities are largely neglected; in fact, the enemy is ignored almost entirely. In lavishly praising the work of the Germans, the treatment of the activities of other military forces, whether nationalist or republican, becomes superfluous for Beumelburg, as does the suffering of the civilian population. The human dimension of the war becomes hopelessly (and deliberately) lost in the detailed consideration of tactics, weaponry, battles and fronts, and of course the glorious deeds of the Condor Legion. This glorification reaches its climax during the description of German participation in the victory parade in Madrid immediately after the war: "Over years they had done their duty, true to their own resolve, obedient to their command, brave and modest like their fathers and brothers, silent and tough in the quiet consciousness that one day history would record their deeds."[51] This praise applied also to those who did not survive the war. The whole of Germany had taken them "in her arms and ranged them among the endless masses of those who have fallen for Germany in the thousands of years of her glorious history."[52]

## TRADITION AND CONTINUITY IN NAZI PROPAGANDA

It is helpful to place the Nazi literature of the Spanish Civil War in the tradition of German war literature in order to appreciate its propaganda function. The last years of the Weimar Republic witnessed the production of a plethora of novels on World War I, and although Erich Maria Remarque's *Im Westen nichts Neues* (*All Quiet on the Western Front*) was and remains the most popular example of this genre, works by anti-pacifist, anti-democratic writers like Werner Beumelburg and Edwin Erich Dwinger were more numerous and ultimately more influential. There is little doubt that "the most powerful myths of the war came from the Right not from the Left."[53] The nature of the impact of these anti-democratic war novels must be understood in the context of the political crisis prior to Hitler's coming to power. As we have seen in the case of Beumelburg, this crisis was viewed by extremist authors as a kind of war, which had to be won in order to save the nation. The stab-in-the-back legend, that is, the myth that German forces had not faced defeat on the field of battle but were effectively sabotaged by the government and the civilian population, was propagated by them with the aim of shaking the foundations of Weimar democracy. The Great War is depicted in an idealising, romanticising light; soldierly virtues such as comradeship and obedience are expounded and the capacity of the German people for individual and collective heroism affirmed. Moreover, these rightist war novels portray forms of social and political existence which served as models for certain principles of authoritarian ideology.[54] For example, the *Kampfgemeinschaft* (fighting community) depicted in them is no more than a miniature version of the Nazi *Volksgemeinschaft* (community of the Volk). The relationship of strict, unquestioning subservience between soldier and superior is identical with that between Volk and Führer. The political function of the rightist war literature is clear: in preparation for what was considered as a war on the domestic front, the reader is inculcated with the military virtues of a glorified German soldier from the Great War and is familiarised with principles of Nazi doctrine presented in fictional form. The domestic political crisis was to be solved through a heroic battle.

The Nazi literature of the Spanish Civil War fulfills a very similar function, but in a different context. Its aim is also the psychological preparation of the German population for war, this time not on the domestic front, where the war had already been won, but on a foreign front, where the final confrontation with the arch-enemy was yet to commence. It is *war* literature, and at the same time it is *prewar* literature, that is, literature which prepares the reader for a war Hitler was soon to set in motion. An enemy is identified, albeit in the broadest, vaguest terms, and an intense, ideologically based hatred of this enemy is provoked. At the same time, Germany's military tradition is recalled and brought into connection with the Condor Legion. It is demonstrated how the enemy is to be confronted and obliterated, namely with the assistance of Germany's technologically superior weaponry, and through the adoption of military qualities such as discipline, obedience and comradeship as practiced individually and collectively by the members of the Condor Legion. In the Third Reich these values did not apply only to the military but also to the civilian population as a whole. Just as the *Kampfgemeinschaft* of the anti-democratic war novels had been converted into the Nazi*Volksgemeinschaft*, so this*Volksgemeinschaft* was now to be reconverted into a massive *Kampfgemeinschaft*, entailing the total mobilisation of the German people. [55] Readers were to be instilled with the qualities of the soldier in order to make them more effective, functioning cogs in the machinery of Nazi society, especially in the case of the hostile application of that machinery.

The Nazi literature of the Spanish Civil War is a combination of agitation and integration propaganda. [56] It is agitation propaganda because it points to an enemy and creates the impression that this enemy posed an immediate threat to Germany. It persuades the reader that every government decision, whether related to domestic or foreign policy, was a necessity in resisting the supposed threat. It appeals above all to that most basic of sentiments, hatred, in order to mobilise the German people in an attack on the enemy in the guise of an act of self-defence. At the same time it is propaganda of integration, since it seeks to instill in its readers important principles of Nazi ideology. [57] In the description and indeed glorification of the wartime activity of German armed forces, even if this was in distant Spain, behavioural models were established which were to apply to the entire German population. Discipline, an unquestioning obedience to the Führer and a sense of solidarity and duty in the face of a common enemy were the key qualities which were to ensure the required functionality and uniformity of society. If this Nazi *Volksgemeinschaft* were to transform itself into an efficient and victorious *Kampfgemeinschaft*, as Hitler had clearly planned, no claim to individual identity could be tolerated. The model citizen of the Third Reich had to be in every respect unswervingly loyal to the Führer and to the collective interests of the German Volk as determined by the Führer.

With the application of this combination of agitation and integration propaganda in the late 1930s, of which the literature of the Spanish Civil War was just one component, Hitler made his final preparations for a war on a much larger scale, one which was to be sparked off by him just a few months after the end of the Spanish conflict, confident that the work of his propagandists had ensured him of the support of the masses. Whether that confidence was fully justified is a moot point. On 3 September 1939, just after the outbreak of World War II, the American journalist William Shirer, staying in Berlin, noted in his diary: "In 1914, I believe, the excitement in Berlin on the first day of the World War was tremendous. Today, no excitement, no hurrahs, no throwing of flowers, no war fever, no war hysteria."[58]

## NOTES

1. Some academic interest in the subject has been shown by historians, who have consulted some of the Nazi works as an important but frequently unreliable primary source. Herbert Southworth, in *Le mythe de la croisade de Franco* Paris: Ruedo ibérico, 1964 (originally in Spanish as *El mito de la cruzada de Franco*. Paris: Ruedo ibérico, 1963), has a short section on Nazi writers (pp. 41-42). For more recent literary scholarship in this area see Peter Monteath. "Die Legion Condor im Spiegel der Literatur." *LiLi. Zeitschrift für Literaturwissenschaft und Linguistik* 15, 60 (1985): pp. 94-111; Peter Moneath and Elke Nicolai. *Zur Spanienkriegsliteratur. Die Literatur des Dritten Reiches zum Spanischen Bürgerkrieg. Mit einer Bibliographie zur internationalen Spanienkriegsliteratur.* Frankfurt a.M., Berne, New York: Peter Lang, 1986; Günther Schmigalle. "Deutsche schreiben für Hitler und Franco. Vierzig bio-bibliographische Porträts." In *Der Spanische Bürgerkrieg. Literatur und Geschichte.* Ed. Günther Schmigalle, 197-243. Frankfurt a.M.: Vervuert, 1986; Christoph Eykman. "The Spanish Civil War in German Publications during the Nazi Years." In *German and International Perspectives on the Spanish Civil War: The Aesthetics of Partisanship.* Ed. Luis Costa, Richard Critchfield, Richard Golsan and Wulf Koepke, 166-78. Columbia SC: Camden House, 1992. The only cases to my knowledge of the re-publication of Nazi literature on the Spanish war are Fritz von Forell's biography *Mölders. Mensch und Flieger. Ein Lebensbild.* Salzburg: Sirius-Verlag, 1951, which contains two chapters on Mölders's participation in Spain, and which was originally published under the title *Mölders und seine Männer. Ein Erlebnisbericht.* Graz: Steirische Verlagsanstalt, 1941; there are extracts from Nazi works in the excellent anthology edited by Hans-Christian Kirsch. *Der Spanische Bürgerkrieg in Augenzeugenberichten.* Düsseldorf: Karl Rauch, 1967. This is not to suggest that Nazi authors were unable to publish after 1945. On the contrary, Werner Beumelburg and Hannes Trautloft, to name just two examples, were able to publish a number of works in the Federal Republic of Germany.

2. The one definite exception is Stefan Andres's novelle *Wir sind Utopia*, first published in Frankfurt in 1942. Its apolitical nature clearly sets it apart from the Nazi literature and perhaps accounts for its popularity in Germany in the 1950s. Andres is sometimes regarded as an exiled author, as he was living in Italy at the time of publication.

3. Adolf Galland. *Die Ersten und die Letzten.* 9th. ed. Munich: Heyne, 1979 (1953). pp. 27-28.

4. Hitler himself is the best example. In the sixth chapter of the first volume of *Mein Kampf* he discusses war propaganda extensively, praising in particular the British propaganda effort in World War I. He is highly critical of the German failure to employ propaganda effectively. Low civilian morale, which Hitler considered partly responsible for the German defeat, is attributed to the absence of a skillful propaganda campaign. Adolf Hitler. Transl. Ralph Manheim. *Mein Kampf.* London: Hutchinson, 1969 (1926). pp. 161-9.

5. Joseph Goebbels. "Die zukünftige Arbeit und Gestaltung des deutschen Rundfunks. Rede vom 23.3.1933." Reproduced in *Goebbels-Reden. Band I.* Ed. H. Heiber, 82-107. Düsseldorf: Droste, 1971. p. 90.

6. On Hitler as peace prophet see Jutta Sywottek. *Mobilmachung für den totalen Krieg. Die propagandistische Vorbereitung der deutschen Bevölkerung auf den Zweiten Weltkrieg.* Opladen: Westdeutscher Verlag, 1976. pp. 49-53.

7. Z. A. B. Zeman. *Nazi Propaganda.* London, New York: Oxford University Press, 1964. p. 93.

8. See Heinz Odermann. "Die vertraulichen Presseanweisungen aus den Konferenzen des Nazi-Propagandaministeriums." *Zeitschrift für Geschichtswissenschaft* 13, 8 (1965): p. 1371.

9. Joseph Goebbels. *Die Wahrheit über Spanien. Rede auf dem Reichsparteitag in Nürnberg 1937.* Berlin: Müller, 1937.

10. *Ibid.* p. 3.

11. *Ibid.* p. 11.

12. *Ibid.* p. 34.

13. *Ibid.* p. 34.

14. Siegfried Bork. *Mißbrauch der Sprache. Tendenzen nationalsozialistischer Sprachregelung.* Berne, Munich: Francke, 1970. p. 71.

15. Goebbels. *op. cit.* pp. 4, 5.

16. *Ibid.* p. 11.

17. *Ibid.* p. 11.

18. *Ibid.* pp. 32-3.

19. *Ibid.* p. 4.

20. See again Bork. *op. cit.* pp. 72-86.

21. Goebbels. *op. cit.* p. 35.

22. *Ibid.* p. 36.

23. For examples of these polemics see *Das Rotbuch über Spanien. Bilder, Dokumente, Zeugenaussagen.* Edited by the Anti-Komintern. Berlin, Leipzig: Nibelungen-Verlag, 1936; Heinrich Baldauf. *Christen im spanischen Sturm. Tatsachenberichte zur Verfolgung der Kirche in Spanien.* Saarbrücken: Saarbrücker Druckerei und Verlag, 1937; Sebastian Cirac. *Hier spricht Spanien. Wahrheit und Klarheit über das heutige Spanien.* Aschaffenburg: Görres-Verlag, 1937; *Moskau – der Henker Spaniens.* Munich, Berlin: Verlag Frz. Eher Nachf., 1936; Johannes Priese. *Hammer und Sichel über Spanien. In rotspanischen Kerkern. Selbsterlebnisse nach den Aufzeichnungen des vom "roten Volkstribunal" zum Tode verurteilt gewesenen griechisch-orthodoxen Geistlichen Wladimir Vicenik.* Leipzig: Helingsche Verlagsanstalt, 1938; Karl Willnitz (pseudonym of Karl Willy Nietzsche). *Bruderkrieg in Spanien.* n. p.: 1937.

24. Most notably the following three novels: Erich Dietrich. *Kriegsschule Toledo. Des jungen Spaniens Heldenkampf vom Alkazar.* Leipzig: Koehler und Amelang, 1937; Hans Roselieb (pseudonym of Konrad Siebel). *Blutender Sommer. Roman aus dem spanischen*

*Bürgerkrieg*. Stuttgart: Deutsche Verlags-Expedition, 1938; Horst Uden. *Trauermarsch. Roman aus Andalusien*. Berlin: Vier Falken Verlag, 1938.

25. Such as Willibrord Menke (pseudonym of Bernhard Menke). *Das Heldenlied vom Alkazar*. Paderborn: Ferdinand Schöningh; Vienna: Raimund Fürlinger; Zürich: B. Göttschmann, 1937.

26. Sywottek. *op. cit.* p. 165.

27. *Ibid.* pp. 176-77.

28.Hellmut Hermann Führing. *Wir funken für Franco. Einer von der Legion Condor erzählt*. Gütersloh: Verlag C. Bertelsmann, 1939; Klaus Köhler. *Kriegsfreiwilliger 1937. Tagebuch eines Kriegsfreiwilligen der Legion Condor*. Leipzig: "Der nationale Aufbau" Verlag Günther Heinig, 1939; Alfred Lent. *Wir kämpften für Spanien. Erlebnisse eines deutschen Freiwilligen im spanischen Bürgerkrieg*. Oldenburg, Berlin: Gerhard Stalling, 1939; Karl Keding. *Feldgeistlicher bei Legion Condor. Spanisches Kriegstagebuch eines evangelischen Pfarrers*. Berlin: Ostwerk-Verlag, 1939.

29. See the following anthologies: Wulf Bley (ed.). *Das Buch der Spanienflieger. Die Feuertaufe der neuen deutschen Luftwaffe*. Leipzig: Von Hase und Koehler, 1939; Legion Condor (ed.). *Deutsche kämpfen in Spanien*. Berlin: Wilhelm Limpert, 1939; Oberkommando der Wehrmacht (ed.). *Männer der deutschen Legion Condor berichten von ihren Erlebnissen auf dem spanischen Kriegsschauplatz*. Berlin: Verlag "Die Wehrmacht," 1939. The last title is a special issue of *Die Wehrmacht* which was released in an edition of 250,000 on 30 May 1939 to coincide with the return of the Condor Legion.

30. See *Deutsche Luftwacht, Ausgabe Luftwehr* 3 (1939) p. 115. Quoted in E. Nowak. "Die 'Legion-Condor'-Propaganda als Bestandteil der psychologischen Aufrüstung im faschistischen Deutschland." In *Interbrigadisten. Der Kampf deutscher Kommunisten und anderer Antifaschisten im national-revolutionären Krieg des spanischen Volkes 1936-1939*. Ed. Lehrstuhl Geschichte der deutschen Arbeiterbewegung an der Fakultät für Gesellschaftswissenschaften der Militärakademie "Friedrich Engels," 283-89, East Berlin: Deutscher Militärverlag, 1966. p. 287.

31. In Hannes Trautloft. *Als Jagdflieger in Spanien. Aus dem Tagebuch eines deutschen Legionärs*. Berlin: Albert Pauck, 1944 (1940). p. 3.

32. *Ibid.* p. 13.

33. *Ibid.* p. 31.

34. *Ibid.* p. 243.

35. Dieter Kühn. *Luftkampf als Abenteuer. Kampfschrift*. Munich: Hanser, 1975. p. 24.

36. Trautloft. *op. cit.* pp. 139-40.

37. Wulf Bley (ed.). *op. cit.* p. 192.

38. Max Graf Hoyos. *Pedros y Pablos. Fliegen, Erleben, Kämpfen in Spanien*. 3rd. ed. Munich: Verlag F. Bruckmann, 1940 (1939) p. 57.

39. Trautloft. *op. cit.* p. 91.

40. The trilogy comprises *Sperrfeuer um Deutschland*. Oldenburg: Stalling, 1929; *Gruppe Bosemüller*. Oldenburg: Stalling, 1930; and *Deutschland in Ketten*. Oldenburg: Stalling, 1931.

41. By 1942 some 70,000 copies had been sold. See Schmigalle. *op. cit.* p. 207.

42. Note once more the preference for the word *Kampf* over *Krieg* in both film and book titles. Note also that the film title avoids naming the *Weltfeind*, though it is obvious that the Soviet Union and communism are meant.

43. Werner Beumelburg. *Kampf um Spanien. Die Geschichte der Legion Condor*. Oldenburg and Berlin: Gerhard Stalling, 1939. p. 10.

44. *Ibid.* p. 7.

45. *Ibid.* p. 10.

46. *Ibid.* p. 7.

47. *Ibid.* p. 7.

48. *Ibid.* p. 98.

49. *Ibid.* p. 31.

50. *Ibid.* p. 49.

51. *Ibid.* pp. 307-8.

52. *Ibid.* p. 309.

53. Martin Patrick Anthony Travers. *German Novels on the First World War and Their Ideological Implications, 1918-1933*. Stuttgart: Akademischer Verlag, 1982. p. 195.

54. See especially Karl Prümm. "Das Erbe der Front. Der antidemokratische Kriegsroman der Weimarer Republik und seine nationalsozialistische Fortsetzung." In *Die deutsche Literatur im Dritten Reich. Themen –Traditionen – Wirkungen* Ed. Horst Denkler and Karl Prümm, 138-64. Stuttgart: Reclam, 1976.

55. One famous event of the Spanish war, discussed widely in pro-nationalist literature, provided the Nazis with an excellent illustration of the conversion of a *Volksgemeinschaft* into a *Kampfgemeinschaft*, namely the successful defence of the Alcázar of Toledo. The event received widespread treatment in the Nazi literature, despite the noninvolvement of the Condor Legion. See Hellmut Boerner. *Die Kadetten von Toledo* Berlin, Leipzig: Franz Schneider, 1942; Erich Dietrich. *op. cit.*; Willibrord Menke. *op. cit.*; Roland Strunk. *"Alcázar. Die Helden von Toledo. Ein Hörspiel nach Tatsachenberichten."* In *Das Hörspielbuch.* Ed. Horst Kriegler. 13-63 Breslau: Ostdeutsche Verlagsanstalt, 1938; Rudolf Timmermans. *Die Helden des Alcázar. Ein Tatsachenbericht aus Toledo.* Olten, Freiburg i. Br.: Otto Walter, 1937; Peter Ujj. transl. Margarethe von Udvary. *Die Kadetten von Alkazar* Budapest: Danubia Verlag, 1941; There is also an Italian film entitled *L'Assedio dell' Alcazar* (1939) which screened in Germany under the title *Alkazar*.

56. These categories of propaganda were formulated by Jacques Ellul, who argues that

when a government wants to galvanize energies to mobilise the entire nation for war, it will use a propaganda of agitation. At that moment the subversion is aimed at the enemy, whose strength must be destroyed by psychological as well as physical means, and whose force must be overcome by the vigor of one's own nation. . . . In all cases, propaganda of agitation tries to stretch energies to the utmost, obtain substantial sacrifices, and induce the individual to bear heavy ordeals. . . . In order to succeed, it need only be addressed to the most simple and violent sentiments through the most elementary means. Hate is generally its most profitable resource.

"Propaganda of integration" on the other hand aims to make the individual a functional member of society, to make him "share the stereotypes, beliefs, and reactions of the group; he must be an active participant in its economic, ethical, esthetic, and political doings. All his activities are dependent on this collectivity. And, as he is often reminded, he can fulfill himself only through this collectivity, as a member of the group. Propaganda of integration thus aims at making the individual participate in his society in every way." See Jacques Ellul. transl. K. Kellen and J. Lerner. *Propaganda. The Formation of Men's Attitudes.* New York: Vintage, 1973 (1962). pp. 71-75.

57. Ellul agreees that "Hitler used two kinds of propaganda simultaneously." *Ibid.* p. 78. Foulkes similarly contends: "As Germany came closer to war, what in fact developed was a situation in which the Germans were subjected simultaneously to agitation and integration propaganda." A. P. Foulkes. *Literature and Propaganda.* London, New York: Methuen, 1983. p. 12.

58. William Shirer. *Berlin Diary.* London: Sphere, 1970. p. 159.

# 3. Politics and Beyond:
# The Rhetoric of the Right

## THE INTERNATIONAL RIGHT

Nazi literature, as the tightly controlled expression of a state ideology, represents just one section of the international pro-Franco cause. In its entirety, however, the international Right, which is defined here as all those forces both within and outside Spain which expressed support for Franco, was by no means a homogeneous ideological entity. It ranged from a moderate conservatism which tacitly approved the restoration of traditional order in Spain and simultaneously opposed active foreign intervention in the war, through to the radicalism of German and Italian fascism, whose adherents threw their military support behind Franco. The international Right was not united by common ideological goals; rather, it was united by shared antipathies. And in the case of the war in Spain, it saw an opportunity to oppose the greatest of the perceived threats of the day – international communism.

The Spanish Civil War serves to highlight one of the great weaknesses of the Right as a political force in the 1930s, namely its lack of solid intellectual support. Two surveys, one in Britain and the other in the United States, were carried out to gauge the level of intellectual commitment to the opposing sides in the war. In a British survey, published by *Left Review* as a 6d pamphlet entitled *Authors Take Sides on the Spanish War*, only five replies, including those of Evelyn Waugh and Edmund Blunden, were "Against the Government," compared with sixteen neutral and 127 pro-government writers.[1] Had they wished, those who conducted the survey could easily have found more than five pro-franquists; nevertheless it remains true that "not only were right-wing opinions held by comparatively few writers at the time but the rightist fringe was an unpleasantly lunatic one."[2] Many members of that fringe were undoubtedly disappointed that such writers as T. S. Eliot and Ezra Pound were amongst those who declared themselves neutral, but that declared neutrality was in itself symptomatic of a lack of firm and unambiguous political commitment in conservative circles. Certainly the Spanish Civil War did not fire the literary imagination of the British Right as much as it did that of the Left. As for the American survey, the result was even more clear-cut. Only one author (Gertrude Atherton) expressed opposition to the Republic.[3] Naturally the proportion of intellectual support for the respective sides varied considerably from country to country, so that for example nationalist support was appreciably higher in France with its higher percentage of Catholic intellectuals. On an international scale, however, the quantitative superiority of pro-republican publications is a clear indication of how ill-matched the two sides were in terms of intellectual support.

Moreover, with the obvious exceptions of the armies sent by Hitler and Mussolini, the willingness of representatives of the Right to support Franco on the field of battle was much more limited than that of the Left for the Republic. Hugh Thomas mentions that some 600 Irishmen under General Eoin O'Duffy fought for the nationalists; a few right-wing Frenchmen volunteered for the carlist *requetés* and the Spanish Foreign Legion, as did some Latin American and White Russian exiles and others. Only four Americans and some twelve Englishmen fought for Franco.[4] Compared with the level of pro-republican volunteer support, most notably in the International Brigades, the pro-Franco total is truly paltry.

Despite the absence of a large and committed intelligentsia and of a volunteer body to rival the International Brigades, the international Right in all its disparity was by no means a negligible force. After all, it did play its role in ensuring that the Western democracies did not intervene in favour of the Republic. Considering the numerical weakness of its intellectual support, there is no doubt that the Right was disproportionately well represented in the international press, in such organs as the *Morning Post*, the *Daily Mail*, the *Observer*, *L'Action Française*, *Le Temps*, *L'Echo de Paris* and *The New York American*, to name just a few of the most famous.

It is impossible here to detail the complexities of right-wing ideologies in the world of the 1930s. What is important to note here, just as in the specific instance of nationalist Spain, is their very diversity. Predictably, support for Franco came from fascist groups such as Mosley's Black Shirts, General O'Duffy's Blue Shirts, Le Croix du Feu and Action Française, who saw in Franco a sort of Spanish version of Hitler or Mussolini. But it also came from a wide range of less radical sources, from moderately conservative groups who in some cases explicitly denied fascist sympathies. Franco for them was not another fascist dictator; rather, he was viewed as a defender of traditional order and values against the threat of radical change posed by the Left. Evelyn Waugh typified much conservative opinion when he wrote in his response to Nancy Cunard's *Authors Take Sides* survey: "If I were a Spaniard I should be fighting for General Franco. As an Englishmen I am not in the predicament of choosing between two evils. I am not a Fascist nor shall I become one unless it were the only alternative to Marxism. It is mischievous to suggest that such a choice is imminent."[5]

In all the Western democracies a large proportion of pro-franquist opinion came from Catholics like Waugh. In Britain this was true of a number of prominent figures whom Nancy Cunard chose not to survey. It applies, for example, to Douglas Jerrold, who was the chairman of the publishing company Eyre and Spottiswoode. Jerrold was important not just as a publisher and writer, but also as a participant in events leading to the outbreak of war in Spain. It was he who helped to organise the charter of an English aeroplane for Franco's crucial flight from the Canaries to Morocco.[6] In his autobiography, *Georgian Adventure*, which was published during the war, Jerrold devotes most of the final chapter (aptly titled "The Last Crusade") to this episode and to a number of others before and after the beginning of the war. He informs his readers: "The action of the generals who saved Spain, and Europe, in July, 1937, was not of course a military revolt."[7] He then proceeds to explain that the outbreak of war "did in fact coincide with the murder of Calvo Sotelo, which was taken by men of all shades of opinion as the signal, not for an army uprising, but for the long expected Communist revolt."[8] During his travels in Spain in the course of 1937 Jerrold was privileged to meet Franco, whom he describes as "a supremely good man, a hero possibly; possibly a saint."[9] Arnold Lunn, like Jerrold a Catholic who visited Spain during the war, expressed a similar admiration for Franco and a similar concern for the fate of the Church in the event of a communist victory in Spain. In Lunn's opinion, "the question of democracy versus dictatorship did not exist, since the Communists had already destroyed Spanish democracy before the revolt began, and the issue was simply whether Spain was to have a Communist dictatorship that would throttle religion or a dictatorship in which the Church could survive and wield influence."[10] The Catholic journalists William Foss and Cecil Gerahty displayed the same sort of anti-communist mania in expressing their view that in Spain the fate of Christian civilization was at stake. They summarised their interpretation of events there in a manner which is reminiscent of Goebbels: "We have shown that Spain was the victim of a vast Communist plot, inspired and controlled by the continental Freemasons, largely Jewish, and international agitators, working with certain Spaniards as their tools and assistants, to establish a world domination for the Comintern, which at present is identified with Stalin and Russia."[11] The authors maintain that Guernica "was burned by the Reds,"[12] and conclude their account with the nationalist slogan, "Viva España! Viva Franco!"[13] Finally, Hilaire Belloc, who also travelled to Spain and was granted a personal audience with Franco, proved to be one of Franco's staunchest supporters. In an article written in 1938 Belloc proclaimed that the struggle in Spain was "between those who would stamp out the Christian religion . . . and those who are determined to defend it."[14]

On the other side of the Atlantic a similar concern for the fate of the Church was to be found amongst some Catholics, though apparently not amongst all or even most of them. A poll carried out in the United States suggested that only 39 percent of Catholics were for General Franco.[15] Even fewer were willing to write in support of the franquist state, so that the majority of pro-franquist books and articles published by Catholic publishers in the United States were written by foreigners.[16] The American novelist Helen Nicholson happened to be living in Spain at the time of the outbreak of war. In *Death in the Morning*[17] she wrote what Arnold Lunn described as "a beautiful and moving account of life in Granada during the first two months of the war."[18] Her novel *The Painted Bed* also deals with the war.[19] It reaches its climax with the depiction of a republican air raid which "causes destruction and death, but also brings a vision of Christ upon the cross."[20]

In Australia the spokesmen for the Catholic Church were unanimous in their condemnation of the republican government. In Sydney the *Catholic Freeman's Journal* "discerned the hideous hand of Soviet Russia and turned on the prejudiced conservative daily press for allowing even a faint spirit of approval to creep into its garbled reports of communistic and atheistic onslaughts on Christianity in far-off Catholic countries."[21] In July 1936 all but three Australian bishops signed the Spanish bishops' thirty-six-page *Joint Letter to the Bishops of the Whole World*, in which they damned the republican government and justified the war as Christian and just.[22] The Reverend Father Leo Dalton told an audience in Croydon in New South Wales: "I have uncontestable evidence of fiendish and lustful torture inflicted by the communists on nuns, priests and all who tried to bar their way in Spain. . . . Had a vast asylum of sexual maniacs been released upon the people, they could not have conceived things more foul than the Communists have done to Catholics in Spain."[23] A steady flow of pamphlet literature propagated the official Church line on events in Spain. Despite this, a 1937 Pastoral Letter of the archbishops and bishops of Australia and New Zealand expressed concern that "too many Catholics were not sufficiently aware of the savage and relentless onslaught on religion by the Reds in Spain."[24]

In France, where a large proportion of intellectuals and writers were Catholic, support for Franco as a defender of Christianity against heathen communism was widespread. A key literary figure of the French Right was Charles Maurras, a convinced monarchist and leader of the ultra-rightist Action Française. The newspaper of the same name began its propaganda campaign on behalf of the nationalists as early as four days after the *pronunciamiento*.[25] Maurras undertook a quasi-official tour of nationalist Spain in April and May of 1938, during which he met Franco and was treated almost as a head of state.[26] In his propaganda work Maurras was supported in France by such prominent Catholics as Robert Brasillach and Maurice Bardèche, who were also members of Action Française, and who together wrote a pro-nationalist historical account of the war.[27] In collaboration with Henri Massis, who, like Maurras, was to travel to Spain and be granted a personal audience with Franco, Brasillach also wrote a book on that central event in nationalist propaganda, the defence of the Alcázar of Toledo.[28] An almost boundless admiration for Franco and the nationalists was displayed by the Catholic journalist Pierre Héricourt, an editor of *L'Action Française*.[29] This was shared conspicuously by the poet, dramatist and diplomat Paul Claudel, who wrote a famous poem to glorify the Spanish clerics who had been killed in republican Spain.[30]

There were, however, some significant "defections" from the Catholic camp in France. The staunchly Catholic Basques had remained loyal to the Republic, and two widely respected French Catholics, François Mauriac and Jacques Maritain, publicly pronounced their support for the Basques. Forming part of what the French pro-franquist press called the *chrétiens rouges*, their case for sympathy with the Basques was strengthened in April 1937 with the bombing of Guernica. By far the most prominent of the French defectors was Georges

Bernanos. Bernanos had been a member of Action Française, and although he had officially resigned from it in 1919, in the early 1930s he cooperated closely with Maurras's organisation. He spoke at some of its political gatherings and wrote for the newspaper *L'Action Française*. Bernanos was a monarchist, "an embittered enemy of democracy and of the principle of political and social equality."[31] When war broke out in Spain, Bernanos was living in Majorca, where his eldest son, Yves, was a member of the Falange.[32] He at first welcomed Franco's *pronunciamiento* and even the Italian intervention. But the experience of the war on the island persuaded him to revise his political views radically, so that he distanced himself from the Right and condemned its role in the war. This break is recorded in *Les grand cimetières sous la lune* (The Great Cemeteries under the Moon), which deals with the brutal tactics of oppression and terror employed on Majorca in the first ten months of the war.[33] In a preface to the English edition Bernanos, refuting a bitter Catholic response to the original French edition, wrote: "I am in no way out to create a scandal. But when so many Catholics try to excuse, or even justify, one of the most atrocious civil wars that has ever been known, in the name of 'Lesser-Evil' policy, it is not much to ask that a denunciation of cowards and rogues should be treated with the same indulgence."[34]

The disparate fascist, conservative and Catholic elements of the international Right did not and could not promote a specific political program. For that the Right was much too poorly organised and too ideologically incoherent. This problem was compounded by the fact that, in the early stages of the conflict in particular, it was impossible to determine the precise nature of Franco's own program. How seriously, for example, was the almost wholesale adoption of the falangist program in April 1937 to be taken? Precisely with the aim of maximising the breadth of domestic and international support, Franco had wisely opted for a deliberately ambiguous political posture.

Under these circumstances, the primary goal of right-wing propaganda had to be to overlook the absence of a commonly shared ideological line and to concentrate on discrediting the enemy. To do this, a particular element of the Left, international communism, was identified as the most acute threat to "Western civilisation," and accordingly was made responsible for the war in Spain and for all the alleged violence and atrocities associated with it. Support for Franco from the rightist viewpoint was justified purely on the grounds that he had sworn to eradicate communism.

In promoting the positive values of the nationalists, the propagandists were obliged to be careful to avoid political specifics, since to do so would only have highlighted the absence of ideological coherence. Instead, the preferred strategy of the Right was to remove the Spanish controversy from the sphere of politics altogether. It willingly adopted a rhetoric devoid of specific political content, one which appealed to the emotions rather than to reason. Walter Benjamin's observation that fascism leads to an aestheticisation of political life is valid for much pro-franquist literature.[35] The aim was to transform the war through propagandistic means from a contest between rival political ideologies into a contest between moral, metaphysical or even mythical elements, the less tangible the better. Above all, the Right relegated political issues to the background by making it a religious war, in which the Christian "crusaders" and "martyrs" battled the invading infidels. The literature of the Right is overflowing with religious rhetoric, to which is added (with particular prominence in the case of Spanish authors) a similarly recondite concept of the Spanish nation, rooted in a highly idealised perception of Spanish history. Even events and figures from the most recent Spanish history (such as José Antonio Primo de Rivera and the siege of the Alcázar of Toledo) are endowed with a mythical status bearing little resemblance to political or military reality. As Barbara Pérez-Ramos puts it, literature "did not serve fascism in the Spanish Civil War as a coming to terms with reality, but to cover it up with rhetorical and aesthetic elements."[36]

The adoption of this strategy of evading political reality (albeit for distinctly political reasons) is to be observed throughout the international pro-franquist literature. For the purposes of this study, the works of one non-Spanish and one Spanish poet are drawn on to illustrate the literary implications of this strategy. The South African-born poet Roy Campbell was one of Franco's most vocal supporters and, if he were to be believed, one of the few foreign volunteers in the nationalist ranks. His epic poem *Flowering Rifle* is a fine example of rightist rhetoric. The prominent Spanish nationalist poet José María Pemán wrote the *Poema de la Bestia y el Angel*, which has predictably been described by a neo-franquist critic as "the poetic highpoint of the Spanish war."[37]

## ROY CAMPBELL AND *FLOWERING RIFLE*

Roy Campbell, "English verse's most bullying blusterer,"[38] is an extraordinarily elusive character who defies ready classification. Throughout his life he willingly played the role of the rugged individual, the outsider. He was born and bred a white in South Africa, but was of British descent, and received the privilege of a thorough education. He lived for a time in England, where he admittedly experienced the friendship of such prominent figures as the Sitwells, T. S. Eliot, Aldous Huxley and, most decisively, Wyndham Lewis, but where he always remained a literary outsider in the age of Bloomsbury and the Oxford poets. He then lived in the Provence, in Spain and finally in Portugal, still an outsider, but one who was at least spiritually at home in bucolic settings which reminded him of his native Natal.

Roy Campbell moreover is an enormously paradoxical figure. He became a devout Catholic but seemed almost to revel in the spectacle of violence. He praised individualism, yet openly expressed admiration for Hitler and Mussolini in the 1930s and lived out the last years of his life under probably the most oppressive regime in Western Europe. He threw his support behind Franco in the Spanish Civil War but fought against the Axis in World War II. He condemned the republicans and all their supporters in the most vitriolic terms in *Flowering Rifle* but also translated some of the works of the great Spanish poet and dramatist Federico García Lorca, who was killed by the nationalists in the early stages of the war.[39]

Bernard Bergonzi goes at least some way towards unravelling this complex persona by daring a comparison with Ernest Hemingway. Apart from a love of bullfighting, Campbell and Hemingway "shared a great capacity for self-dramatisation, which expressed itself in a love of violent activity and displays of physical prowess; they both appeared before the world as men of action and tried to hide the fact that they were highly cultivated literary artists."[40]

Where the comparison breaks down is, of course, in the area of political commitment, which saw Campbell and Hemingway support opposing sides during the Spanish Civil War. In the 1930s Roy Campbell's political sympathies became so blatantly and radically right-wing as to earn him the label "fascist" from many quarters.[41] More generous critics, though, have tended to give Campbell the benefit of the doubt. His countryman Alan Paton, for example, writes: "Was Campbell a fascist? Of course he was not. I don't think for a moment he understood the true nature of Nazism and Fascism, though I think he should have done. Campbell lived, he did not think."[42]

The truth is that Campbell's mind was illsuited to dealing in political abstractions. He himself confesses in his first autobiography, *Broken Record*: "I have never had many political ideas."[43] Campbell never joined a political party and in his second autobiography, *Light on a Dark Horse*, he furthermore admits that he never voted, except under compulsion.[44] This is not to suggest that the general direction of Campbell's political thinking was at all ambiguous. *Broken Record*, published in 1934, bears testimony to Campbell's admiration for Hitler and Mussolini, his strident anti-Semitism, his preference for the bourgeoisie over the working class, his contempt for such terms as "Humanity," "Liberty" and "Rights," and his preference for a cultured élite over the common person. Campbell abhorred Charlie Chaplin, the representative of the common man, and he declared himself "all on the side of the natural human relationship of slave and master."[45] But these expressions of political allegiance were not so much the result of an intellectual grappling with contemporaneous political trends; rather, they were the result of heart-felt sympathies and, more importantly, antipathies. In *Broken Record* he comments: "My reactions came out of personal contacts, and not group urges."[46] Campbell, as one critic suggests, is one of those writers "whom it seems impossible to discuss on literary grounds without including a great deal about his personality, his philosophy, his politics and other seemingly irrelevant matters."[47] To deal with the politics of Roy Campbell is not to deal with a cogent set of views, but with a highly idiosyncratic set of likes and dislikes.

It so happened that Campbell was living with his family in Toledo when the war in Spain broke out. They had originally moved from Provence to Barcelona in late 1933, from there to Valencia for a short time, and then to Altea, a village near Alicante, with which the Campbells were immediately enchanted. It was here that their conversion to Catholicism took place, and this conversion was without doubt an important factor in confirming the inclination of Campbell's political thinking towards the Right. The anti-clericalism of many sections of the Spanish Left was renowned, so that openly to proclaim allegiance to the Church, as the Campbells did, could (not unjustifiably) be interpreted as a political gesture.

In 1935, shortly after being rebaptised and remarried, the Campbells moved to Toledo. Campbell's response to the city is well summed up in *Light on a Dark Horse*: "Toledo was the whole embodiment of the crusade for Christianity against Communism and I felt it the minute I set foot in the city."[48] (Toledo had been the site of the forced baptism and expulsion of Jews in the Middle Ages.) The Campbells established a close relationship with the Carmelite friars of Toledo, some of whom they were known to shelter during the period of escalating civil violence after the February 1936 elections. In March 1936 Campbell himself was severely beaten and then thrown into prison by two Assault Guards. It was an incident which, according to his biographer Peter Alexander, "merely increased Campbell's religious enthusiasm."[49]

The conversion to Catholicism, albeit a markedly belligerent Catholicism tinged with mithraic and other pagan elements, coupled with the direct experience of anti-clerical violence in Toledo, provide one key motive for Campbell's decision to support Franco when war broke out in July. Another motive, and one whose relative significance is impossible to measure, stems from an enmity which predates Campbell's conversion by several years. Campbell had never been able to find a niche in the mainstream British intellectual community, which was populated largely by sympathisers with the Left and which, rather than disapproving of Campbell's poetry, had tended to adopt the far more infuriating tactic of ignoring it altogether. The publication in 1936 of *Mithraic Emblems*, the volume of poetry which immediately preceded *Flowering Rifle* and for which Campbell held high hopes, went almost unnoticed.[50] It may be argued that Campbell's right-wing convictions, which were expressed most clearly in July 1936 with his decision to support the military rebellion, were founded at least in part on his disdain for the British intellectual Left, which unanimously favoured the Republic. As he had done in 1931 in *The Georgiad*, Campbell's response was to mock those who, so he believed, had conspired to deprive him of his rightful place in British letters.[51] In his decision to offer his services to Franco he was motivated, John Povey suggests, "by an element of sheer defiance; a cussed refusal to be in the same camp with those who had belittled him while he was in London, no matter what the grounds of the quarrel. His choice of the side opposing the London intelligentsia was ardent and automatic."[52]

It was Campbell himself who started the rumour that he fought in Spain, and it is a point which has been raised frequently.[53] Peter Alexander shows convincingly, though, that Campbell did not play a military role. The Campbells fled Spain soon after the outbreak of war and returned to England. With the credentials of a journalist for the Catholic-conservative paper *The Tablet* Campbell returned to Spain in June 1937. In Salamanca he offered (according to his own account) to fight in the ranks of the *requetés* but was instructed by the chief of the Nationalist Press Service that what the Right needed was good propaganda, not good soldiers. His only actual experience of the battlefield of Spain was a tour by car on 1 July 1937.[54]

Campbell's poem *Flowering Rifle*, subtitled *A Poem from the Battlefield of Spain*, was his main contribution to the nationalist campaign. Its 5,000 lines were written in Portugal, the bulk of them within the space of a couple of weeks in March 1938. Having been refused by Faber, it was published by Longman's on 6 February 1939. The impact of the poem was to convince all those who read it "that Campbell was a thorough-going Fascist; it was a slur from which he was never fully to free himself."[55] A toned-down version was released in 1957, but the damage had already been done.[56]

The reception of the poem went predictably along political lines. The reviewer in *The Tablet*, the paper for which Campbell himself had reported, described the poem as "genuine Rabelais," whilst the Catholic historian Arthur Bryant, who wrote a weekly column in the *Illustrated London News*, eulogised: "In the light of this magnificent epic of civil war, criticism is dumb, for poetry such as this has not been written in English since Julian Grenfell fell in battle."[57] More recently the Spanish scholar Esteban Pujals has described *Flowering Rifle* as "the most important poem on the Spanish war" but concedes that it is "not always convincing from a poetic viewpoint."[58] At the other extreme Campbell's traditional foe Stephen Spender labelled the work "an incoherent, biased, unobjective, highly coloured and distorted account of one man's experiences of the Spanish Civil War, seen through the eye of a passionate partisan of Franco."[59] Campbell himself was known publicly to count the work amongst his best, but in a letter dating from shortly before the poem's publication he confided to a friend: "I should have kept it by for revision for a year at least but preferred to strike while the iron's hot."[60]

The poem was conceived and written with the intention of influencing British public opinion in favour of the franquist cause. For Campbell it was perhaps even a sort of literary substitute for active military service. He openly proclaims his pro-nationalist bias in his "Author's Note," which he tellingly ends with the slogan "VIVA FRANCO! VIVA ESPAÑA!"[61] As for the poem itself, the issues to be addressed here concern the nature of the ideas and emotions expressed in it and the choice of a literary form or genre, namely that of satire, through which those ideas and emotions could be conveyed.

Widely acknowledged as being a poet of considerable technical proficiency, Campbell unquestionably possessed a great talent for satire, and one which he had exercised on many occasions before the Spanish Civil War. *Flowering Rifle*, written in the traditional form of heroic couplets, is above all a satirical poem, and even Campbell's bitterest intellectual opponent, Stephen Spender, praises the satirical qualities of such passages as the following:

And, see, the Bullring to its use restored,
Where late the loud, half-hourly "Meeting", roared
For every time the bolsheviks are routed,
Why, sure, a Meeting must be held about it,
Which held, and many resolutions passed,
They seek a bigger meeting than the beating,
And so the endless rigmarole repeating,
From meeting to defeat, defeat to meeting,
From rout to rout so rapidly they switch
That nobody could tell you which was which.[62]

Campbell is at his best as a practitioner of Horatian satire, as in the above example, where the narrator expresses wry amusement at the process of democratic consensus.[63] But in switching on so many occasions to the Juvenalian mode, which demands the expression of contempt and indignation rather than amusement, Campbell reveals the lack of discipline which vitiates his work.[64] Rather than occupying the moral highground, he proves himself a bigot, and rather than ridiculing the targets of his satire, he abuses them in the coarsest terms. Whereas Jonathan Swift wrote of himself, "Yet malice never was his aim; / He lashed the vice, but spared the name," Campbell has no intention of apportioning malice sparingly.[65]

The abusive satire in *Flowering Rifle* has several targets, many of which are only indirectly related to Spain and the Spanish Civil War. Many of them are notably identical with the targets of Nazi vitriol: the poem is explicitly anti-communist, anti-Semitic, anti-Freemason, anti-democratic and, as in the following extract, anti-humanitarian:

The Inquisition in six hundred years
Pumped not a thousandth of the blood and tears
As, in some twenty, has the world-reforming,
Free-thinking, Rational, Cathedral-storming
Humanitarian, with his brother love,
To whom Tsarism was a sucking dove
And Hitler was to this degrading sham,
As to a rabid skunk, a snow-white lamb.[66]

"Humanitarianism," Campbell claims in his "Author's Note," is "a form of moral perversion due to overdomestication, protestantism gone bad, just as are the other perversions with which our intellectuals are riddled."[67]

Campbell's abuse is aimed at specific figures of the Spanish Left (such as Largo Caballero, Prieto and Negrín), at the International Brigades and at those who circulated the "lie" that Guernica had been destroyed by the nationalists.[68] But much applies to an international or even specifically non-Spanish context. It concerns Marx, Lenin, Freud and Léon Blum, but above all it pertains to the British intellectuals with whom Campbell had feuded for years. Campbell at times employs proper names (Auden, Spender, Bates, Huxley, Read) but generally prefers collective terms such as "Bloomsbury," "Charlies" or "Wowsers."[69] He ridicules the supposed softness of their upbringing by contrasting it to the toughness of his own. As is the case with Beumelburg, the struggle, the *Kampf*, possesses for Campbell a superior moral quality:

Since my existence has been lived and fought
As theirs at Oxford ready-made was bought
And in my teens I'd shed like threadbare trousers
Every experience possible to Wowsers;
I know what wrings their withers night and morn
To wish (quite rightly) they had not been born
Since of the English poets on your shelf
The only sort of "Worker" is myself.[70]

The satire on all those elements which Campbell associates with the Spanish Republic is accompanied by a similarly illogical pro-nationalist panegyric, thus creating a distinctly manichaean scheme not unlike that employed by Nazi authors. The second of the poem's six parts, for example, begins with the lines:

A hundred years of strife with warring vans
Had winnowed Spain in two distinctive clans
Upon the left, inflammable, the chaff,
Corn to the right, the vulnerable half,
And thus in Spanish history began
The struggle between the Wowser and the Man – 71

Although in this instance too proper names are provided (Mola, Moscardó, Sanjurjo, José Antonio, Hitler, Mussolini), "the Man" refers to *all* those who backed Franco. Campbell's archetypal franquist is "Armed chiefly with a sense of Bad and Good," and is "In labour proud, in worship most devout."72 Whereas the enemy is defined in racial, social or political terms with blatantly negative connotations, the nationalists are attributed with positive moral and religious qualities.

In *Flowering Rifle* these moral and religious qualities are rewarded with divine favour. According to Campbell's scheme, as in so much of the literature of the Right, the Spanish Civil War is the crucial battle between belief and atheism, and even God and nature have intervened to ensure the victory of "the Heroes, and the Martyrs, and the Saints."73 A recurrent theme of the poem is the harvest, super-abundant in nationalist territory, where there are "A million tons, a sickle for each ton / Of surplus wheat refulgent in the sun,"74 whereas in republican territory nature sabotages the Jewish-bolshevist crop:

But nature's elements, except for gold,
Will shun the Yiddisher's convulsive hold,
And it's an axiom that mere eyesight yields –
Grass hates to grow on communistic fields!
The plains and valleys fought upon our side
And rivers to our victory were allied. 75

Just as nature rebels against the republican war effort, the pious nationalists' prayers for assistance are answered with miracles:

For even their machinery rebelled
And as by miracles, our armouries swelled:
Till we could almost pray for what we wanted
And take the answer to the prayer for granted,
And with our Pater nosters and Hail Marys
Were liming Aeroplanes like tame canaries. 76

Apart from elements of satire and panegyric, *Flowering Rifle* also possesses epic qualities. As an epic it lacks a central figure; instead it elevates a vague conception of a renascent Spanish nation to that role. Campbell explains in his

"Author's Note" that his aim is to provide "an account in terms of everyday life, from my own experiences at the front and in both rearguards, of what must be the most extraordinary awakening of a national consciousness in a ruined and prostrate country that the world has yet seen."[77] The poem's second major shortcoming as an epic is its repetitiveness and disjointedness. The narrative is episodic and is punctuated by lengthy satirical and panegyrical passages, as well as by prolonged descriptive sections.

Predictably, a key episode in Campbell's epic, as in much of the Nazi literature and other literature of the Right, is the siege of the Alcázar of Toledo. The resoluteness of the Alcázar's defenders was for Campbell the quintessence of the spirit of the "New Spain," but the event also acquired a deeply religious significance. Campbell had been living in Toledo at the time of the outbreak of war but was not a witness to the siege by republican forces and the ultimate relief of the defenders by Franco's army. He did, however, return to Toledo during the war to view the half-ruined town and to describe it in the following, intensely religious terms:

Over the blood of martyrs scarcely dry
Toledo, there, against the morning sky
Like some great battle-cruiser from the fight
Returned with Victory (terrific sight!).
God's flagship she, with shattered sides, presents
Her leaning funnels and her gaping rents,
In high salute uplifts her steepled guns,
And far the deep reverberation runs —[78]

The most famous single incident in the franquist mythification of the siege of the Alcázar concerns Colonel José Moscardó, the commander of the besieged fortress. Although details vary enormously depending on the author, the story goes that the "reds", having captured Moscardó's son, attempted to bargain with the colonel by offering his son's life in return for the surrender of the Alcázar. Moscardó refused, instructed his son to commend himself to God and then, so the franquist version usually goes, immediately heard over the telephone the shot that killed his son. Campbell clothes the incident in religious significance by employing a simile which borders dangerously on blasphemy: "That God was never brilliantined or curled / Who out of Chaos saw his battles won, / And gave, like Moscardó, his only Son, / To save the charred Alcázar of the world."[79]

As befits an epic poem, *Flowering Rifle* contains numerous narrative moments devoted to the description of battle. The narrator counts himself amongst the protagonists in these war scenes. Campbell himself had not been a combatant, but what his detractors find even more reprehensible is the narrator's insensitivity to the horrors of war, his apparently casual acceptance of violence. At some points indeed the narrator, in a manner certainly comparable with Nazi texts such as that of Trautloft, appears to relish the spectacle of human suffering and death: "And by Brunete you may see in stacks / Dead Charlies climbing on each other's backs / To make a huge paella of the plains, / A dish of rice, with corpses for the grains."[80] This, presumably, is one of the passages in the poem which made Stephen Spender feel physically ill.[81]

*Flowering Rifle* was popular enough for Longman's to bring out a second edition in July 1941, but whether it did anything to improve the British image of the nationalists is dubious. Peter Alexander suggests that "it almost certainly did more harm than good to the Francoist cause."[82] The poem is too crudely abusive to be effective satire, too blatantly biased and illogical to be a credible panegyric, and too lacking in narrative substance or coherence to impress as an epic. Its vitriol might have possessed the capacity to reinforce existing opinions or prejudices, but precisely this quality deprives the work of the capacity to persuade. Campbell does not permit even the slightest ambivalence towards the Spanish question. Rather than constructing a cogent argument to address pertinent political circumstances, Campbell's tactic is to declare as axiomatic the dialectic of nationalist good and republican evil. By thus denying the war a genuine political framework and placing it into a moral-religious one, he puts himself in a position to trivialise the suffering and death caused by it. In a "holy war" the deaths of "martyrs" and "heroes" pale into insignificance against the background of a struggle on a cosmic scale.

## NATIONALIST SPAIN AND JOSÉ MARÍA PEMÁN

Although he lived in Spain for some time, Campbell did not acquire a broad literary reputation there. This, however, applies to most of the non-Spanish writers who supported Franco. In stark contrast to the political Left, the writers of the Right failed to generate a sense of solidarity and common purpose on an international scale. Unlike the Left they did not attend international congresses or launch collaborative projects. Nevertheless, it is apparent in several ways that in terms both of literary form and content, the literature produced in nationalist Spain had much in common with the outpourings of the non-Spanish Right.

Firstly, it can be observed that the Spanish nationalist writers in the 1930s, like their international supporters, believed firmly in a politically committed literature, in a literature which addressed the social and political issues of the day. Spain since the turn of the century had been experiencing a second "Golden Age" of Spanish literature, which in the 1920s had become closely associated with a rejection of mimetic, realist traditions and a willingness to experiment boldly with new literary forms. This Spanish version of literary modernism generally preferred not to address political questions but to explore issues of individual sensibility and imagination. The literary élite of the 1920s "concerned themselves only marginally with party politics – at least until 1930."[83] As from about 1930, however, modernist *poesía pura* was gradually replaced by *poesía comprometida*, committed poetry, which increasingly *did* explicitly address social and political issues and which *was* concerned with party politics.[84] This development in the 1930s was one which is evident on both sides of the political spectrum.[85] The political commitment in the literature of the Right, like that of the Left, culminated in the war. Although it assumed forms which differed from the literature of the Left, its presence can nevertheless be easily illustrated. Erneste Giménez Caballero, who had been one of the representatives of a Spanish literary avantgarde during the 1920s, became one of the key initiators of a Spanish fascist movement. In his important theoretical work *Arte y Estado* (Art and the State), published in 1935, Giménez insists that art must fulfil a political function: "Every work of art is always political. Every literary work is always partisan."[86] A year before the outbreak of war he was suggesting that art "is simply a technique of conquest. A military technique."[87] Four years later, and looking back on the war, Jorge Villén reaffirmed Giménez Caballero's rejection of the modernist art of the preceding era and his insistence on a poetry of (military) commitment. In his foreword to an anthology of nationalist war poetry he writes: "And because it was a war of spirit, the poets wrote their songs from the first hour, and the cold and sceptical era which preceded ours was succeeded by a new rebirth, a new age, in which the battle and the poetry were manifestations of faith, of enthusiasm for eternal principles and values."[88] In order to emphasize the military dimension of poetic commitment, Villén concludes his foreword with the words: "This book is in reality nothing more than this: a book of war."[89]

Secondly, just as Campbell opted for the traditional form of the heroic couplet, the Spanish nationalists tended to adopt traditional literary forms in order to express their commitment. This entailed therefore not just a rejection of the thematic concerns of modernism but also of the more formal implications of the *poesía pura* of the 1920s. In particular, nationalist poets showed a preference for the form of the *romance*, a traditional Spanish form with roots dating back to medieval times. It consisted of octosyllabic verses with assonance in the even lines only. Jorge Villén in his foreword notes that a variety of forms was present in the nationalist poetry of the war, but that the more classical forms, "the *romance* and the sonnet," predominated.[90] Indeed, in nationalist Spain the decline of the *romance* in Spanish literature since the sixteenth century was attributed to the decline of the Spanish empire.[91] But in these formal matters, as in other areas in the nationalist zone, a distinct hierarchy existed. Despite the revival of the *romance*, a kind of ranking of poetic forms took place, "with the sonnet at the top and the *romance* at the bottom, viewed as a lesser verse form, most appropriate for ignorant people."[92]

Thirdly, it is apparent that, despite the widespread adoption of traditional forms such as the *romance*, the Spanish nationalist writers, like their non-Spanish counterparts, could not match the literary Left in popularity. Popularity here can be assessed in two ways, namely in terms of reception and production. The two outstanding literary journals of nationalist Spain, *Jerarquía* (Hierarchy, of which just four issues were published in the period 1936-39) and *Vértice* (Vertex, of which only sixteen issues appeared in the period 1937-46), never gained the readership enjoyed by the war-time republican journals such as *Hora de España* (Spain's Hour) or *El Mono Azul* (The Blue Monkey). As José-Carlos Mainer has pointed out, "*Vértice* was, fundamentally, a luxurious and expensive magazine (it cost three pesetas; despite everything two less than *Jerarquía*)."[93] (*Hora de España* cost just one peseta.) The prices alone indicated that these were publications which were not designed to expand the reading public beyond a wealthy élite. As far as participation in production is concerned, they were similarly unpopular, publishing only about one-tenth of the number of poems that were published in *El Mono Azul* and *Hora de España*.[94] In his study of the *romance* genre in the war, Serge Salaün estimates that of some 20 000 poems published during the war, only about a quarter were published in nationalist territory.[95]

Fourthly, there is a range of thematic similarities betwen the literature of the Spanish and the non-Spanish Right. The Spanish nationalists concentrate on the same events during the war, on the alleged atrocities committed by republicans, and on the acts of heroism performed by nationalists. Like Roy Campbell they focus great attention on the defence of the Alcázar of Toledo, and like Campbell they adopt a manichaean scheme which portrays the nationalists as the forces of goodness, the republicans as the embodiment of evil. They seek the causes of Spain's woes outside Spain: in communism (particularly the Russian variety), in western materialism, in freemasonry and Judaism. Having taken up the struggle against these invading forces, they were profoundly interested in the value of the struggle itself. In other words, like the Nazis, and like Roy Campbell, they saw the battle not just as a means to an end, but as an end in itself, a realisation of desirable soldierly virtues. In tracing the course of the war, nationalist poetry tends not to celebrate the collective heroism of nationalist forces, but to focus on the achievements of certain individuals, on José Antonio, or on famous military figures such as Generals Mola, Moscardó or Quiepo de Llano. Above all they focus on the Caudillo Franco, who is portrayed as Spain's infallible saviour.

Spanish nationalist poets were just as ideologically heterogeneous as the international Right and consequently tended to adopt the same obfuscation tactics. The eclecticism of franquist doctrine rendered a cogent discussion of political issues difficult, if not impossible. In drawing attention away from their exigent heterogeneity, the nationalists looked to a supra-political realm in which agreement *could* be reached. In particular they looked to religion as a unifying force, and they labelled their war a *cruzada*.[96] For them it was not "a war between bourgeoisie and proletariat, or between Right and Left; it was above all a war between those who wanted to preserve their faith in God and those without God."[97] One contributor to *Jerarquía* even spoke of the necessity of a "crusade against politics."[98]

In pursuing this tactic of obfuscation, of deflecting attention away from the explicilty political realm, the Spaniards added a dimension which was generally lacking in non-Spanish literature. They constructed an image of a Spanish *imperio*, in much the same way as Mussolini and the Italian fascists had constructed a vision of an Italian empire. The war was depicted as an effort to reconstruct a glorious empire, similar to that which had existed centuries earlier. The extent to which the imperial vision that the franquists propagated coincided with the reality of Spain's imperial past is debatable. In any case, terms like *imperio*, *patria* and of course *España* possessed for them the connotation "not of an existing, but of an *ideal* Spain, which was to be created through victory in the *cruzada*."[99] With the widespread employment of terminology relating to the religious and historico-mythical dimensions of the franquist cause, the descriptions in nationalist literature of present political and military circumstances either became very vague or disappeared altogether. Nationalist poetry was distinguished by "the exaltation of the past and of traditional values, the epic and triumphant tone which ignores harsh reality, its insistence on the 'dreams of grandeur in order to forget real problems,' its vague, abstract, empty and confused ideology, reduced almost to an irrational emotionalism, and its 'high-sounding, bombastic, antiquated' style."[100] In this "content-less rhetoric"[101] there is no mention of the specific political aims of the war, no indication of a program by which the restoration of an empire in all its past glory could be achieved.

One of the most famous practitioners of this kind of rhetoric in nationalist Spain was José María Pemán. It is some indication of the eclecticism of franquism that Pemán is ideologically so different from Giménez Caballero. Unlike the latter, Pemán is not a fascist in any narrow sense of the word, and during the 1920s he had nothing to do with the literary modernism in which Giménez Cabellero was playing a major role. In aesthetics and in political beliefs Pemán was distinctly conservative, writing poetry, prose and drama in traditional forms and expressing political opinions which unambiguously identified him as a supporter of the Primo de Rivera dictatorship. In fact, Pemán published a number of panegyric works on behalf of the regime, such as *El hecho y la idea de la Unión Patriótica* (The Fact and the Idea of the Patriotic Union) and the anthology *El pensamiento de Primo de Rivera* (The Thought of Primo de Rivera). [102] During the Republic he was a delegate to the Cortes, where he achieved prominence by publicly defending General Sanjurjo's failed 1932 coup attempt. He participated in various conservative and monarchist (traditionalist) political bodies and activities in the 1930s. After the outbreak of war he was proclaimed *poeta alférez* (poet-ensign) by the nationalists, much as Werner Beumelburg was the quasi-official historian of the Condor Legion, and he held a number of official positions in nationalist Spain. He travelled overseas on propaganda missions for the Franco government, for which he wrote abundantly. [103]

Much of Pemán's wartime writing was of a journalistic nature, both in radio and in the print medium. In it he sought to establish an ideological basis for the franquist regime, much as he had done for Primo de Rivera a decade earlier. For example, in a radio address delivered a few days after the Generals' attempted coup, Pemán sought to provide a justification for the coup and for the (now inevitable) lengthy civil war. A quick and successful coup, Pemán contends, would have been "too low a price for a great, revitalised Spain, for this gleaming treasure which we are fervently demanding. It ought not be so cheap! We should pay for Spain according to its value – pay with the suffering of a war."[104] In a later radio address on the war Pemán insisted that it was "not a class struggle: this is the eternal battle between the two supernatural powers of good and evil; this is satanic will against divine grace."[105] In a 1937 article on the role of the intellectuals in the "New State," Pemán wrote of a state which "excluded those who opted for the anti-national, the masonic, the Jewish or the marxist, or those who were the cause of the revolution."[106] Finally, in an article written almost a year later, he demonstrates the respect with which he held Franco: "From the official car, followed by a single adjutant, the Caudillo descended rapidly. . . .

And right away he went inside; he went inside with that austere haste to which he is accustomed in reducing to a minimum the time spent on the street. . . . The Caudillo passed doors and curtains like a dagger in search of a heart; like an incisive glance searching for the truth."[107]

As a poet during the war, Pemán deserves the epithet *poeta del Nacional-Catolicismo Español* (Poet of Spanish National-Catholicism).[108] In Jorge Villén's already mentioned 1939 anthology of nationalist poetry, *Antología poética del Alzamiento* (Poetic Anthology of the Uprising), six of the poems are by Pemán. Four of them are in fact extracts from his epic and famous *Poema de la Bestia y el Angel* (Poem of the Beast and the Angel), which in April 1938 had been published in a lavishly illustrated edition by the publishers of *Jerarquía*.[109]

Before turning attention to the poem itself, it is useful to consider Pemán's lengthy prose introduction, since it reveals much about his views on aesthetics. In it, Pemán makes a plea for a committed art, for art which is directly related to life and which, to recall Goebbels's terminology, would mobilise the people. In time of war in particular, he contends, the link between art and life is obligatory: "To this alliance [i.e., of life and art] the raw and energetic realism of war challenges us fatefully. Everything is now mobilised; and to this mobilisation Poetry also has been called. Consequently that which I offer you, reader, is not a work written in a study, but in the sunshine and the open air. Poetry in action. Poetry . . . of the 'avantgarde' in the most direct and military sense of the term."[110] In insisting on a poetry of direct relevance to life, Pemán also explicitly rejected "avant-garde" poetry in the more usual sense of the word. That is, he rejected the *poesía pura* of the 1920s, accusing it of failing to perform the necessary task of depicting objective reality. The trend away from objectivity he traces back to Immanuel Kant and the concept of "pure reason." It was this philosophical subjectivism which had infected the poets with a faith in "pure poetry." Both poetry and philosophy had "betrayed being [*Ser*]; both turned their backs on reality and life. Both reached, as just reward, complete *nihilism*."[111]

Pemán saw the epic form as a means of overcoming the false and unhealthy subjectivism in poetry, of re-uniting spirit and being. But Pemán's understanding of the kind of objective reality he was to depict in his epic work is unusual. Objective reality for Pemán consists of intangible qualities which many would prefer to assign to the realm of metaphysics. Adopting a characteristic manichaeism, he describes the supposedly objective reality in the following way:

The Angel and the Beast are locked in battle before us. Being and Nothingness, the powers of Evil and of Good are fighting before our eyes. Let us not retreat inside ourselves when the reality is so great and so important.

Spain's War was waiting for us, now, at the end of this apprenticeship which these twenty years of poetic purification and formal intensification have been. . . . It was for this – supreme theme, ultimate triumph of being – that we poets, without knowing it, spent years sharpening our pencils with such patience.[112]

To justify this curious, metaphysically based conception of objectivity, Pemán calls on the seventeenth-century French classical painter Nicolas Poussin for assistance. He differentiates between "realist" and "real," between "prospect" and "aspect," between an inner reality and a superficial reality.[113] His concern as a poet is allegedly not to depict the superficial reality of war, but to uncover an inner reality. Referring to this important distinction and also to the prophetic function of his work, Pemán declares: "This is the image of the Spanish Civil War I have wanted to convey to my contemporaries. Not just the present, anecdotal, immediate fact, but all the profound apocalyptic meaning in the revelation of the eternal fight between the Beast and the Angel, its entire prophetic and imperial anticipation of a glowing future."[114]

An examination of the poem itself soon reveals the eccentricity of its supposed objectivity. Covering just over 200 pages, it is an epic work which adopts a variety of traditional poetic forms, including the *romance*. Incorporated into it are short prose interludes which commentate and interpret the course of events, depriving the readers of the possibility of "decoding" the wealth of allegorical figures for themselves. The work is divided into three *cantos*, three being, as Pemán points out in his Introduction, a mystical, round and perfect number. Above all, though, it is the number of God, that is, of God the Father, God the Son and God the Holy Ghost.[115]

The first *canto* is entitled "*En el principio de los tiempos*" (At the Beginning of Time). As the title suggests, it deals with the past, but not with a specific, historically locatable past. Although a number of actual figures from Spanish history are mentioned, the tendency is towards ahistorical allegory. Amongst a whole range of allegorical figures the two central ones are the beast, representing the material world and the forces of evil, and the angel, representing the spiritual world and the forces of goodness. Aided by this tendency to allegory, the precise nature of good and evil in Spain remains conveniently vague, but Pemán litters the text with some obvious clues. Thus there are specific references to the Lodge and the synagogue as well as to the "red East."[116] Predictably the dominant symbol of goodness is the cross, which, along with the falangist yoke and arrows, was the favourite icon of nationalist Spain.

Nuestra Cruz no es de piedra ni de leño.
Nuestra Cruz es de idea y geometría
    y es anhelo y poesía
y es inviolable como el sueño
y es inmortal como la alegoria.

    No es preciso que hiera
nuestra mano su peso de hierro o de madera.
Basta soñarla: basta con un trazo
    de espíritu o de luz. . . .
¡donde existe un suspiro y un abrazo
    existirá una Cruz!

(Our Cross is not of stone nor of wood. / Our Cross is of idea and geometry / and is longing and poetry / and is inviolable like sleep / and is immortal like allegory. // It is not necessary that it strike / our hand its weight of iron or of wood. / It is enough to dream of it: a trace / of spirit or light is enough. . . . / where there exists a sigh and a hug / there will exist a Cross!) [117]

Goodness is personified literally for Pemán by *los mártires de julio* (the July Martyrs) and, in particular, by the assassinated monarchist leader José Calvo Sotelo, who receives the epithet *protomártir de la gran Cruzada española* (Proto-martyr of the Great Spanish Crusade). [118] In the nationalist version of history Calvo Sotelo led the battle against "the great powers of international Jewish finance," [119] and, as in other pro-franquist interpretations of Spanish history, it was the murder of Calvo Sotelo which brought about the civil war. [120]

The second *canto*, "*En el centro de la historia*" (In the Centre of History) deals with the historical present, but with the same allegorising tendencies as the first *canto*. It begins with the birth of Franco, which, much like the birth of Jesus Christ, is commemorated with the presentation of gifts, on this occasion from three fairies. [121] The battle Franco wages on behalf of the forces of good is depicted as the culminating point of all past history, in which good and evil finally confront each other and do battle to the death. As in Roy Campbell's poem and many other nationalist works, a central incident in this decisive battle is the heroic defence of the Alcázar of Toledo. An entire section of the second *canto* is devoted to the episode, but in such a way as to remove it from any precise historical or military context. It begins with an evocation of El Greco's painting *El entierro del Conde de Orgaz* (The Funeral of the Count of Orgaz), which serves Pemán as a symbol of events in Spain. Just as in the painting light is separated from blackness, so in the Alcázar these two forces stand in opposition:

Mis ojos de poeta
la alta Ciudad Primada vieron partida en dos.
En dos como en profética figura
ya el Griego la pintaba: el alba pura
de la Resurrección sobre la Cruz. . . .
Por abajo la Muerte, la Pena, la Negrura:
¡por encima el Alcázar glorioso de la Luz!

(My poet's eyes / saw the noble Supreme City divided in two. / In two as in the prophetic figure / already painted by El Greco: the pristine dawn / of the Resurrection on the Cross. . . . / Below the death, the pain, the blackness: / Above the glorious Alcázar of Light!) [122]

The victory achieved by the defenders of the Alcázar is seen by Pemán not merely as a victory for nationalist Spain but as a triumph for the Western, Christian tradition. Addressing General Moscardó, the commander of the Alcázar, Pemán writes: "Le has devuelto a Occidente la Verdad y la Idea / de que otra vez los pueblos de Europa vivirán." (You have brought back to the West the Truth and the Idea that once again the peoples of Europe shall live.) [123]

As the accounts of the birth of Franco and the siege of the Alcázar suggest, the description of the war offered here has little in common with the realism in the image of war constructed by prorepublican soldiers and journalists. Here there are no descriptions of the privations suffered in trench warfare, the injuries and deaths caused by aerial bombardments, or the dread of military engagement experienced by the soldiers. In fact, there is very little mention of the modern machinery of war at all, and then only in connection with the enemy. The decisive battle described in this second *canto* is not the siege of the Alcázar, but an encounter between an enemy tank and a young soldier from Aragón. It is this duel which bears the symbolic weight of the entire poem. The enemy tank is described as

Sonido de materia triunfadora
sin el más leve toque de la Gracia
ni el más leve reflejo del Espíritu.

Sonido de dinero
en la desmesurada
escarcela sin fondo de algún cíclope.

Sonido, sin sintaxis,
de prosa dura y proletaria.

(The sound of triumphant matter / without the slightest touch of Grace / or the slightest reflection of spirit. // The sound of money / in the bottomless pouch of some Cyclops. // The sound, without syntax, / of harsh and proletarian prose.)[124]

The nationalist soldier is the precise opposite.

Es rubio como una espiga
a punto de madurar.
Tiene una sonrisa clara
y alegre como la paz.

Sano es como una amapola
y puro como un San Juan.

El carro es toda materia,
él es toda idealidad:
San Jorge frente al dragón,
San Miguel frente a Satán.

(He is golden like an ear of grain / about to ripen. / He has a smile which is clear / and happy like peace. // He is healthy like a poppy / and pure like a Saint John. // The tank is all matter, / he is all ideality: / Saint George confronting the dragon, / Saint Michael confronting Satan.)[125]

This allegorical treatment of the confrontation of the two armies in Spain is quite different from that of the Nazi pilots examined earlier. The latter strictly avoid allegory, preferring to recount their own particular experiences of the war. Despite this difference, the function of these quite different modes of writing is similar. Both Pemán and the pilots can be accused of trivialising the effects of war by creating distance from it. Pemán employs allegory and the pilots report events from the safe perspective of their aircraft; both in their own ways manage to avoid the task of communicating the horror and the suffering caused by the war. There is no suggestion of resolving the antagonism which had enveloped Spain in a community of death and suffering. One of the *romances* in the second *canto* describes a battlefield in which the dead of both sides, the blue and the red, appear to become equal in death. But even here the appearance deceives, because "God knows the names – and separates them in the clouds."[126]

Pemán concludes the second *canto* with a prophecy of the victory of the angel over the beast. In its prophetic function the poem goes so far as to anticipate the celebrations held in the main square of Salamanca. It is attended by an Italian emissary who proclaims: "I believe in Spain."[127]

The third and final *canto*, entitled "*Hacia los tiempos nuevos*" (Towards New Times) is an extended prophecy of timeless peace and Spanish imperial glory. It anticipates a grand age of Spain, which in its cultivation of traditional values and qualities is not noticeably different from the construction of an idealised past in the first *canto*. Here Pemán constructs a distinctly non-dynamic conception of history (and as such quite different from liberal, Marxist or even anarchist teleology). The future is nothing more than the re-creation of an idealised past. As one critic has put it, Pemán "envisions a sort of uchronia: a future not yet lived that will be the nostalgic recreation of a mythical and idealised past, that never really existed."[128] Specifically, the vision of the future it promotes is one of an abundance of natural products; in fact it opens with an "*Himno de la Abundancia*" (Hymn of Abundance). The new Spain, "feliz y prodiga, / tiene el aceite para su lámpara, / y tiene el duro pino, y el álamo, / que será luego mesa de amor" (happy and abundant, / has oil for its lamp, / and has the hard pine, and the poplar, / which will soon be a table of love).[129] There is no hint here of the application of modern science or technology, which in the second *canto* had been so closely associated with the enemy, or of the disruptions within Spanish society which had led to turmoil. Instead, a state of perfect harmony prevails. In a parable centred on the figures of Queen Isabel and Cardinal Mendoza, a perfect marriage of the Spanish Church and the State is achieved. A new world is created which is characterised by "Libertad y Realeza; Jerarquía entre hermanos." (Liberty and Royalty; Hierarchy among brothers.)[130] The poem concludes with lines pronounced by the allegorical figure Alegría (Happiness):

Todo el mar se ha rayado de una luz infinita.
El palo de mesana se ha vestido de sol.
¡Aureos pilotos de la España Nueva!
¡Levad los remos!
    ¡¡A la vista Dios!!

(All the sea is streaked with an infinite light. / The mizzen mast is clothed in sunlight. / Golden pilots of the New Spain! / Raise the oars! / God is in sight!!)[131]

The vision of harmony projected here could hardly be further removed from the belligerent circumstances during which the poem was written. Rather than representing the war, Pemán was more concerned to justify it, to disseminate confidence in a nationalist victory, and to play down the unsavoury side of war. Given that the war had been started by a military uprising, these were literary functions of which all Spanish nationalist writers must have been acutely aware.

## NOTES

1. *Authors Take Sides on the Spanish War*. Ed. Nancy Cunard. London: Left Review, 1937.

2. Valentine Cunningham. "Introduction." In *The Penguin Book of Spanish Civil War Verse*. Ed. Valentine Cunningham, 25-94. Harmondsworth: Penguin, 1980. p. 53.

3. *Writers Take Sides. Letters about the War in Spain from 418 American Writers*. New York: League of American Writers, 1938.

4. Hugh Thomas. *The Spanish Civil War*. 3rd. ed. Harmondsworth: Penguin, 1986. p. 980.

5. Quoted in Valentine Cunningham. *op. cit.* p.51.

6. Thomas. *op. cit.* pp. 203-4.

7. Douglas Jerrold. *Georgian Adventure*. London: Collins, 1937. p. 374.

8. *Ibid.* p. 374. The murder of Calvo Sotelo took place on July 13, several days before the outbreak of war.

9. *Ibid.* p. 384.

10. Katharine Bail Hoskins. *Today the Struggle. Literature and Politics in England During the Spanish Civil War*. Austin and London: University of Texas Press, 1969. p. 17. Lunn's visit to nationalist Spain is recounted in his *Spanish Rehearsal*. Boston: Sheed and Ward, 1937.

11. William Foss and Cecil Gerahty. *The Spanish Arena*. London: The Right Book Club, 1938. p. 429.

12. *Ibid.* p. 334.

13. *Ibid.* p. 502.

14. Hilaire Belloc. "The Issue in Spain." *Spain* 44 (July 1938) p. 100. Quoted in Hugh D. Ford. *A Poets' War: British Poets and the Spanish Civil War*. Philadelphia: University of Pennsylvania Press; London: Oxford University Press, 1965. p. 21.

15. Allen Guttmann. *The Wound in the Heart. America and the Spanish Civil War*. New York: Free Press of Glencoe, 1962. p. 65. The corresponding figure for Protestants was 9 percent, for Jews 2 percent.

16. *Ibid.* p. 37.

17. Helen Nicholson. *Death in the Morning*. London: L. Dickson, 1937. Nicholson's real name was Helen de Zglinitzki.

18. Quoted (unsourced) in Stanley Weintraub. *The Last Great Cause. The Intellectuals and the Spanish Civil War*. London: W. H. Allen, 1968. p. 171.

19. Helen Nicholson. *The Painted Bed*. London: L. Dickson, 1937.

20. Weintraub. *op. cit.* p. 171.

21. Amirah Inglis. *Australians in the Spanish Civil War*. Sydney, Wellington, London, Boston: Allen & Unwin, 1987. p. 43.

22. *Ibid.* p. 43.

23. Quoted (unsourced) *ibid.* p. 45.

24. *Ibid.* p. 48.

25. Gottfried Pfeffer. "Der Niederschlag des Spanischen Bürgerkrieges 1936-1939 in der französischen Literatur." Doctoral dissertation, Tübingen, 1961. p. 16.

26. *Ibid.* pp. 16-17.

27. Robert Brasillach and Maurice Bardèche. *Histoire de la guerre d'Espagne.* Paris: Plon, 1939. By Brasillach see also his novel *Les sept couleurs.* Paris: Plon, 1939.

28. Robert Brasillach and Henri Massis. *Les cadets de l'Alcázar.* Paris: Plon, 1936. See also (by the same authors) *Le siège de l'Alcázar.* Paris: Plon, 1939.

29. See Pierre Héricourt. *Pourquoi Franco vaincra.* Paris: Editions de la Baudinière, 1936. A new version, entitled *Pourquoi Franco a vaincu,* was published in 1939. It contained a preface by Franco himself, who wrote that Héricourt was "the first French journalist to announce without hesitation the triumph of our cause, which was not merely that of Spain . . . but also that of civilized Europe." *Pourquoi Franco a vaincu.* Paris: Editions de la Baudinière, 1939. p. 7. Quoted in Maryse Bertrand de Muñoz. *La guerre civile espagnole et la littérature française.* Montreal: Didier, 1972. p. 77.

30. The poem "Aux martyrs espagnols" appeared first as a preface to Joan Estelrich's book *La persécution religieuse en Espagne.* Paris: Plon, 1937. The Pope had officially declared all those priests who had been murdered to be martyrs.

31. Pfeffer. *op. cit.* p. 74.

32. *Ibid.* p. 75.

33. Georges Bernanos. *Les grands cimetières sous la lune.* Paris: Plon, 1938. In English, transl. Pamela Morris, as *A Diary of My Times.* New York: Macmillan, 1938.

34. *Ibid.* p. 7.

35. Walter Benjamin. "Das Kunstwerk im Zeitalter seiner technischen Reproduzierbarkeit." In Walter Benjamin. 471-508. *Gesammelte Schriften I, 2.* Frankfurt a.M.: 1974. p. 506.

36. Barbara Pérez-Ramos. "Aspekte faschistischer Rhetorik im Spanischen Bürgerkrieg." In *Der Spanische Bürgerkrieg. Literatur und Geschichte.* Ed. Günther Schmigalle, 147-79. Frankfurt a.M.: Vervuert, 1986. p. 179.

37. Ricardo de la Cierva y de Hoces. *Cien libros básicos sobre la Guerra de España.* Madrid: Publicaciones Españolas, 1966. p. 312.

38. Valentine Cunningham. *op. cit.* p. 52.

39. Roy Campbell. *Flowering Rifle. A Poem from the Battlefield of Spain.* London, New York, Toronto: Longman's, Green and Co., 1939. Campbell's critical work *Lorca. An Appreciation of His Poetry.* New Haven: Yale University Press, 1952, contains his Lorca translations.

40. Bernard Bergonzi. "Roy Campbell: Outsider on the Right." In *Literature and Politics in the Twentieth Century.* Ed. Walter Laqueur and George L. Mosse, 128-42. New York: Harper and Row, 1967. p. 129. John Povey similarly speaks of a "life identity" between Hemingway and Campbell. John Povey. *Roy Campbell.* Boston: Twayne, 1977. p. 105.

41. For example Herbert Southworth in *Le mythe de la croisade de Franco.* Paris: Ruedo ibérico, 1964. p. 114 and Stanley Weintraub. *op. cit.* p. 11 call him a fascist; John Povey too in "A Lyre of Savage Thunder: A Study of the Poetry of Roy Campbell." *Wisconsin Studies in Contemporary Literature* 7 (1966): p. 97 speaks of "Campbell's Fascism."

42. Alan Paton. "Roy Campbell: Poet and Man." *Theoria* 9 (1957): pp. 28-29. Similar judgements are made by biographer Peter Alexander in *Roy Campbell. A Critical Biography.* Oxford, New York, Toronto, London: Oxford University Press, 1982. p. 178, Harold R. Collins in "Roy Campbell: The Talking Bronco." *Boston University Studies in*

*English* 4 (1960): p. 50, and Edith Sitwell. Untitled piece in *Hommage à Roy Campbell*. Ed. Armand Guibert, 47-51. n.p.: 1958. p. 48.

43. Roy Campbell. *Broken Record. Reminiscences*. Michigan: Scholarly Press, 1978 (1934). p. 206.

44. Roy Campbell. *Light on a Dark Horse. An Autobiography (1901-1935)*. London: Hollis and Carter, 1951. p. 334.

45. Campbell. *Broken Record*. p. 144.

46. *Ibid*. p. 202.

47. C. J. D. Harvey. "The Poetry of Roy Campbell." *Standpunte* (October 1950): p. 53. Quoted in Povey. *op. cit*. p. 215.

48. Campbell. *Light on a Dark Horse*. pp. 324-25.

49. Alexander. *op. cit*. p. 161.

50. Roy Campbell. *Mithraic Emblems*. London: Boriswood, 1936. The collection included four poems which were written after the outbreak of the war, but which are not considered here. For the critical response see especially Alexander. *op. cit*. pp. 167-68.

51. Roy Campbell. *The Georgiad*. London: Boriswood, 1931.

52. Povey. *op. cit*. p. 96.

53. Campbell in *Light on a Dark Horse*. p. 226, claims to have "fought" against bolshevism and killed bolsheviks in self-defence; Collins. *op. cit*. p. 49 suggests that he was a soldier in the ranks of the *requetés*. Rafael Calvo Serer beats even that – Campbell fought amongst the *requetés* and then in the Legion. Rafael Calvo Serer. *La literatura universal sobre la Guerra de España*. Madrid: Ateneo, 1962. p. 46.

54. Alexander. *op. cit*. pp. 172-3.

55. *Ibid*. p. 174.

56. Revised version in *The Collected Poems of Roy Campbell. Volume 2*. London: Bodley Head, 1957. pp. 135-256. For the differences between the 1939 and 1957 editions see Southworth. *op. cit*. pp. 114-24.

57. "Viator" in *The Tablet* 11 December 1939; Arthur Bryant quoted (exact source not provided) in Alexander. *op. cit*. p. 177.

58. Esteban Pujals. *España y la guerra de 1936 en la poesía de Roy Campbell*. Madrid: Ateneo, 1959. p. 65.

59. Stephen Spender. "A Review of Roy Campbell, *Flowering Rifle*, 1939." *New Statesman and Nation* 11 March 1939. In *The Penguin Book of Spanish Civil War Verse*. Ed. Valentine Cunningham, 440-43. Harmondsworth: Penguin, 1980. pp. 440-1.

60. Unpublished letter Roy Campbell to F. C. Slater. Nov.-Dec. 1938. Quoted in Alexander. *op. cit*. p. 174.

61. Campbell. *Flowering Rifle*. pp. 8-9.

62. *Ibid*. pp. 145-6. Quoted also in Spender. *op. cit*. p. 442.

63. In Horatian satire "the character of the speaker is that of an urbane, witty, and tolerant man of the world, who is moved more often to wry amusement than to indignation at the spectacle of human folly, pretentiousness, and hypocrisy, and who uses a relaxed and informal language to evoke a smile at human follies and absurdities – sometimes including his own." M. H. Abrams. *A Glossary of Literary Terms*. 3rd. ed. New York: Holt, Rinehart and Winston, 1971. pp. 154-55.

64. In Juvenalian satire "the character of the speaker is that of a serious moralist who uses a dignified and public style of utterance to decry modes of vice and error which are no less dangerous because they are ridiculous, and who undertakes to evoke contempt, moral indignation, or an unillusioned sadness at the aberrations of men." *Ibid*. p. 155.

65. Jonathan Swift. "Verses on the Death of Dr. Swift." In Jonathan Swift. *Satires and Personal Writings*, 478-95. London, New York: Oxford University Press, 1932. p. 494.

66. Campbell. *Flowering Rifle*. p. 55.

67. *Ibid.* p. 8.

68. *Ibid.* p. 115.

69. A "Wowser" is defined by Campbell in the footnotes to the 1957 edition of the poem as "any kind of puritan killjoy, socialist and fabian, or pedant." Roy Campbell. *The Collected Poems of Roy Campbell. Volume 2.* p. 139.

70. Campbell. *Flowering Rifle.* p. 18.

71. *Ibid.* p. 31.

72. *Ibid.* p. 32.

73. *Ibid.* p. 28.

74. *Ibid.* p. 44.

75. *Ibid.* p. 15.

76. *Ibid.* p. 56.

77. *Ibid.* p. 9.

78. *Ibid.* p. 28.

79. *Ibid.* p. 64. The charge of blasphemy is made explicitly by Herbert Southworth. *op. cit.* pp. 115, 123.

80. *Ibid.* p. 52.

81. Spender. *op. cit.* p. 442.

82. Alexander. *op. cit.* p. 174.

83. John Butt. *Writers and Politics in Modern Spain.* London, Sydney, Auckland, Toronto: Hodder and Stoughton, 1978. p. 7.

84. For an examination of the trend from *poesía pura* to *poesía comprometida* in the period up until the outbreak of the war see especially Jean Bécarud and Evelyne López Campillo. *Los intelectuales españoles durante la II. República.* Madrid: 1978. passim; John Butt. *op. cit.* 7-32; Juan Cano Ballesta. *La poesía española entre pureza y revolución (1930-1936).* Madrid: Ed. Gredos, 1972. *passim*; Anthony Leo Geist. *La poética de la generación del 27 y las revistas literarias: de la vanguardia al compromiso (1918-1936).* Barcelona: 1980. *passim*; J. Lechner. *El compromiso en la poesía española del siglo XX. Parte Primera. De la Generación de 1898 a 1939.* Leiden: Universitaire Pers, 1968. 1-142. Manfred Lentzen. *Der spanische Bürgerkrieg und die Dichter. Beispiele des politischen Engagements in der Literatur.* Heidelberg: Carl Winter, 1985. 9-23; Barbara Pérez-Ramos. *Intelligenz und Politik im Spanischen Bürgerkrieg 1936-1939.* Bonn: Bouvier Verlag Herbert Grundmann, 1982. 1-66.

85. In asserting that this trend affected both Left and Right, I am rejecting a thesis put forward by Juan Cano Ballesta. The latter suggests: "Whilst materialist thought and that of the Left accuses 'pure art' of the crime of high treason and attempts to convert the artist into a zealous propagandist, the conservative groups wish to continue assigning [the artist] the function of providing society with a decorative element." Cano Ballesta. *op. cit.* 104-5. I find myself supported by Barbara Pérez-Ramos, who discusses in some detail the politically committed literature of the Spanish Right. Barbara Pérez-Ramos. "Poesie und Politik: Aspekte faschistischer Rhetorik im Spanischen Bürgerkrieg." In *Der Spanische Bürgerkrieg. Literatur und Geschichte.* Ed. Günther Schmigalle, 147-80. Frankfurt a.M.: Vervuert, 1986. *passim*.

86. Ernesto Giménez Caballero. *Arte y Estado.* Madrid: Gráfica universal, 1935. p. 83. Quoted in Pérez-Ramos. *Intelligenz und Politik im Spanischen Bürgerkrieg 1936-1939.* p. 173.

87. *Ibid.* p. 173.

88. Jorge Villén. "Prólogo." In *Antología poética del Alzamiento. 1936-1939.* Ed. Jorge Villén. Cádiz: 1939. Reproduced in J. Lechner. *op. cit.* p. 275. The second important anthology of nationalist war poetry is *Corona de sonetos en honor de José Antonio Primo de Rivera.* Barcelona: 1939.

89. *Ibid.* p. 275.

90. *Ibid.* p. 275.

91. Anthony Geist. "Popular Poetry in the Fascist Front During the Spanish Civil War." In *Fascismo y Experiencia Literaria: Reflexiones para una Recanonización*. Ed. Hernán Vidal, 145-53. Minneapolis: Institute for the Study of Ideologies and Literature, 1985. p. 147.

92. *Ibid.* p. 147.

93. José-Carlos Mainer. "Introducción: Historia Literaria de una Vocación Política (1930-1950)." In *Falange y Literatura*. Ed. José-Carlos Mainer, 13-65. Barcelona: Editorial Labor, 1971. p. 42.

94. Pérez-Ramos. "Poesie und Politik." p. 156.

95. Serge Salaün. "L'expression poétique pendant la guerre d'Espagne." In *Les écrivains et la Guerre d'Espagne*. Ed. Marc Hanrez, 105-13. Paris: Pantheon Press France, 1975. p. 106.

96. For an examination of religious terminology in franquist writings see especially Michael Scotti-Rosin. *Die Sprache der Falange und des Salazarismus. Eine vergleichende Untersuchung zur politischen Lexikologie des Spanischen und Portugiesischen*. Frankfurt a.M., Berne: Lang, 1982. *passim*.

97. Vicente Marrero. *La guerra española y el trust de cerebros*. 2nd. ed. Madrid: Ediciones Punta Europa, 1962 (1961). p. 23.

98. Fermín Yzurdiaga Lorca. "Para la Política." *Jerarquía* 2 (1936): pp. 151-52. Quoted in Pérez-Ramos. "Poesie und Politik." p. 165.

99. Pérez-Ramos. *Intelligenz und Politik im Spanischen Bürgerkrieg 1936-1939*. p. 176.

100. Juan Cano Ballesta. "El enfrentamiento de dos retóricas: la poesía de la guerra civil." In *Entre la Cruz y la Espalda: En Torno a la España de Posguerra. Homenaje a Eugenio G. de Nora*. Ed. José Manuel López de Abiada, 75-85. Madrid: Ed. Gredos, 1984. p. 85.

101. Pérez-Ramos. "Poesie und Politik." p. 168.

102. Both published in Madrid in 1929. This biographical information on Pemán based on Julio Rodriguez Puertolas. *Literatura Fascista Española. Volumen 1. Historia*. Madrid: Akal, 1986. p. 81.

103. *Ibid.* p. 201.

104. José María Pemán. "Militärstreich? Vernichtungskrieg gegen marxistischen Vernichtungswillen!" Radio Address 24 July 1936. In José María Pemán. Transl. Irene Behn. *Flammendes Spanien. Der Freiheitskampf des spanischen Volkes in Ansprachen und Aufsätzen*. 2nd. ed. Salzburg, Leipzig: Otto Müller, 1938. p. 71.

105. José María Pemán. "Heilige und nationale Frohbotschaft." *Ibid.* pp. 119-20.

106. José María Pemán. "Los intelectuales y el Nuevo Estado." *ABC*. 13 March 1937. Quoted in Rodriguez Puértolas. *op. cit.* p. 201.

107. *ABC*. 9 January 1938. Quoted *ibid.* pp. 201-2.

108. The term is used by Eutimio Martín in his article "José María Pemán: Poeta del Nacional-Catolicismo Español." *Cahiers d'Etudes Romanes* 5 (1979): 117-38.

109. José María Pemán. *Poema de la Bestia y el Angel*. Saragossa: Ediciones Jerarquía, 1938.

110. *Ibid.* p. 7.

111. *Ibid.* p. 10.

112. *Ibid.* p. 11.

113. *Ibid.* p. 16.

114. *Ibid.* p. 17.

115. *Ibid.*

116. *Ibid.* pp. 47, 26. Pemán's anti-Semitism, like Roy Campbell's, was renowned and becomes explicit on a number of occasions.

117. *Ibid.* p. 53.

118. *Ibid.* pp. 81, 66.

119. *Ibid.* p. 66.

120. Calvo Sotelo, the outspoken leader of the opposition in the Cortes, was killed on the morning of 13 July 1936 whilst being held by the police, several days before the attempted military coup. See Hugh Thomas. *The Spanish Civil War.* 3rd. ed. Harmondsworth: Penguin, 1986. pp. 207-8.

121. Pemán. *Poema de la Bestia y el Angel.* pp. 79-81.

122. *Ibid.* p. 114.

123. *Ibid.* p. 122.

124. *Ibid.* pp. 155-56.

125. *Ibid.* p. 157.

126. *Ibid.* p. 136.

127. *Ibid.* p. 171.

128. Anthony L. Geist. "The Angel and the Beast: The Poetics of Politics." In *LA CHISPA '83. Selected Proceedings. The Fourth Louisiana Conference on Hispanic Languages and Literatures.* Ed. Gilbert Paolini, 105-13. New Orleans: Tulane University, 1983. p. 108.

129. Pemán. *op. cit.* pp. 177-78.

130. *Ibid.* p. 196.

131. *Ibid.* p. 202.

# 4. Literature and the Popular Front

## THE WRITERS' CONGRESS IN VALENCIA AND MADRID

The policy of a Popular Front, that is, of a coalition of communist, socialist, liberal and other anti-fascist forces with the goal of halting the spread of European fascism, was officially pronounced by the Bulgarian communist leader Georgi Dimitrov at the Seventh Congress of the Comintern in 1935. In fact, Dimitrov was doing little more than expressing official approval of a fait accompli, since the move toward a Popular Front had begun in the previous year in France, where socialists and communists had signed a pact of unity of action. Thus the Popular Front concept was "that very rare thing in Communist history – a spontaneous initiative from a national party that was only later endorsed by Moscow."[1]

Above all else the Popular Front was a political strategy which took the form of party coalitions in Western Europe. In Spain in February and then in France in June 1936 these Popular Front coalitions assumed control of government. From the Soviet viewpoint, the great advantage of the Popular Front policy was that it curbed the spread of fascism and so helped to preserve "socialism in one country." For the more moderate participants in the Popular Front coalitions, that is, for many socialists, liberals and even for anti-fascist conservatives, the great advantage lay in the Communist Party's abandonment of agitation against the democratic state. Cooperation was the key word for all parties, at least as long as fascism continued to be perceived as a threat to Western democracy and to communism's Soviet bulwark.

Political cooperation between communists and other anti-fascist groupings was reinforced in other areas. In the sphere of cultural activity too there was to be on all sides an attempt to overlook, if not to overcome, differences of opinion; it was universally acknowledged by all participants in the Popular Front that cultural activity had to be devoted to bringing fascism to its knees.

The extent but also the limitations of the cultural solidarity of the Popular Front were best illustrated by the International Writers' Congresses for the Defence of Culture. The first was held in June 1935 in Paris, where such questions as the role of the writer in society, humanism, cultural heritage and problems of literary creativity were discussed. At that congress the Spanish delegate proposed that the next congress should take place in Madrid two years later. Despite the intervening outbreak of war in Spain, the republican government affirmed its desire to host the congress in July 1937, although it had become apparent that it would not be possible to conduct all the proceedings in besieged Madrid.

After an unofficial session in Barcelona on 3 July 1937, the Second International Writers' Congress for the Defence of Culture was officially opened by the then Prime Minister of republican Spain, Juan Negrín, on the following day. The list of delegates reads almost like a "Who's Who" of European and American literature in the 1930s. It included Antonio Machado, José Bergamín, Rafael Alberti, Jacinto Benavente, León Felipe, Margarita Nelken, María Theresa León (Spain); André Malraux, Julien Benda, André Chamson, Tristan Tzara (France); Ambrogio Donini (Italy); W. H. Auden, Stephen Spender, Ralph Bates, Edgell Rickword (England); Louis Fischer, Malcolm Cowley, Anna Louise Strong (USA); Pablo Neruda (Chile); César Vallejo (Peru); Raúl González Tuñón (Argentina); Carlos Pellicer, Octavio Paz, Silvestre Revueltas (Mexico); Alejo Carpentier, Nicolas Guillén (Cuba); Ilya Ehrenburg, Mikhail Koltsov, Alexei Tolstoy (USSR); Nordahl Grieg (Norway); Martin Andersen Nexö (Denmark); Willi Bredel, Bertolt Brecht, Ludwig Renn, Anna Seghers, Lion Feuchtwanger, Egon Erwin Kisch, Hans Marchwitza, Heinrich Mann (Germany); Denis Marion (Belgium) and Jef Last (Holland). [2]

The official topics for discussion in Spain did not vary substantially from those of the 1935 congress: the role of the individual in society, the individual, humanism, nation and culture, the problems of Spanish culture, cultural heritage, literary creation, reinforcement of cultural ties, support for Spanish republican writers.[3] Such topics were not designed to provoke long and heated discussions on political matters, but to promote solidarity. All of the topics were chosen in such a way "that the situation in Spain, the burning questions concerning policy towards the social revolution, external influences and the organisation of the war effort, would not be discussed. The organisers of the congress did not want discussion, they wanted acclamation."[4] One of the participants in the Spanish congress, the British delegate Edgell Rickword, noted that there was "not much discussion of particular cultural problems,"[5] whilst the German delegate Willi Bredel observed that it was "not a congress of long theoretical disputes, not a congress concerned with abstract problems, rather it was a congress of unanimous indictment of fascist abominations and of general willingness to support the Spanish people in their struggle for the defence of their culture and their freedom."[6] In a similar vein Bredel's compatriot Anna Seghers compared the Spanish congress with the Paris congress of two years earlier: "Our congress [i.e., in Spain] was conceived from the beginning as a demonstrative congress. Whereas at the first congress it was a matter of working out, of formulating our terms, in this congress it was a matter of bearing witness: namely to the defence of culture, which today is identical with the defence of Spain."[7] Madrid and Valencia undoubtedly provided precisely the right circumstances for bearing witness, for being acutely aware of the threat of fascism. Seghers also noted that the staircase of the town hall in Valencia had been damaged by a bomb – the evidence of "fascist abominations" was literally on the delegates' doorstep.[8]

As an exercise in the public expression of left-wing solidarity the congress enjoyed considerable success. Collectively the speeches delivered in Valencia, Madrid and finally in Paris, much like the responses to Nancy Cunard's *Authors Take Sides* survey, are an expression of the widely felt need for the unified commitment of writers, whether communists, socialists, liberals or whatever else, to the anti-fascist cause.[9] Unanimously the congress delegates condemned the actions of the franquist forces, most notably the destruction of Guernica just over two months earlier, and unanimously the delegates agreed that culture could only be rescued if fascism were defeated. On these issues genuine unanimity did exist. And precisely because so many known and respected writers attended the Spanish congress, much was achieved to draw world attention to the plight of the Republic and to boost the morale of all Spaniards and others who supported the Republic.[10]

It was no coincidence that the Spanish government, fully aware of this political dimension of the staging of the congress, gave it its full support. As mentioned, the communist-sympathetic Prime Minister Juan Negrín opened the congress in Valencia; amongst those present were no less than five ministers of Negrín's cabinet.[11] More than just an expression of intellectual solidarity, the congress was also appropriated as "a propaganda instrument for the newly-formed (on May 19) Negrín government."[12] The best evidence of this is the manifesto which was passed at the end of the congress, and which was widely published in the communist press in many countries. It explicitly praises the "brotherly assistance" accorded to the Spanish Republic by the Soviet Union.[13] Furthermore, there is a suggestion that, in order to maximise the propaganda value of the congress, the government timed the attack and subsequent pyrrhic victory at Brunete on July 6 to coincide with the staging of the congress, to place the scent of battle in the nostrils of the assembled writers.[14] The Soviet delegate and *Pravda* correspondent Mikhail Koltsov wrote in his diary: "In the middle of the meeting a delegation suddenly came into the room, direct from the trenches, with the news that Brunete had been taken. They were carrying flags they had just captured from the fascists. Indescribable jubilation."[15] It was an incident which showed that the Left, too, was at times guilty of aestheticising politics, of resorting to ritual in order to gain political advantage.[16]

Despite these public displays of solidarity, whether genuine or more cynically motivated, the Writers' Congress of 1937 was not in all respects an overwhelming success. Presumably because of a common desire to avoid issues which could prove divisive, the French writer André Chamson declared that the intellectual level of the congress was "appallingly low."[17] More importantly, though, the image of left-wing intellectual solidarity was vitiated by tensions which arose along ideological lines and which could not always be confined to the backrooms. Most telling were the responses to André Gide in his new role as critic of Stalinist Russia, and to those long-established opponents of the Stalinist brand of communism, namely the Trotskyists.

Stephen Spender recalled in 1951 that the congress in Spain "was divided over the issue of Gide."[18] In November of 1936 Gide had published his book *Retour de l'URSS*, which was an account of Gide's travels through the Soviet Union in the summer of that year.[19] Controversy surrounding the book was not entirely new – it had sent shock waves through the French Left immediately upon its appearance. In it Gide dared to express open criticism of Stalinist policies, to the point of even comparing Stalin's Soviet Union unfavourably with Hitler's Germany. He wrote: "And I doubt whether in any other country in the world, even Hitler's Germany, thought be less free, more fearful (terrorised), more vassalised."[20] Rather than seeking to heal the rift that his book caused, Gide in his sequel, *Retouches à mon Retour de l'URSS*, only rubbed salt into the wound by repeating and even strengthening his criticisms.[21] This sequel appeared just days before the opening of the Spanish congress.

Inevitably the display of intellectual solidarity under the banner of the Popular Front was eroded by the private but at times also the public discussion of Gide's blatant anti-Stalinist stance. According to Spender, even more sensational than Gide's book itself was "the fury with which it was received by Communists."[22] Within a short time Gide's reputation in the communist press had changed dramatically from "the greatest living French writer" to "Fascist monster" and "self-confessed decadent bourgeois."[23] At the congress the Soviet delegates reportedly went to great lengths to praise the Soviet Union's role in the Popular Front and simultaneously to denounce Gide. The Dutch writer Jef Last, who had accompanied Gide on his travels through the Soviet Union, reported that the Soviet delegation attempted to have a motion passed against Gide. Last, supported by two eminent (but unnamed) French writers, "protested against this attempt on the simple ground that the books of André Gide had not yet been translated in Spanish and could not be obtained anywhere in Madrid."[24] Finally, and ironically, the Soviets had to be content with a private statement by the Spanish Catholic writer José Bergamín, in which the latter praised the Soviet Union and chided Gide for his excessive and unbalanced criticism. Even this attempt at appeasement proved only partially successful. At the final sitting of the congress in Paris, Louis Aragon continued the criticism of Gide, who was denounced as a Trotskyist and accused of collaboration with the fascists. André Malraux declared such accusations groundless and subsequently refused to offer an address.[25]

The second thorn in the side of the Stalinists at the congress were the real Trotskyists, to whom the notion of Popular Front solidarity did not extend. The feeling was mutual; Trotsky for his part had denounced the Popular Front as a doomed alliance with the enemies of social revolution. The Trotskyists had been present in small number at the 1935 Writers' Congress, but by the time of the Spanish congress, when the notorious Moscow trials had already begun, they were absent altogether. Consequently they were in no position to defend themselves against the accusations levelled by the Soviet delegates, who demanded the "liquidation" of such enemies. Whether the Stalinist diatribes served to reinforce the official communist/Stalinist line appears highly dubious.

Certainly many of the delegates to the congress were loyal Communist Party members, who had welcomed the installment of the Negrín government less than two months earlier. But there also existed widespread support or at least sympathy amongst the non-communist Left for the anarchists and the POUM. For these delegates the "May events" in Barcelona, occurring just two months before the staging of the Writers' Congress, were a fresh and painful memory. To revive that memory through the remorseless condemnation of Trotskyism might have been a grave political miscalculation on the part of the communists. Even the Soviet delegate and *Izvestia* correspondent Ilya Ehrenburg mentions in his memoirs that the calls by Soviet delegates to "liquidate" the enemy "perplexed and alarmed" many Spaniards. [26] Jef Last similarly observed that the Soviets "began by upsetting even the Spaniards by their entirely gratuitous attack upon the Trotskyists." [27] Furthermore, Last drew attention to the hypocrisy of Soviet tactics precisely in the age of the Moscow trials. It was good, Last argued, that the congress should espouse "the cause of all the great writers who have been exiled from the Fascist countries or have lost their civic rights. But in the course of the proceedings other names were not so much as mentioned; such names as Ottwald, Günther, Tarassov, Rodianov, Rom, Mandelstam, Tretiakov, Bezunienski, Jossiensky, Gronski, Kliuiev? Why?" [28]

Although the Writers' Congress gave the impression of anti-fascist solidarity, the first important conclusion to draw from it is that there were underlying tensions and antagonisms which gave the lie to that impression. To a certain extent, in other words, the solidarity was feigned. The Popular Front was not an ideologically homogeneous entity, and although it could identify a common foe and direct the bulk of its energies against that foe, it was incapable of smoothing over deep-rooted ideological differences in its own camp.

Although some criticised the standard of aesthetic discourse at the congress as being disappointingly low, it is in this area that the second major lesson from the congress is to be learned. Despite latent ideological divisions, participants appear to have reached general agreement that art needed to be politically committed, and that in being committed it needed to abandon the radical experimentation of avantgarde and modernist art and to adopt widely accessible forms. In this context a *Ponencia Colectiva* (Collective Pronouncement), which was read at the congress by Arturo Serrano Plaja and published in the August 1937 edition of the journal *Hora de España*, possesses rare significance for aesthetic discourse, precisely because it was a *collective* pronouncement. In it the signatories declared:

The abstract art of recent years appeared false to us. But we could not admit as revolutionary, as authentic, a painting, for example, for the simple fact that its purpose was to portray a worker with a raised fist, or with a red flag, or with some other symbol, leaving the most essential reality unexpressed. . . . We declare that our greatest aspiration is to express fundamentally that reality with which we feel ourselves in agreement poetically, politically and philosophically. . . . We say, and we consider ourselves certain of it, that, ultimately, there is no clash between objective reality and the private world. [29]

Despite the presence of such figures as Louis Aragon[30] and Tristan Tzara (by now a member of the French Communist Party[31]) at the congress, the intellectuals clearly decided *against* abstract art. At the same time, though, they rejected purely propagandistic art forms which, in their judgment, failed to contain the essence of reality. Instead, in an attempt to unite moderate and revolutionary elements, which was entirely in the spirit of the Popular Front, and in adopting the banner of a kind of revolutionary humanism, the intellectuals pledged their support for a realism which would strike a balance between notions of an objective and a subjective reality.

## SPENDER'S LIBERAL DILEMMA

One of the most prominent of the British participants in the Writers' Congress was the poet Stephen Spender. Shortly after the congress, Spender had an article published in *New Writing*, in which he reviewed the proceedings in glowing terms. He describes his relations with the Spanish-American delegates, with whom he "was on back-slapping terms,"[32] and with André Malraux, whom Spender regarded as a hero.[33] He recalls that the most memorable incident of all occurred during the journey from Valencia to Madrid. The delegates stopped for lunch at a village called Minglanilla, where their meal was accompanied by the singing of the village children:

First they sang the International, then they sang other songs, of the Spanish Republic. We got up and stood at the windows to thank and applaud them. When we had finished eating we went down the stone steps of the Fonda where the children had cleared a little space in their crowd in the square and they were dancing a dance which consisted of running up and down from one end of this oblong space to the other. There were no men in the village – they were all either in the fields or fighting – and the women stood watching their children, suddenly weeping. When we went into the square to get back into our cars, the women began talking to us about the war and they asked us that one of us should speak from the balcony of the Fonda in order to show that we understood their fate (these were their words). One of the Mexicans spoke, very effectively. After that one of the women took Pablo Neruda and me back to her house, which was beautifully clean, and showed us photographs of her two sons at the front, and, in spite of our earnest protestations, insisted on our taking about half of all the sausages she had, because we would be hungry on the rest of the journey. We were all of us more moved by our few hours in Minglanilla than by any other single incident of our stay in Spain.[34]

Although unquestionably an avid supporter of the concept of a Popular Front, Spender is not entirely uncritical of the congress. On the contrary, as has been shown, it was Spender who reported Chamson's unflattering opinion of the intellectual standard of the congress, and Spender does make mention of the discord caused by the Gide controversy. He judges most of the speeches to have been ineffective and confesses a private antipathy towards the manner in which many of the Spanish poets depicted the heroism of war in their *romances*, "I myself, because I am not a writer of heroics, have felt rather isolated from the cause and the people I greatly care for, because I could not share this uncritical attitude."[35]

As early as this 1937 congress review, therefore, it is possible to detect in Spender a discrepancy between his public commitment and his private beliefs. Spender's mere presence in Spain (albeit in a nonmilitary capacity) and his participation in the congress were tangible evidence of his support for the republican cause and his opposition to fascism. Privately, though, Spender held certain reservations. He could accept the desirability of the ends, but he was troubled by the means employed in the name of the Popular Front.

This unresolved tension between the public and the private spheres is evident in Spender's other prose writing on the Spanish Civil War. Apart from the 1937 *New Writing* review, there are two other reviews of the Writers' Congress, both written approximately a decade after the war. One is in an essay in Richard Crossman's 1949 collection *The God That Failed*;[36] the other is in the already-mentioned 1951 autobiography *World Within World*. In both these accounts, the enthusiasm evident in the original congress review is missing. Here Spender writes of the "hysterical conceitedness" which had seized some of the delegates, and of Chamson's "fanatical self-importance."[37] Without revealing her name, he writes of a female communist writer, whose "sentences usually began, 'Wouldn't it be less selfish, comrade', which she followed by recommending some course of action highly convenient from her point of view."[38] The congress had "something about it of a Spoiled Children's Party, something which brought out the worst in many delegates."[39] The Russian delegates in particular "were impressive only for their arrogance and mental torpidity."[40] The incident at Minglanilla also is described in terms quite different from his earlier account. Introducing the course of events at the village, Spender writes:

The circus of intellectuals, treated like princes or ministers, carried for hundreds of miles through beautiful scenery and war-torn towns, to the sound of cheering voices, amid broken hearts, riding in Rolls-Royces, banqueted, fêted, sung and danced to, photographed and drawn, had something grotesque about it. Occasionally we were confronted with some incident which seemed a reproach, a mockery, emerging with a sharp edge from the reality which had been so carefully disguised for us. One such occurred at Minglanilla, on the single road connecting Valencia with three-quarters-surrounded Madrid.[41]

Other prose documents similarly point to a discrepancy between Spender's public and private world. Of particular importance is a letter which Spender wrote to Virginia Woolf in April 1937. It predates the Writers' Congress; in fact, it dates from the very end of Spender's second visit to Spain, during which he spent time in Barcelona, Madrid and Valencia.[42] During this visit one of Spender's tasks was to secure the release of his friend T. A. R. Hyndman from service in the communist-controlled International Brigades.[43] In attempting to achieve this, Spender was for a long time foiled by communist stubbornness and implacability.[44] He was concerned about Hyndman just as Virginia Woolf was worried about her nephew Julian Bell, who similarly had gone to Spain to fight (and die) for the Republic.[45] In his letter, Spender reports that he had not seen

Julian Bell at Albacete and therefore assumed that he had not joined the
International Brigades. He adds: "In any case, I hope he will not do so."[46] For
someone who publicly lent his unqualified support to the republican
government, this seems a quite extraordinary statement. Especially revealing in
the letter is Spender's critical attitude to the war and to the role being played by
the communists, whose implacability would have been fresh in his memory.
Publicly of course Spender supported the Popular Front and communist
participation in the Popular Front. Privately, though, he was prepared to admit
that the war was "horrible," that politicians everywhere were "detestable" and
that the pro-republican propaganda "depressed me a good deal."[47] Of the
communists specifically he wrote:

The political commissars are mostly Scotch Presbyterians who bully so much that even
people who were quite enthusiastic Party Members have been driven into hating the
whole thing. One man fighting at the Front complained to me bitterly about the
inquisitorial methods of the Party. Some of these methods are lies, for instance it is a lie
to say as the *Daily Worker* does that people can leave the Brigade whenever they like. On
the contrary, one is completely trapped there, and illness, nervous breakdown, bad
wounds are no excuse for getting away unless one belongs to the Party élite and is sent
home as a propagandist to show one's arm in a sling to audiences.[48]

Symptomatic of the discrepancies between Spender's public and private
attitudes to the war is his request to Virginia Woolf at the end of the letter:
"Quote this letter to any pacifist or democrat who wants to fight, but please do
not mention my name."[49] Spender was later to complain in the *New Statesman*
that volunteers for the International Brigade were not being told in advance that
it was a communist-controlled organisation.[50]

Spender's article "Heroes in Spain" is not overtly critical of the Communist
Party, but it does take issue strongly with the kind of propaganda which was
being produced in left-wing circles in Britain. Written after his first visit, it
praises the courage of the Spanish people and the unity of the anti-fascist cause.
Although recognising the existence of ideological differences between the
political parties, Spender affirms that in practice both anarchists and members of
the International Brigade "fight side by side and the boundaries between political
movements are broken down at the front."[51] At the same time, the article was
written with the intention to "counteract the propaganda about heroes in wars."[52]
Spender was prepared to accept that the war in Spain was necessary, but he
could not accept a portrayal of war which was too heroic, as was to be found in
British left-wing newspapers. The overwhelming impression Spender received
of war was its horror. "The final horror of war is the complete isolation of a man
dying alone in a world whose reality is violence. The dead in wars are not
heroes: they are freezing or rotting lumps of isolated insanity."[53]

As the evidence of the prose writings which deal with the Spanish Civil War
suggests, Spender's relationship with communism and with the Communist Party
was a highly problematical one. In the context of the times, though, the
attraction to communism was by no means unusual. Many of the socially
committed British writers and poets of the 1930s looked to communism as a

solution to the problems of the age. As Spender himself later explained, "The slump of the 1930s, the catastrophe of the Weimar Republic, the fall of Socialist Vienna, all of them events which I witnessed more or less from the outside, had forced me to accept a theoretically Communist position."[54] This theoretical acceptance of communism is evident in his book *Forward from Liberalism*, which was published by Victor Gollancz and chosen by the Left Book Club as Book of the Month in January 1937. In it Spender forecast that the liberal democratic state would collapse and be replaced by communism, which he saw as being essentially an advanced form of liberalism. Thus Spender was able to claim: "I am a communist because I am a liberal."[55] Even at this time Spender was prepared to concede that there were certain problems associated with the process by which communism would supersede liberalism. He was critical, for example, of the staging of the Moscow trials, the first of which were taking place at that time. Nevertheless he accepted the orthodox view that a transitional period of dictatorship would be necessary. In short, *Forward from Liberalism* documents a stage in Spender's intellectual development in which he valued the potential public good of the implementation of communism above the individual suffering which would result in the process.

It was shortly after the publication of *Forward from Liberalism* that Spender visited Harry Pollitt, the secretary of the British Communist Party, at the latter's request. A key topic of conversation was inevitably the Spanish Civil War. Having established that he agreed to differ with Spender on certain points, but concurred on the need to support the Spanish Republic, Pollitt proposed that Spender join the Communist Party in order to help the Republic.[56] Pollitt would be prepared to accept Spender's disagreement on certain points but would allow him to publish his point of view in the *Daily Worker* at the time of him joining the Party. Spender accepted the offer, joined the Party in February 1937, and published an article in the *Daily Worker* a few days later.[57] It concluded with the words: "It seems to me that the most important political aim of our time should be the United Front, organised so that it has a common interest with the Soviet and the Popular Fronts of Spain and France. I wish to belong to the party which is most active in working towards this end, and so I have joined the Communist Party."[58]

Just as the Spanish Civil War provided the impetus for Spender's decision to join the Communist Party, so Spender's visits to Spain in 1937 persuaded him that he had made the wrong choice. As has been indicated, the prose writings by Spender which deal with the period reveal an underlying discontent with Party recruitment activities and with the Party's heroism propaganda. Above all, they show that, although Spender maintained public support for the republican cause, he had been deeply affected by the horrible reality of war. It seems that Spender never publicly announced his exit from the Party; his membership was allowed to lapse.

It was the Spanish experience which exacerbated Spender's liberal dilemma. In *Forward from Liberalism* Spender had been willing to accept that long-term public good must rank higher than short-term private suffering. He accepted the superiority of end over means. In Spain, the experience of the mode of operation of the Communist Party combined with the direct contact with the horror of war convinced him otherwise. In short, he came to abhor the means and to affirm the ultimate validity of the private conscience. Spender himself fully recognised the nature of the dilemma which confronted his generation and was later to articulate it as follows: "The impulse to act was not mistaken. But the action we took may not have been the right kind. It was, for the most part, the half-and-half action of people divided between their artistic and their public conscience, and unable to fuse the two."[59]

Although it is possible to detect this dilemma of being unable to fuse the public and the private conscience in Spender's prose writings, it rarely emerges in his poetry of the war. As a poet, Spender opted quite consistently for the presentation of the private conscience.

In only a couple of instances in the body of his Spanish Civil War poetry does Spender adopt what could be described as a public mode. Very rarely does he express ideological orthodoxy in the form of an explicit condemnation of fascism or capitalism. "Ultima Ratio Regum" begins with lines which link capitalism with militarism: "The guns spell money's ultimate reason / In letters of lead on the Spring hillside."[60] Similarly, "At Castellon" is explicit in articulating an anger at the nationalist strategy of bombing the Spanish people into submission.

In the vast majority of Spender's Spanish Civil War poems, however, the reader looks in vain for signs of commitment to the revolution or to the republican cause. Rather than affirming faith in the necessity of the battle against fascism, Spender's poetry devotes itself consistently to the themes of death and the futility of war. Though the first two lines of "Ultima Ratio Regum" might reflect Marxist orthodoxy in linking capitalism with militarism, the following lines confront the senselessness of the destruction of innocent youth: "But the boy lying dead under the olive trees / Was too young and too silly / To have been notable to their important eye. / He was a better for a kiss."[61] "The Coward" also deals with Spender's related themes of death and innocence. With attention focussed here also on the corpse of a soldier beneath the grey olive trees, the poem rebuffs the idea of heroism and demands love and pity for the dead:

Here one died, not like a soldier
Of lead, but of lead rings of terror.
His final moment was the birth
Of naked revelatory truth:
He saw the flagship at the quay,
His mother's care, his lover's kiss,
The white accompaniment of spray,
Lead to the bullet and to this.[62]

In dealing with these prominent themes, Spender does little to hint even that his sympathies rested with the republicans. On the contrary, it often appears that he goes to considerable lengths not just to avoid any sense of partisanship but to promote a strict impartiality in political matters. The poem "Two Armies," for example, establishes a setting in which two armies confront each other on a "winter plain," but no attempt is made to identify the armies or to discriminate between them. The sense of futile suffering applies equally to both of them. Finally the two sides cease to hate each other, and in death they become as one in No-Man's-Land:

When the machines are stilled, a common suffering
Whitens the air with breath and makes both one
As though these enemies slept in each other's arms.

Only the lucid friend to aerial raiders
The brilliant pilot moon, stares down
Upon this plain she makes a shining bone
Cut by the shadows of many thousand bones.
Where amber clouds scatter on No-Man's-Land
She regards death and time throw up
The furious words and minerals which destroy. 63

Tellingly, one of Spender's poems describing the struggle between time and a soldier's corpse is entitled "In No Man's Land."[64] Here, too, a rigid impartiality is observed, as is the case in "Port Bou." In this poem the narrator, who describes himself as "the coward of cowards," is careful to adopt the perspective of precise and detached impartiality: "I am left alone on the parapet at the exact centre / Above the river trickling through the gulley, like that old man's saliva. / The exact centre, solitary as the bull's eye in a target."[65]

Spender's important contribution to the popularisation of much Spanish Civil War poetry will be discussed in more detail shortly. As an editor of *Poems for Spain* he was in a position to promote the *romances* of Spanish poets. For his own purposes, however, Spender opted not to employ public and popular poetic forms to voice his very private response to the war. It is evident from the examples given above that Spender continued to write in the free verse which had been a hallmark of poetic modernism, both in Britain and elsewhere. Moreover, Spender's language was often rendered barely accessible by its wealth of metaphor. This, too, is already evident from extracts already provided. It is not easy task to decode such complex metaphors as "No-Man's-Land" or "the parapet at the exact centre." The entire poem "Till Death Completes Their Arc" is equally elusive in its metaphorical intensity and in its apparent distance from the direct context of the war.

Spender's war poetry was not the poetry of an unreserved political commitment but of a heightened individual sensibility to the horror of war and the reality of death. As in Wilfred Owen's World War I poems, the poetry was very much in the pity.[66] Spender himself was not a combatant as Owen had been, but he applied his creative energy to empathise with the soldiers. Clearly, though, it was not the kind of poetry which would generate enthusiasm for the war and persuade young men to join the International Brigades. It was a brand of poetry which attracted harsh criticism from communist circles, where Spender's claims of having advanced from liberalism to communism had been treated with considerable scepticism. Spender's war poems served to reinforce the suspicion that the "liberal," "Oxford" poets like Spender (and W. H. Auden, Cecil Day

Lewis, Louis MacNeice and others) were too "bourgeois" to unite their private and public consciences. With some justification, the communist critic Randall Swingler wrote of Spender's war poems: "Not one of them is about the Spanish War. They are all about Spender and his detachment from history in the making of Spain. He objectifies his own rejection of the historical issue in the Deserter, the Coward, the Wounded getting a little respite from the war. To those who had any part in that war, whether fighting or actively supporting, these poems mean very little."[67]

Whether, like Valentine Cunningham, one extols Spender's war poetry for its honesty,[68] or whether, like Randall Swingler, one condemns it for favouring the private at the cost of the public conscience, the ideological implications are apparent. Although written by an enthusiastic supporter of the Popular Front, the content and the reception of Spender's poems reveal fundamental differences of opinion within the Popular Front coalition. Whereas Spender insisted on separating the public from the private sphere and thematicising the latter in his poetry, the communists expounded the unity of the spheres and the feasibility of a kind of honest collectivity in literature. It may not have been the kind of issue to bring the Popular Front to its knees, but, like the Writers' Congress, it revealed that there were irreconcilable differences which challenged the image of solidarity.

## POEMS FOR SPAIN

Although it is not difficult to locate dissent and antagonism amongst elements of the Popular Front, outwardly its adherents were determined to project an image of confident solidarity. In the literary sphere a number of anthologies helped to perform this function, not just because of the content of the individual items they contained but also because they were able to bring together anti-fascist writers representing a broad range of the political spectrum. In effect these anthologies were the Popular Front in aesthetic form.

Not surprisingly, the first of these anthologies was a Spanish production, a collection of thirty-five *romances*, that is, poems in a traditional Spanish form of eight-syllable lines employing assonance rather than rhyme. It presented the work of twenty poets, most of whom, such as Rafael Alberti, Miguel Hernández and Spender's acquaintance Manuel Altolaguirre, had a well-established reputation before the outbreak of war. Bearing the title *Romancero de la Guerra Civil (Serie 1)* (Romancero of the Civil War, Series 1), it was published at the time of the siege of Madrid in November 1936 under the editorship of the Literary Section of the *Alianza de Intelectuales* (Alliance of Intellectuals).[69] The second major Spanish anthology was occasioned by the 1937 Writers' Congress. To commemorate the event, Emilio Prados collected 302 *romances* by 101 poets, the choice having been made from some 900 *romances* which had been submitted for publication in the journal *El Mono Azul* (The Blue Monkey or The Blue Overalls).[70] The volume was dedicated to García Lorca, the most famous of the modern writers of *romances*, who had been killed by the nationalists in the early days of the war. Like the first anthology, this collection reflected the range of ideologies which supported the concept of a Popular Front, including a few nonprofessional poets, who in many cases preferred to remain anonymous or signed their poems only with their initials. One of the best represented poets, with twelve poems, was the anarchist Antonio Agraz, a spokesman for an ideology which officially was outside the Popular Front. At the same time, and to perform the identical function of commemorating the 1937 Writers' Congress, the editors of the journal *Hora de España* (Spain's Hour) published a volume entitled *Poetas en España leal* (Poets in Loyal Spain). This was an anthology of forty-four poems, most of which had appeared in *Hora de España*.[71]

During the war an anthology was published which transcended not only ideological but also some national boundaries, and that was *Poems for Spain*, edited by Stephen Spender and John Lehmann.[72] It did not appear until 1939, when the cause of Spain and the Popular Front had been almost fought and certainly lost, but many of the fifty-three poems date from the early part of the war, when hopes for a crushing victory over fascism were still high. Most of the poems are by British poets, some of whom had little or no literary profile. But the volume also contains works by prominent non-British poets, by Spaniards such as Hernández, Agraz and Altolaguirre, by the Chilean poet Pablo Neruda, and by the young Irishman Charles Donnelly. The ideological range of the collection is seen in the inclusion of poems by communists (such as Tom Wintringham, John Cornford, Edgell Rickword and Charles Donnelly), by non-communist leftists (such as Auden, MacNeice and Spender himself, at this time no longer a member of the Party) and even by anarchists (Antonio Agraz, Herbert Read). The poems are divided into six sections: "Action," "Death," "The Map," "Satire," "Romances" and "Lorca," and are preceded by an introduction written by Spender.

When one considers the predominance of private concerns in his own war poetry, Spender's introduction is a remarkable document. It is an unabashed plea for a poetry which plays a role in the battle *for* culture and *against* fascist barbarism. Although Spender's own distinctly anti-heroic war poetry bears the unmistakable influence of Owen, in his introduction Spender hints at the inadequacy of Owenesque poetry in the Spanish context: "'All a poet can do to-day is to warn,' the greatest of the English war poets, Wilfred Owen, wrote in 1918. That is true always of poetry written in the midst of a great social upheaval; but the poets of the International Brigade have a different warning to give from that of the best poets of the Great War. It is a warning that it is necessary for civilisation to defend and renew itself."[73] To strengthen this claim, Spender refers back beyond Owen to the tradition of a politically committed British romantic poetry. He cites the words Keats used of Peterloo: "No contest between Whig and Tory – but between Right and Wrong."[74] In writing of the "poets of the English Liberal tradition" who "responded to Spain crushed by Napoleon", he quotes in full Wordsworth's sonnet "Indignation of a High-minded Spaniard".[75]

Spender's intention, however, is not to claim for the poets of the Spanish Civil War the same literary status as that of a Keats or a Wordsworth. Although the political function of the *Poems for Spain* links them with the poetry of the

Romantics, Spender is conscious that the value of his anthology rests not in aesthetic quality but in historical representativeness. He perceives the collection as "a document of our times."[76] Many of the poems in it "were written by men for whom poetry scarcely existed before the Spanish War."[77] The fact that a struggle for freedom, education and leisure was taking place meant that there was "little time for the maturing of poetry in minds which are violent and unsettled."[78]

In short, and in contrast to his own poetic practice, Spender's introduction is an appeal for a popular and public poetry, tailored to the particular political needs of the day. He argues that "occasionally, in a revolution, a national resurgence, a war against an aggressor, there is a revival of the fundamental ideas and there is actually an identity of public policy and poetry. This is the sense in which poetry is political; it is always concerned with the fundamental ideas, either because they are being realised in action, or, satirically, to show that they are totally removed from public policy."[79] Spender offers no indication of division amongst the Popular Front forces, and it is true to say that neither the introduction nor indeed any of the poems collected in *Poems for Spain* contains any suggestion of divided aims. One poem by Pedro Garfias indeed emphasises the unity of purpose of anarchists and marxists:

When the enemy pours out
his barrage on our parapet
shoulder close to shoulder,
courage beside courage too,
we grip hands with nothing said.
And Marx and Bakunin . . . hug each other warmly
as brothers swearing loyalty
there where lie our dead.[80]

The poems do not delight in war, and indeed many depict its horror. But they accept its necessity, praise the courage of those who defended the Republic and condemn the greed or stupidity of those who sought to destroy it.

Even a cursory glance at the table of contents reveals that the anthology contains a number of poems by representatives of two "groups" of British poets in the 1930s. The first of these is the so-called "Auden group," which is represented here by all its members: Auden himself, Spender, MacNeice and Day Lewis. The second group is perhaps less readily definable, but it contains committed communist poets such as John Cornford and Charles Donnelly. Key figures in this group, although not represented here, were Christopher Caudwell and Ralph Fox, both of whom, like Donnelly and Cornford, lost their lives in Spain.[81] Although literary history has tended to accord more attention to the Auden group, both groups were of central importance to the left-wing literary movement in Britain in the 1930s.

The existence of two distinct groups is not merely a historical construct imposed by literary historians for the sake of convenience. Young communist writers demonstrably *did* hold a genuine antagonism towards the Auden group, an antagonism expressing itself in attacks which in their acerbity rivalled those launched by Roy Campbell from the other end of the spectrum. The communists were inclined to accuse the Auden group of being "too bourgeois," of not being prepared to break with their privileged class roots. John Cornford, for example, accused Spender, Auden and company of trying to make a "literary fashion of 'revolution' among bourgeois intellectuals whilst denying the possibility of the growth of a genuinely revolutionary literature with a new class basis."[82] Similarly Christopher Caudwell labelled the Auden group "bourgeois revolutionaries", although he did express the belief that "they will escape from the bourgeois round; they will become complete Communists and help to create a new vital poetry, instead of galvanising with mechanical formulae a dead body."[83]

Despite this demonstrable antagonism, to identify differences between the groups on ideological or aesthetic grounds is no easy task. While it is true that the members of the Auden group shared privileged social backgrounds and educations, this holds true also for many communists. The communists were firmly committed to Marxist ideology, and the strength of that commitment manifested itself in the theoretical works of Fox and Caudwell.[84] But the Auden group was also attracted to Marxism, even if that attraction was somewhat tenuous. Spender, it will be remembered, did join the Communist Party for a short time, and Day Lewis was a member for several years. Auden was attracted to Marxism without actually joining the Party. He was greatly impressed by Caudwell's *Illusion and Reality*, which he described in *New Verse* as "the most important book on poetry since the books of Dr. Richards, and, in my opinion, provides a more satisfactory answer to the many problems which poetry raises."[85] In aesthetic matters, both groups expressed a firm belief in a socially and politically committed poetry, in the capacity of poetry to influence objective reality.

On close inspection, therefore, the image of two clearly defined groups constantly at loggerheads in matters of aesthetics and political ideology does not always hold true. Hugh Ford suggests that "a fairly relaxed relationship, based on respect for each other's independence, existed between left-wing poets and politicians. It is true that Cornford, Caudwell and Julian Bell were condemning the Auden group as too 'bourgeois'. But this internecine feud seemed peripheral."[86] Ford goes on to observe that the situation became more tense after the outbreak of war in Spain in 1936, because "there was increasing pressure upon writers to state their attitudes toward the struggle and, if possible, to persuade them to work for the Popular Front."[87] On the one hand, the predominantly private poetry produced by Stephen Spender and the unfavourable response to it by communists suggested that the relationship had become strained. On the other hand, the publication of *Poems for Spain*, of Nancy Cunard's already-mentioned *Authors Take Sides* and of countless poems by communists and non-communists in journals such as *Left Review*, *New Writing* and *Volunteer for Liberty* demonstrated that cooperation between ideologically disparate elements of the Left was still viable. Moreover, although Spender's poetry reveals a clear preference for the private over the public, the other "Auden group" contributors to *Poems for Spain* display a willingness in their work to openly espouse the cause of the Republic. Both technically and substantively, much of the poetry produced by the members of the Auden group is not remarkably different from that written by their alleged opponents.

Louis MacNeice was politically the least committed of the Auden group. Like the others, he was disdainful of capitalism, but less inclined to opt for the Marxist solution. *Poems for Spain* contains an extract from his long 1938 poem "Autumn Journal." It records the seemingly disinterested impressions of a group of "trippers" touring Spain before the outbreak of war. (MacNeice had been in Spain at Easter in 1936.) They leave Spain ignorant of the decisive role that it is about to play in their lives, providing them with a cause which would focus their previously vague hopes. It concludes with the lines:

And next day took the boat
For home, forgetting Spain, not realizing
That Spain would soon denote
Our grief, our aspirations;
Not knowing that our blunt
Ideals would find their whetstone, that our spirit
Would find its frontier on the Spanish front,
Its body in a rag-time army.[88]

Whether for reasons of copyright or of length, Cecil Day Lewis's poem "The Nabara," which Katharine Bail Hoskins describes as being probably his "most valuable contribution to the cause of the Spanish Republic,"[89] is not included in *Poems for Spain*. Based on an episode in George Lowther Steer's book *The Tree of Gernika*, it deals with the heroism of Basque seamen who protect a freighter loaded with ammunition from a nationalist attack.[90] The poem by Day Lewis which Spender and Lehmann did include is "Bombers," a work which in richly metaphorical language depicts the mechanised horror generated by enemy aircraft. When it is considered that this poem appeared in *Poems for Spain* and that the bombing of republican towns had been widely reported in Britain, it is inevitable that "Bombers" was interpreted as an anti-nationalist poem. Interestingly, though, the identity of the bombers is not revealed, and the final stanza presents the reader with a moral choice with distinctly pacifist overtones. It may be seen to foreshadow the suffering which was to be endured by the English population in the near future when it ask the reader to make a choice "between your child and this fatal embryo."[91]

The best-known poem by a member of the Auden group in *Poems for Spain*, and arguably the most famous poem of the war in any language, is Auden's "Spain." It had in fact already appeared long before its inclusion in *Poems for Spain*, Faber and Faber having published it as a sixteen-page pamphlet in May 1937. It sold for one shilling; all proceeds went to "Medical Aid for Spain."

The fame of the poem is partly attributable to the controversy surrounding it. That controversy begins with Auden himself and the circumstances under which he acquired his knowledge of the war in Spain. Unlike Day Lewis, Auden certainly did visit Spain during the war, but the visit is shrouded in mystery because of Auden's extraordinary reticence on the subject. One of his biographers, Humphrey Carpenter, observes that Auden "seems to have written no letters home from Spain; on his return he rarely discussed what had happened to him, and he wrote no connected account of his experiences."[92] The *Daily Worker* reported on 12 January 1937 that Auden had left for Spain "to serve as an ambulance driver."[93] He spent time in Barcelona and in Valencia, from where he sent a report for publication in the *New Statesman & Nation*. For the most part it contains an array of seemingly disconnected, almost flippant observations of the seat of the republican government. This apparently casual tone of the bulk of the article is corrected in the final paragraph, which conveys a sense of pugnacious commitment:

For a revolution is really taking place, not an odd shuffle or two in cabinet appointments. In the last six months these people have been learning what it is to inherit their own country, and once a man has tasted freedom he will not lightly give it up; freedom to choose for himself and to organise his life, freedom not to depend for good fortune on a clever and outrageous piece of overcharging or a windfall of drunken charity. That is why, only eight hours away at the gates of Madrid where this wish to live has no possible alternative expression than the power to kill, General Franco has already lost two professional armies and is in the process of losing a third.[94]

This piece was published on 30 January 1937, and so is a product of Auden's early impressions of Spain. It appears that Auden did not work as an ambulance driver as he had hoped, but he might have been involved in propaganda work with one of the Valencia broadcasting stations. Possibly Auden did spend a brief period at the front, but by March 4 he was back in London.[95] Valentine Cunningham speculates that there might have been a second, brief visit in April or May 1937.[96]

Controversy similarly surrounds the history of the poem. The 1939 *Poems for Spain* version is identical with the original May 1937 version. When the poem was included in the 1940 collection *Another Time*, three stanzas were omitted and some words and phrases were altered. Most famously, the words "conscious acceptance of guilt in the necessary murder" were changed to "conscious acceptance of guilt in the fact of murder." The poem did appear in the 1950 *Collected Shorter Poems*, but otherwise Auden preferred to omit it from postwar anthologies. When permission was sought to include it in an anthology of poetry of the 1930s, Auden agreed only on the condition that the editor make it absolutely clear that "Mr W. H. Auden considers [it] to be trash which he is ashamed to have written."[97] In the foreword to the 1966 *Collected Shorter Poems* Auden quoted the last two lines of "Spain," which suggested that history could at best say "alas" but "cannot help nor pardon" the defeated. In a tone of deep regret he then wrote: "To say this is to equate goodness with success. It would have been bad enough if I had ever held this wicked doctrine, but that I should have stated it simply because it sounded to me rhetorically effective is quite inexcusable."[98]

Finally, considerable controversy is to be found in the reception and interpretation of the poem, both during the war and in the postwar period. Included in the reception history is of course Auden's own later negative response, but also a mass of secondary literature which has praised "Spain" as "the most satisfactory poem anyone wrote about the Spanish Civil War" and condemned it as "a reflection of the poet's continuing isolation, falsifying the perspective of social development and delaying the re-integration of the poet into the body of society."[99]

Yet another detailed examination of the text need not be undertaken here. What is important in this context is that Auden *does* adopt a public voice in a poem which was intended to inspire commitment to the republican cause. In its twenty-six tightly structured stanzas it presents a series of images of the past, the present and the future. They all revolve around the central fourteenth stanza: "'What's your proposal? To build the just city? I will. / I agree. Or is it the suicide pact, the romantic / Death? Very well, I accept, for / I am your choice, your decision. Yes, I am Spain.'"[100] The poem demands the making of a moral choice, namely a choice *for* the struggle in Spain in the present, in order to ensure a better future. To make this decision in favour of progress means an acceptance that today there will be a struggle. It means an acceptance of all the exigencies of the struggle, that is, "the expending of powers / On the flat ephemeral pamphlet and the boring meeting"[101] More than that, it entails "the deliberate increase in the chances of death, / The conscious acceptance of guilt in the necessary murder"[102] There is no sense here of the delight in participation in war that has been observed in the pro-nationalist literature of the war; on the contrary, Auden acknowledges the burden of guilt that participation inevitably brings with it. Furthermore, he does not attempt to play down the significance of that burden. Murder is murder, but is necessary murder at this point of history. Should this struggle be unsuccessful, should this unique opportunity be lost, it would be lost forever. "We are left alone with our day, and the time is short, and / History to the defeated / May say Alas but cannot help nor pardon."[103]

The political implications of the poem as a call to action were recognised immediately by its readers. Spender places it in the tradition of Wordsworth's sonnets on Spain, claiming that it "translates a political action into terms of the imagination and thus tests the implications of a particular, contemporary situation by the whole tradition of values which exists in poetry."[104] Elsewhere, and noting the dominance of the public over the private in the poem, Spender paid it a somewhat backhanded compliment when he observed: "Within these limits, in which the element of personal experience and direct emotional response is rigorously excluded, the poem is a remarkable interpretation of the issues and implications of the struggle in Spain."[105] John Lehmann was similarly apprehensive about the dominance of the public at the expense of the private, claiming that the poem had a "suspicion of rhetoric" clinging to it.[106]

Despite the poem's explicit commitment to the Spanish cause, and despite the presence in it of a kind of Marxian dialectic of past, present and future, the communist response to the poem was mixed. Whereas Spender and Lehmann were cautiously critical of its overwhelmingly public mode, Edgell Rickword adopted the opposite tack. He accused the "flat ephemeral pamphlet" lines of being "an extraordinary example of what used to be accepted as the aloofness proper to the intellectual, in one who has recently been to Spain and had the opportunity of observing the immense vitality which the people are bringing to the task of simultaneously defeating the invaders and creating a free culture".[107]

Richard Goodman in the *Daily Worker* was more generous, although he too was not convinced that the combination of the public and the private was entirely successful:

"Spain" – the best poem that Auden has yet written and, with Spender's "Vienna", the only poem by an Englishman anywhere near being a revolutionary poem – still deals with Auden's own personal reactions and personal interpretation of the Spanish struggle, although it is very near realizing the fusion of this personal interpretation with the objective interpretation, which is essential for the realization of true revolutionary poetry.[108]

Whereas Spender and Lehmann found the public element too strong, the communists were objecting to the poem being too personal.

Ironically, the harshest criticism of the poem was that it was too blatantly communist. That criticism came from George Orwell, originally in a relatively mild form in the journal *The Adelphi* in December 1938, and then much more caustically in his 1940 essay "Inside the Whale".[109] Referring specifically to the stanza which included the words "conscious acceptance of guilt in the necessary murder", Orwell wrote that it was

intended as a sort of thumbnail sketch of a day in the life of a "good party man". In the morning a couple of political murders, a ten-minutes' interlude to stifle "bourgeois" remorse, and then a hurried luncheon and a busy afternoon and evening chalking walls and distributing leaflets. All very edifying. But notice the phrase "necessary murder". It could only be written by a person to whom murder is at most a *word*. Personally I would not speak so lightly of murder. It so happens that I have seen the bodies of numbers of murdered men - I don't mean killed in battle, I mean murdered. . . . Mr. Auden's brand of amoralism is only possible if you are the kind of person who is always somewhere else when the trigger is pulled. So much of left-wing thought is a kind of playing with fire by people who don't even know that fire is hot.[110]

It is often overlooked that Orwell had prefaced these remarks by saying that "Spain" was "one of the few decent things that have been written about the Spanish war."[111] Nevertheless, Orwell's criticism is interesting in that it is based on substantive rather than aesthetic grounds. He is not concerned with whether the poem offers a successful fusion of public and private elements; instead, he reaches beyond the poem and accuses the poet of downright hypocrisy.[112]

Like Auden's poem, and like much of the poetry by members of the Auden group in *Poems for Spain*, the poems by communist poets combine public and private elements in varying proportions. This is certainly true of the war poetry of John Cornford, who is often regarded as the leading British communist poet of the Spanish Civil War. The communist literature of the war must be dealt with in detail in the next chapter, but here an examination of the work of Cornford can serve to highlight the limitations of a construction of literary history which arbitrarily distinguishes between the literature of the communist and that of the non-communist Left.

To begin with, the case of Cornford's involvement in the war illustrates the mythical dimensions of the notion that all communists were permanently subjected to party discipline, and that the history of foreign pro-republican involvement in the war is synonymous with the history of the International Brigades. Cornford had just graduated from Cambridge University when the war broke out. He set off to Spain, arriving in Barcelona on 8 August 1936. As his travelling companion in Spain, Franz Borkenau, relates, Cornford joined the POUM militia at a time when the International Brigades had not yet been formed.[113] Under the circumstances it would have been expected for Cornford to join the ranks of the United Socialist Party of Catalonia militia rather than that of the dissident POUM, which Orwell was to join in January of the following year. What is even more surprising is that when Cornford returned to England in the middle of September to recuperate, it was apparently with the intention of returning to Spain to rejoin the same POUM militia. On October 4 he wrote to his college tutor to resign his scholarships, "as by the time this reaches you I shall already be on the way to rejoin the unit of the Anti-Fascist Militia with which I have been fighting this summer."[114] On returning to Spain, he became aware of the formation of the International Brigades and signed up with them. In late December 1936, in fact on the day after his twenty-first birthday, Cornford was killed in battle.[115]

The poetic fruits of Cornford's Spanish experience are three poems. "Full Moon at Tierz" was written at the Huesca front during his first sojourn in Spain, as was "Poem," which is sometimes known by its first line, "Heart of the Heartless World." It is these two poems which are included in *Poems for Spain*. The third, "A Letter from Aragon," was probably written when Cornford was about to depart from Spain.[116]

In his introduction Spender is moderate in his praise of Cornford. The essential quality of his poems, he suggests, lies in that they were "written from *inside* Spain; they have the merits and defects of being extremely close to experience." He adds:

Cornford's few poems have remarkable and insistent qualities which may indicate one of the directions in which an orthodox communist poetry might develop. His problem is to attain just this orthodoxy, to express in poetry the unity of thought and action, to translate necessity into terms of the poetic imagination. Most contemporary literature seems to be written from the sensibility, Cornford's poems seem to be written by the will.[117]

Whether Spender considered the achievement of communist orthodoxy a desirable goal in poetry is of course dubious. Nevertheless, it is a measure of Spender's perceptiveness that he recognised that in communist orthodoxy a fusion of elements was essential – a fusion of thought and action, of imagination and necessity, ultimately of the private and the public.[118]

"Poem" is accorded the considerable honour of opening *Poems for Spain*. Just sixteen lines in length, it is a love poem in the first person.[119] The first- and second-person personal pronouns and possessive adjectives occur no less than twelve times, a statistic which gives some indication of the deeply personal nature of the poem. The narrative "I" expresses fear of losing his lover, as well as the fear of fear itself: "I am afraid to lose you, / I am afraid of my fear."[120] He then reveals that the source of his fear is the possibility of death, and bids that, in the case of his death, his love should be remembered: "And if bad luck should lay my strength / Into the shallow grave, / Remember all the good you can; / Don't forget my love."[121] Only a single word, "Huesca," indicates a Spanish setting, and only one line, "The last fence for our pride"[122], points to a supra-personal concern. With its frank and overriding expression of individual sensibility and fear, however, it is no wonder that Spender admired it.

"Full Moon at Tierz," subtitled "Before the Storming of Huesca," in stark contrast to "Poem," is *not* an intensely personal poem. It even incorporates explicitly communist terminology, speaking, for example, of the "dialectic's point of change," "the Seventh Congress," "Dimitrov," "Maurice Thorez," "Communism" and "my Party."[123] It concludes with a rhetorical flourish which pleas for communism, liberty and the triumphant raising of the red flag. This is not to suggest that there is no longer any consideration of private concerns here. On the contrary, as in "Poem," Cornford expresses his personal fears, but they are fears which are allayed through the recognition of the collective purpose to which he has dedicated himself.

In this suggestion of the primacy of the collective or the public sphere, Cornford's poem bears comparison with Auden's "Spain." Both poems clearly perform the function of attracting support to the republican cause, even if Cornford's allegiance is more specifically communist. Both poems stress the necessity to overcome private fears or reservations for the sake of historical progress. On this precise point regarding the nature of historical progress, the two poems are remarkably similar. Cornford begins his poem by establishing a dialectical scheme of history which is much like that of "Spain." Like Auden, Cornford emphasises the vital importance of collective and committed action in the present in order to shape the future.

Whether or not this poem and the other poems of John Cornford offer a successful combination of the public and the private is a question of aesthetic evaluation which is of no concern here. The point is that in the communist poetry of the war and in most of the poetry of the non-communist Left (with the exception of the bulk of Spender's poetic work) such a combination is attempted. It is true that communist critics and reviewers differed from their non-communist counterparts in insisting on a fusion of public and private, to the extent of condemning work (such as the greater part of Spender's) which favoured the depiction of private sensibility at the expense of public commitment. It is true also that privately many non-communist writers (like Auden and Spender) baulked at the notion of ranking the long-term common good over the necessarily evil means and individual suffering of the present. But in *aesthetic practice* there is very little to distinguish the communists from the non-communists; in aesthetic practice there really was a kind of Popular Front, which for a time at least helped to hide, but not to bury, the deep and genuine ideological divisions within the Front.

# NOTES

1. H. Stuart Hughes. *Contemporary Europe: A History*. 2nd. ed. Englewood Cliffs, NJ: Prentice-Hall, 1966. p. 251.

2. This list is based on Robert S. Thornberry. "Der Zweite Internationale Schriftstellerkongreß zur Verteidigung der Kultur (1937)." In *Der Spanische Bürgerkrieg. Literatur und Geschichte*. Ed. Günther Schmigalle, 115-28. Frankfurt a.M.: Vervuert, 1986. p. 117. From Thornberry's list I exclude John Lehmann, who did not attend. See John Lehmann. *The Whispering Gallery*. London, New York, Toronto: Longman's, Green and Co., 1955. p. 283. The list includes only the authors who officially represented their countries. Some writers, including Bertolt Brecht, Heinrich Mann, Ramón Sender, Louis Aragon and Langston Hughes, participated only in the special Paris sessions of the congress held on 16 and 17 July. George Orwell, Ernest Hemingway, Thomas Mann and John Dos Passos were just a few of the well-known pro-republican writers who did not attend at all.

3. *Solidaridad Obrero*. 3 July 1936. p. 6. Quoted *ibid*. p. 118.

4. Reinhold Görling. *"Dinamita Cerebral." Politischer Prozeß und ästhetische Praxis im Spanischen Bürgerkrieg (1936-1939)*. Frankfurt a.M.: Vervuert, 1986. pp. 295-96.

5. Edgell Rickword. "In Defence of Culture. The Second Congress of the International Association of Writers. Madrid July 1937." *Left Review* 3, 6 (July 1937): p. 381.

6. Willi Bredel. *Spanienkrieg. Begegnung am Ebro. Schriften – Dokumente. Vol. 2*. East Berlin, Weimar: Aufbau, 1977. p. 244.

7. Anna Seghers. "Zum Schriftstellerkongreß in Madrid." In Anna Seghers, 180-86. *Willkommen, Zukunft! Reden und Aufsätze über Kunst und Wirklichkeit*. Munich: Damnitz, 1975. pp. 181-82.

8. *Ibid*. p. 181.

9. Contributions to the congress were published in such journals as *Das Wort, Left Review, Nueva Cultura* and *Hora de España*. The best collection of documentation on the congress is *II congreso internacional de escritores antifascistas (1937). Volumen 3. Actas, ponencias, documentos y testimonios*. Ed. Manuel Aznar Soler and Luis Mario Schneider. Barcelona: Laia, 1979.

10. For a pro-communist account of the congress, which predictably stresses the solidarity of its participants and plays down the elements of dissent which are discussed here, see Kurt Schelle. "Überlegungen zum II. Internationalen Schriftstellerkongreß zur Verteidigung der Kultur während des nationalrevolutionären Krieges in Spanien 1937. Ein Beitrag zum Verhältnis von Literatur und Geschichte." *Beiträge zur Romanischen Philologie* 19, 1 (1980): pp. 7-29.

11. Thornberry. *op. cit*. p. 118.

12. *Ibid*. p. 120.

13. Text of the manifesto in *Left Review* 3, 8 (Sept. 1937): pp. 445f. and in *Commune* 48 (August 1937): pp. 1409f. Reproduced in full in Thornberry. *op. cit*. p. 121.

14. Görling. *op. cit*. p. 300.

15. Mikhail Koltsov. *Die rote Schlacht*. Berlin: Deutscher Militärverlag, 1965. pp. 602-3.

16. See especially Görling. *op. cit*. pp. 299-301.

17. As reported by Stephen Spender in "Spain Invites the World's Writers. Notes on the International Congress, Summer 1937." *New Writing* 4 (Autumn 1937): pp. 245-51. Reproduced in *Spanish Front. Writers on the Civil War*. Ed. Valentine Cunningham, 85-91. Oxford: Oxford Univ. Press, 1986. p. 90.

18. Stephen Spender. *World Within World*. London: Hamish Hamilton, 1951. p. 241.

19. André Gide. *Retour de l'URSS*. Paris: Gallimard, 1936.

20. André Gide. Transl. Dorothy Bussy. *Back from the U.S.S.R.* London: Martin Secker and Warburg, 1937. pp. 62-63.

21. André Gide. *Retouches à mon Retour de l'URSS*. Paris: Gallimard, 1937.

22. Spender. *World Within World*. p. 241.

23. *Ibid.*

24. Jef Last. Transl. David Hadett. *The Spanish Tragedy*. London: G. Routledge and Sons, 1939. Quoted in Cunningham, 94-101. *op. cit.* p. 96.

25. Thornberry. *op. cit.* p. 125.

26. Ilya Ehrenburg. *Menschen, Jahre, Leben. II. 1923-41*. Munich: Kindler, 1965. p. 489.

27. Last. *op. cit.* p. 96.

28. *Ibid.* p. 95.

29. Arturo Serrano Plaja. "*Ponencia Colectiva.*" *Hora de España* 8 (August 1937): pp. 87-89. The pronouncement was presented by A. Sánchez Barbudo, Angel Gaos, Antonio Aparicio, A. Serrano Plaja, Arturo Souto, Emilio Prados, Eduardo Vicente, Juan Gil-Albert, J. Herrera Petere, Lorenzo Varela, Miguel Hernández, Miguel Prieto and Ramón Gaya.

30. Aragon took part only in the Paris sessions.

31. Tzara was Romanian by birth but had been living in Paris since 1920 and attended the congress as an official French delegate. Of the four French speakers only he was a member of the French Communist Party. For an account of French participation in the Congress, see Gabriel Jacobs. "A Picture of French Unity: The 1937 Writers' Congress and the 'Just War.'" *Romance Studies* 3 (1983): pp. 87-102.

32. Stephen Spender. "Spain Invites the World's Writers." p. 86.

33. *Ibid.*

34. *Ibid.* pp. 88-89.

35. *Ibid.* p. 90.

36. Stephen Spender. "Stephen Spender." In *The God That Failed*. Ed. Richard Crossman, 229-73. New York: Books for Libraries, 1949.

37. Spender. *World Within World*. pp. 241-42.

38. *Ibid.* p. 245.

39. *Ibid.* p. 241.

40. Spender. "Stephen Spender." p. 251.

41. Spender. *World Within World*. pp. 241-42.

42. Spender's first of altogether three visits to Spain had been a very brief one. He had been commissioned by the *Daily Worker* to investigate the disappearance of a Russian ship, a task which had taken him to Gibraltar, Oran and Tangier. On his return to London he spent just a few days in Barcelona.

43. In *World Within World* Hyndman is referred to as "Jimmy Younger." Spender had recently married, which probably was an important factor in Hyndman's decision to enlist in the Brigades. In any case, it is apparent that Spender was motivated by a bad conscience in trying to secure the release of his friend.

44. The matter went so far as to be referred to the republican Foreign Minister Alvarez del Vayo. After much pressure Hyndman was finally allowed to return to England.

45. For an account of Julian Bell's participation in the war, see Peter Stansky and William Abrahams. *Journey to the Frontier: Julian Bell and John Cornford: Their Lives and the 1930s*. London: Constable, 1966.

46. Stephen Spender. "Letter to Virginia Woolf." In Cunningham (ed.), 307-9. *op. cit.* p. 308.

47. *Ibid.* p. 307.

48. *Ibid.* p. 308.

49. *Ibid.* p. 309.

50. David Caute. *The Fellow-Travellers: A Postscript to the Enlightenment.* New York: Macmillan, 1973. p. 174. Details of Spender's article are not provided.

51. Stephen Spender. "Heroes in Spain." *New Statesman and Nation* 13, 323 (1 May 1937). Reprinted in Stephen Spender. *The Thirties and After: Poetry, Politics, People – 1933-1970*, 46-50. New York: Random House, 1978. p. 48.

52. *Ibid.* p. 49.

53. *Ibid.*

54. Spender. "Stephen Spender." p. 247.

55. Stephen Spender. *Forward from Liberalism.* London: Gollancz, 1937. p. 202.

56. Spender. *World Within World.* p. 211.

57. *Ibid.*

58. Stephen Spender. "I Join the Communist Party." *Daily Worker.* 19 February 1937. Reprinted in Cunningham (ed.). *op.cit..* pp. 7-9.

59. Spender. *World Within World.* p. 202.

60. Stephen Spender. "Ultima Ratio Regum," ll. 1-2. In *The Penguin Book of Spanish Civil War Verse.* Ed. Valentine Cunningham. Harmondsworth: Penguin, 1980. p. 341. The title was originally "Regum Ultima Ratio" when it appeared in *New Statesman* 13 (15 May 1937): p. 811, but it was changed for inclusion in *The Still Centre.* It comes from the motto embossed on the cannons of Louis XIV. Spender's war poetry was published in various publications during the war, as well as in later anthologies. Here I have chosen to use Cunningham's anthology because it has the most comprehensive collection of Spender's war poetry. According to A. T. Tolley, however, there is one Spanish war poem by Spender, namely "The Town Shore at Barcelona," which has never been collected. See A. T. Tolley. *The Poetry of the Thirties.* London: Gollancz, 1975. p. 340.

61. Spender. "Ultima Ratio Regum."

62. Stephen Spender. "The Coward," ll. 8-15. In Valentine Cunningham (ed.) *The Penguin Book of Spanish Civil War Verse.* 338-39.

63. Stephen Spender. "Two Armies," ll. 29-38. *Ibid.* 333-4.

64. Stephen Spender. "No Man's Land." *Ibid.* p. 196.

65. Stephen Spender. "Port Bou," ll. 45, 33-35. *Ibid.* 354-5.

66. This observation of a similarity between the war poetry of Spender and that of Wilfred Owen is certainly not new, and indeed can be traced back to Spender himself. As Samuel Hynes, for example, points out, of the English poets of the Spanish war, "Spender was most clearly indebted to the example of Owen, and he was clearly conscious of his debt." Samuel Hynes. *The Auden Generation. Literature and Politics in England in the 1930s.* London, Sydney, Toronto: Bodley Head, 1976. p. 249. Hugh Ford agrees that, like Owen, "Spender conceives of war itself as the great destroyer, a kind of impersonal entity indiscriminately brutalising and maiming humanity." Hugh D. Ford. *A Poets' War: British Poets and the Spanish Civil War.* Philadelphia: University of Pennsylvania Press; London: Oxford University Press, 1965. p. 226.

67. Randall Swingler. "History and the Poet." *New Writing* 3 (Christmas 1939). Quoted in Valentine Cunningham. *British Writers of the Thirties.* Oxford, New York: Oxford University Press, 1988. pp. 440-1.

68. "The honesty of Spender's Spanish Poems is what's compelling." *Ibid.* p. 442.

69. *Romancero de la Guerra Civil (Serie 1).* Madrid: Ministerio de Instrucción Pública y Bellas Artes. Sección de Publicaciones, November 1936. Reprinted Madrid: Visor, 1984.

70. *Romancero General de la Guerra de España.* Ed. Emilio Prados. Madrid, Valencia: Ediciones Españolas, 1937.

71. *Poetas en la España leal*. Madrid: Ediciones Españolas, July 1937. Some of the poems from this collection and from the *Romancero de la Guerra Civil (Serie 1)* are to be found collected and translated into English in *Cries from a Wounded Madrid: Poetry of the Spanish Civil War. Bilingual Edition*. Ed. Carlos Bauer. Athens, Ohio; Chicago, London: Swallow Press, 1984.

72. Stephen Spender and John Lehmann (eds.). *Poems for Spain*. London: Hogarth Press, 1939.

73. Spender. "Introduction." *Ibid*. p. 8.

74. *Ibid*. p. 9.

75. *Ibid*. pp. 9-10.

76. *Ibid*. p. 7.

77. *Ibid*.

78. *Ibid*.

79. *Ibid*. p. 10.

80. Pedro Garfias. Transl. Tom Wintringham. "Single Front," ll. 26-33. *Ibid*. p. 94.

81. The absence of the prose writer Ralph Fox is self-explanatory. Caudwell (whose real name was Christopher St. John Sprigg) was a poet, but to my knowledge no poetry by Caudwell on the war was ever published.

82. John Cornford. "Left?" *Cambridge Left* 1 (Winter 1933-4) p. 25. Quoted in A. Kingsley Weatherhead. *Stephen Spender and the Thirties*. Lewisburg PA: Bucknell University Press; London: Associated University Press, 1975. p. 48.

83. Christopher Caudwell. *Romance and Realism. A Study in English Bourgeois Literature*. Ed. Samuel Hynes. Princeton NJ: Princeton University Press, 1970. pp. 130, 138.

84. Fox and Caudwell were two of the leading Marxist literary theorists of the 1930s. Fox was best known for *The Novel and the People*. London: Lawrence & Wishart, 1937. Caudwell became noted for the posthumously published *Illusion and Reality*. London: Macmillan, 1937.

85. *New Verse* 25 (May 1937): p. 22. Quoted in Samuel Hynes. *The Auden Generation. Literature and Politics in England in the 1930s*. London, Sydney, Toronto: Bodley Head, 1976. p. 258.

86. Ford. *op. cit.* p. 86.

87. *Ibid*. p. 87.

88. Louis MacNeice. "Autumn Journal," ll. 93-100. In Spender and Lehmann (eds.). *op. cit.* p. 100.

89. Katharine Bail Hoskins. *Today the Struggle. Literature and Politics in England During the Spanish Civil War*. Austin and London: University of Texas Press, 1969. p. 222.

90. George Lowther Steer. *The Tree of Gernika*. London: Hodder and Stoughton, 1938. Steer, a great admirer of the Basques, was the British journalist who broke the Guernica story.

91. Cecil Day Lewis. "Bombers," l. 21. In Spender (ed.). *op. cit.* p. 83. Samuel Hynes goes so far as to label "Bombers" one of Day Lewis's "poems of passive waiting for disaster that one might call his 'post-political poems.'" Hynes *op. cit.* p. 335.

92. Humphrey Carpenter. *W. H. Auden. A Biography*. London: Allen and Unwin, 1981. p. 209.

93. Quoted in Valentine Cunningham. "Introduction." In *The Penguin Book of Spanish Civil War Verse*. Ed. Valentine Cunningham, 25-94. Harmondsworth: Penguin, 1980. p. 67.

94. W.H. Auden. "Impressions of Valencia." *New Statesman & Nation* 30 January 1937. Reproduced in *Spanish Front. Writers on the Civil War*. Ed. Valentine Cunningham, 115-17. Oxford, New York: Oxford University Press, 1986. pp. 116-17.

95. The reason Auden was later to give was that the CP was running everything and he was not a member of it. Other conceivable reasons for his nonemployment are an administrative muddle, overstaffing, or even Auden's erratic driving skills. One commentator suggested that Auden's not being allowed to drive was "a mercy for the wounded." See Carpenter. *op. cit.* pp. 210-11. Possibly the CP was concerned that Auden should not be exposed to any kind of danger at all. The communist Claud Cockburn, who during the war wrote under the pseudonym Frank Pitcairn, said of Auden in 1964 that "what we really wanted him for was to go to the front, write some pieces saying hurrah for the Republic, and then go away and write some poems, also saying hurrah for the Republic; and that would be his job in the war – and bloody important at that. Instead of which, unfortunately, he took the whole thing terribly seriously; he wanted to do something. "A Conversation with Claud Cockburn." *The Review* 11-12 (1964): p. 51. Quoted in Frederick Buell. *W. H. Auden as a Social Poet*. Ithaca and London: Cornell University Press, 1973. pp. 146-47. For Auden's possible time at the front see Carpenter. *op. cit.* pp. 211, 215 and Charles Osbourne. *W. H. Auden. The Life of a Poet*. London: Eyre Methuen, 1980. p. 134. For his return to England see Cunningham. "Introduction." p. 68.

96. Cunningham. "Introduction." p. 68.

97. Robin Skelton (ed.). *Poetry of the Thirties*. London: Penguin, 1964. p. 41.

98. W. H. Auden. "Foreword." In *Collected Shorter Poems, 1927-1957*. London: Faber and Faber, 1966. p. 15.

99. Buell. *op. cit.* p. 148, and quoted (unsourced) in Carpenter. *op. cit.* p. 219.

100. W. H. Auden. "Spain," ll. 53-56. In Spender and Lehmann. *op. cit.* 55-58. p. 57.

101. *Ibid.* ll. 95-96.

102. *Ibid.* ll. 93-94.

103. *Ibid.* ll. 102-4.

104. Spender. "Introduction." p. 11.

105. Stephen Spender. "Review of Spain." *New Statesman* 21 November 1936. pp. 801-3. Quoted in Cunningham. *op. cit.* p. 69.

106. John Lehmann. *The Whispering Gallery* London: Longmans Green, 1955. p. 281.

107. Edgell Rickword. "Auden and Politics." *New Verse* 26-27 (November 1937): p. 21. Quoted in Cunningham. *op. cit.* p. 70.

108. "Richard Goodman Foresees True Revolutionary Poetry, From Perspectives for Poetry." *Daily Worker* 2 June 1937. p. 7. Reprinted in *W. H. Auden. The Critical Heritage*. Ed. John Haffenden, 237-38. London, Boston, Melbourne, Henley: Routledge & Kegan Paul, 1983. pp. 237-38.

109. George Orwell. "Political Reflections on the Crisis." *The Adelphi* (December 1938). Here Orwell wrote: "Mr. Auden can write about 'the acceptance of guilt for the necessary murder' because he has never committed a murder, perhaps never had one of his friends murdered, possibly never even seen a murdered man's corpse." Quoted in Edward Mendelson. *Early Auden*. London, Boston: Faber & Faber, 1981. p. 321.

110. George Orwell. "Inside the Whale." In *The Collected Essays, Journalism and Letters of George Orwell. Volume 1. An Age Like This 1920-1940*. Ed. Sonia Orwell and Ian Angus, 540-78. Harmondsworth: Penguin, 1970. p. 566. If nowhere else, Orwell is being unfair to Auden here. By "necessary murder" Auden in all likelihood *did* mean "killed in battle" and not the kind of "liquidation" campaigns carried out by Hitler and Stalin that Orwell was referring to.

111. *Ibid.* p. 565.

112. A convincing rebuttal of Orwell's accusations, and of a tradition of interpretation of the poem which seeks to invalidate the public dimension of the poem by claiming that it did not correspond to Auden's actual attitude to the war, is offered by Stan Smith. Referring specifically to Orwell's claims, he writes: "But Orwell is pulling rank here, as someone who had himself shot and killed fellow human beings, and agonised over it in *Homage to Catalonia.* For Auden is precisely *not* being dishonest. He calls murder 'murder', and not some salving euphemism. And the original versions, the 'necessary murder', 'the deliberate increase', are more honest than the revisions, 'the fact of murder', 'the inevitable increase', because they emphasise that dimension of personal, willed responsibility by casting death as an objective process, a *fait accompli* detached from subjective involvement. It is Orwell who is dishonest, projecting his own guilt on to what he called elsewhere "the nancy poets", and those sandal-wearing vegetarian pacifists who believed Fascism could be overthrown by good intentions instead of bullets." Stan Smith. "Missing Dates: From *Spain 1937* to 'September 1, 1939.'" *Literature and History* 13, 2 (Autumn 1987): p. 167. To my knowledge there is no evidence to support Smith's claim here that Orwell shot and killed people in Spain. He is certainly correct, however, in refuting the claim in liberal criticism that Auden "was never really a public, political poet; he was always, *really*, a private and personal one. An ideological preconception of this magnitude precludes argument because its very premise will always return us to the same point: for the liberal critic there is always an uncrossable gulf between public 'life' and private *living*." *Ibid.* p. 161.

113. "We arrived in Barcelona late at night, with the exception of Mr. J. Cornford, who had enlisted in Leciñana." Franz Borkenau. *The Spanish Cockpit: An Eye-Witness Account of the Political and Social Conflicts of the Spanish Civil War*. Ann Arbor: University of Michigan Press, 1963 (1937). p. 108.

114. Pat Sloan (ed.). *John Cornford: A Memoir.* London: 1938. Quoted in Cunningham. *op. cit.* p. 37.

115. For a detailed account of Cornford's involvement in the Spanish war, see Stansky and Abrahams. *op. cit.* pp. 311-90.

116. *Ibid.* p. 352. John Lehmann mentions a fourth poem by Cornford, "As our Might Lessens." Lehmann. *op. cit.* p. 282. To my knowledge it is not anthologised.

117. Spender. "Introduction." pp. 11-12.

118. Spender's admiration for Cornford's work was certainly shared by co-editor John Lehmann, who later wrote of Cornford's poems: "Though I now entirely reject the specific creed that inspired them, I still find them, for all their faults, among the most remarkable poems that came of the Spanish war." Lehmann. *op. cit.* p. 281.

119. Cornford's friend at the time was Margot Heinemann, who is represented in the anthology with three poems.

120. John Cornford. "Poem," ll. 7-8. In Spender and Lehmann (eds.). *op. cit.* p. 21.

121. *Ibid.* ll. 13-16.

122. *Ibid.* l. 10.

123. John Cornford. "Full Moon at Tierz," ll. 4, 23, 26, 32, 36, 40. In Spender and Lehmann (eds.). *op. cit.* 26-9.

# 5. Literature and Marxism

## *DAS WORT* AND MARXIST AESTHETICS IN THE 1930s

Just as *Poems for Spain* was a child of the Popular Front, so too was the German-language Moscow journal *Das Wort*. Its conception dates back to the Writers' Congress of June 1935 in Paris, and with substantial Soviet moral and material support (most notably from Mikhail Koltsov and his Jourgaz publishing company) it came to fruition in 1936. The first issue appeared in July of that year, the last in March 1939,[1] so that the publication dates coincide almost precisely with the length of the Spanish Civil War.[2] The value of a study of the journal in this work however does not rest entirely on that coincidence. *Das Wort* is worth examination because it provided a forum for the most important literary debate of the late 1930s.

The journal's brief was to support in the cultural sphere the political strategy of the Popular Front. Even the choice of editors was to reflect the earnestness of the Soviets' bid to promote actively the cooperation of a broad spectrum of anti-fascist forces. After attempts to engage Heinrich Mann and Thomas Mann had failed,[3] the choice fell on a panel of three – Willi Bredel, Bertolt Brecht and Lion Feuchtwanger. Bredel was a communist, Brecht unquestionably a Marxist without being a member of the Communist Party, and Feuchtwanger was a non-Marxist.[4] Amongst the contributors to the journal there were "liberals, anarchists, communists with and without a Party card, reformists, revolutionary socialists and all those whose political faith cannot be understood in terms of these broad categories."[5] This ideological scope is apparent for example in the many pieces on the Spanish Civil War, which, after Germany, was the second most popular topic.[6] They range from the orthodox Marxist content of Mikhail Koltsov's diary to the barely definable, nondoctrinaire liberalism of Hermann Kesten's novel *Die Kinder von Gernika*.[7]

*Das Wort* readily employed the key slogans of the Popular Front – "humanism," "cultural heritage," "*Volkstümlichkeit*"[8] – and yet it was never able to conceal that it was from beginning to end a Soviet publication, albeit in German. In the early stages the bulk of the editorial work fell on the shoulders of the communist Bredel, largely for quite practical reasons. (Brecht was living in Denmark, Feuchtwanger in France.) When Bredel left for Spain in early 1937, the editorship was effectively assumed by Fritz Erpenbeck, often in cooperation with Alfred Kurella. Both Erpenbeck and Kurella were exiled Germans resident in Moscow; both were followers and allies of the influential Hungarian theorist Georg Lukács, who was also living in Moscow. In Bredel's absence, key editorial decisions were made by Erpenbeck or even Kurella, so that Brecht's and Feuchtwanger's actual editorial function was severely limited. Communist influence on (or control of) editorial policy thus assured, it is not surprising that the journal did *not* adopt a critical attitude to Soviet politics. Most obviously it failed to criticise the conduct of the Moscow trials, the first of which began in August 1936, just a month after the journal's first appearance. Although in principle an organ of the Popular Front, *Das Wort* tolerated and even justified a series of events which at the time was rocking the Popular Front in Western Europe. Similarly the journal denounced André Gide and the latter's scathing attacks on the Soviet Union. Finally, it was symptomatic of Soviet influence on editorial policy that, although the Spanish Civil War broke out in July of 1936, it was not mentioned until the October issue of that year (in Bredel's Foreword), and was not made a focus of attention until the November issue, shortly after the Soviet government had opted to send material support to the Republic.[9]

One of the functions of *Das Wort* was to propagate current Soviet interpretations of Marxist aesthetics. In the context of the Popular Front and the period of the journal's publication (1936-39), this meant above all the discussion and promotion of "realism," more specifically of "socialist realism."

The emergence of the aesthetic doctrine of socialist realism in the Soviet Union coincides with the demise of the radical programme of the Russian Association of Proletarian Writers (RAPP). The latter had argued for a literary production which was committed to the proletarian revolution; the writer was required to write from a consciously Marxist standpoint. The dialectical-materialist rhetoric of the RAPP gradually disappeared over a period of some six years, from 1928 to 1934, and the RAPP itself was dissolved in April 1932. The radicalism of the RAPP was replaced by a cultural policy which argued for the cooperation of communists and socialists, ultimately even of all anti-fascist forces. Cooperation on a political level demanded a commensurate cultural policy, and that policy was to go under the label "socialist realism."

The first use of the term can be traced back to May 1932 and to the *Izvestia* editor Ivan Gronsky, who, in attacking the radical RAPP programme, argued that a knowledge of the theory of dialectical materialism was not a precondition for literary creativity. "The basic demand that we make on the writer is: write the truth, portray truthfully our reality that is in itself dialectic. Therefore the basic method of Soviet literature is the method of socialist realism."[10] Within a few months the formulation of the term was generally accredited to Stalin.[11] The official sanctioning of the term came at the First All-Union Congress of Writers in Moscow in 1934. Andrey Zhdanov, a member of the Central Committee of the Communist Party, gave the term its classic definition: "In the process the truthful and historically concrete artistic presentation [of reality in its revolutionary development] must be combined with the task of ideologically reshaping and educating the working person in the spirit of socialism. This is the method which we call socialist realism in the *belles-lettres* and in literary criticism."[12]

With the dissolution of the RAPP and the introduction of a new formula for artistic production, it is hardly surprising that Soviet aesthetic discourse in the 1930s focussed on the problematics of "socialist realism." There was by no means unanimity in the interpretation of the term - in essence there had developed two rival schools, the Voprekisti and the Blagodaristi.[13] By 1936, however, "the situation began to change and the party's inclinations grew clearer. Socialist realism was outfitted with a set of new prescriptions and injunctions demanding 'simplicity and plebeianism' in art and excluding 'formalism and naturalism'."[14] This signalled a victory for the more moderate Voprekisti, in the ranks of whom Georg Lukács was to be found.

That the decision fell against the vulgar sociology of the Blagodaristi and in favour of Lukács and the Voprekisti, that is, in favour of a form of socialist realism which was pro-simplicity and pro-Volkstümlichkeit, anti-formalist and anti-nationalist, inevitably had a political background. The Party considered that an aesthetic doctrine which paid tribute to the cultural heritage of the bourgeoisie and which rejected a more recent, blatantly Marxist and proletarian heritage, was better suited to the political strategy of the Popular Front. Bourgeois anti-fascist elements had to be attracted to the Popular Front, not repulsed by it.

This political background to the course and resolution of the socialist realism debate in the Soviet Union was of some considerable significance for *Das Wort*. The *de facto* editors Bredel, Erpenbeck and to a degree Kurella were living in Moscow and would have been well aware of the state of the debate. Erpenbeck in particular saw it as the role of the journal to help to bring to western Europe the doctrine of socialist realism as advocated by the Voprekisti and as approved by the Party as the doctrine most appropriate to the needs of the Popular Front.

To do this, a debate was staged in the pages of *Das Wort*, which had as its subject the nature of realism and the relationship to the cultural heritage of the immediate and distant past. Generally it now goes under the names "Expressionism Debate," "Realism Debate" or "Brecht-Lukács Debate."[15] The debate was started, or rather provoked, by Alfred Kurella in the September 1937 issue of *Das Wort*. Klaus Mann in the same issue wrote an article on Gottfried Benn, the expressionist who had declared his support for the Nazi regime. Kurella, writing under the pseudonym of Bernhard Ziegler, added to Mann's article a contribution of his own in which he put forward the famous thesis: "It is clearly recognisable today whose child expressionism was and to where this spirit, followed to its end, leads: to fascism."[16] He went on to plead for a rejection of expressionism and of "formalism," and to argue for an art of *Volksnähe* and *Volkstümlichkeit*.[17]

Considering that, as Alfred Kantorowicz points out, "from Johannes R. Becher to Alfred Wolfenstein, some four-fifths of the expressionist poets who had survived the First World War and the twenties were in exile,"[18] Kurella's accusation of a natural affiliation between expressionism and fascism could be nothing *but* provocative. Especially the fact that expressionism should be denounced in *Das Wort* "meant at least a psychological affront to those former expressionists who were living as anti-fascists in exile and who could have and should have been won for the Popular Front."[19]

The first reaction to Kurella's provocation seems to have been stunned silence. In October 1937 Ernst Bloch, resident at the time in Prague, sent a letter to the editors of *Das Wort* in which he posed the potentially embarrassing question as to whether Kurella's article had been written before or after Hitler's renowned Munich speech, in which the Führer had branded expressionism as *entartete Kunst* (degenerate art). [20] Erpenbeck answered that Kurella's article had been written before Hitler's speech and then asked Bloch to contribute an article to the journal. [21]

Thus began what for German authors was "undoubtedly the most significant and most comprehensive, but at the same time also the most problematical battle of opinion of the exile period."[22] Fifteen writers, literary theorists and artists participated, including such figures as Lukács, Franz Leschnitzer, Hanns Eisler, Rudolf Leonhard, Klaus Mann, Gustav von Wangenheim, Herwath Walden and Heinrich Vogeler. It overflowed from the pages of *Das Wort*, spilling into other German-language exile publications: *Neue Weltbühne*, *Internationale Literatur* and the *Deutsche Zentral-Zeitung*. As a general rule those who supported the anti-expressionist, that is, the pro-Soviet or pro-Stalinist line (most notably Lukács and Kurella), were living in Soviet exile, while those who came to the defence of expressionism (like Eisler, Bloch and Bertolt Brecht, a special case) were former expressionists living in exile outside the Soviet Union.

The proponent of the Soviet line with the highest profile and the greatest influence was Lukács. There is no suggestion that Lukács had to be persuaded to represent the official Soviet viewpoint. His enthusiasm for the Popular Front was genuine; "he seems honestly to have believed that the inception of popular front politics in France, Spain, and Germany betokened a new era for bourgeois writers, one that would change history and reverse the process of cultural disintegration."[23] Lukács's opposition to expressionism and the cultural avantgarde was already known to German readers from essays published in the journal *Linkskurve* in 1931 and 1932, in which he had criticised the proletarian novels of Ernst Ottwalt and Willi Bredel and the theatrical techniques of Bertolt Brecht, as well as from the 1934 essay "'*Größe und Verfall*' des *Expressionismus*" ("'Greatness and Decline' of Expressionism") which he published in *Internationale Literatur*. Lukács had the perfect credentials to present the Soviet line. As David Pike puts it, Lukács "was the right man at the right time. Had there been no Lukács in 1933 to 1939, he would have had to be invented."[24]

His position already well known, Lukács made just one contribution to the debate in *Das Wort*, albeit a very lengthy one (the longest) and strategically located at the end of proceedings. With the significant title "*Es geht um den Realismus*" (It Is a Question of Realism), it appeared in the June 1938 issue of the journal. It was followed only by Ziegler's (that is, Kurella's) conclusion to the debate in the following issue. In all likelihood it had been agreed beforehand by the Moscow editors that Lukács would be allowed the final say in the matter.[25] In any case Hanns Eisler's "*Antwort an Lukács*" (Reply to Lukács) was rejected by Erpenbeck on the grounds that the debate had already been concluded. [26]

Lukács's position on realism can be presented here only in outline. For Lukács, the work of art was to perform a mimetic function, that is, it was to be a reflection of a total, objective reality. It was insufficient to present only surface reality (hence his rejection of naturalism) or only the subjective aspect of reality (rejection of expressionism and surrealism). Instead, in the Lukácsian system the work of art had to achieve a harmonious merging of outward appearance (*Erscheinung*) and inner reality or essence (*Wesen*). "This is the artistic dialectic of outward appearance and inner reality. The more diverse, the richer, the more intertwined, the more "cunning" (Lenin) it is, the stronger it grasps life's contradiction, the living wholeness of the contradiction of wealth and the wholeness of the social determinants, the greater and the more profound the realism will be."[27] This dialectic unity of *Erscheinung* and *Wesen* was best achieved, in Lukács's estimation, in the novels of the great bourgeois realists (especially Honoré de Balzac, Leo Tolstoy and Sir Walter Scott) in the first half of the nineteenth century, that is, in the era of the ascendant bourgeoisie. Consequently, Lukács adopted the novels of Balzac, Tolstoy and Scott as permanently valid models of realism and recommended them to his contemporaries.

Of developments in literature after the phase of the ascendant or progressive bourgeoisie Lukács was hypercritical. The decline of the bourgeoisie, culminating in the age of imperialism, brought with it literary decadence. Symptomatic of that decadence for Lukács were all types of "formalism", that is, experimentation with literary forms. Thus he rejected outright such literary techniques as the interior monologue or change of styles (as practiced, for example, by Joyce), alienation (Brecht) or montage (Dos Passos). The latter in particular represented for Lukács "the fall from grace of the modern artist."[28]

Lukács did not reject the form of reportage outright; in fact he praised the work of the American journalist Herbert Knickerbocker (who later was to report the Spanish Civil War). [29] But he refused to grant reportage the status of an art form, because in his view reportage did not present reality in its totality. In reportage the writer describes (*beschreibt*) a section of reality; the novelist, in contrast, shapes or narrates (*gestaltet*) a totality. Reportage therefore was consigned to the category of journalism (*Publizistik*).[30] The novel of reportage (*Reportageroman*) as practiced by Ernst Ottwalt, which sought to combine fictional and documentary elements, was rejected outright by Lukács as an unacceptable mixture of art and journalism, a form experiment which provided the reader with only part of the truth. [31]

Lukács rejected naturalism, expressionism and *Neue Sachlichkeit* (New Objectivity); he criticised the works of Emile Zola, James Joyce, Franz Kafka, John Dos Passos and Bertolt Brecht. And yet he did find some modern literature worthy of praise. In "*Es geht um den Realismus*" he praises the works of four novelists: Maxim Gorky, Thomas Mann and Heinrich Mann and Romain Rolland.[32] Although he dismissed the idea of an avantgarde, as long as that entailed an experimentation with literary forms, he affirmed the possibility of a genuine avantgarde of realists.[33]

The positions of Lukács's opponents similarly can only be presented in outline here. As early as the 1934 Soviet All-Union Writers' Congress (at which the doctrine of socialist realism was officially proclaimed), the German writers Willi Bredel (whose proletarian novels had been criticised by Lukács) and the dramatist Friedrich Wolf took exception to the new development in aesthetic discourse. Bredel accused the Soviets of overlooking the contribution of an aggressive proletarian literature before Hitler's coming to power; Wolf argued that the situation of confrontation between progressive and nonprogressive elements in capitalist society in Western Europe demanded literary forms which would inevitably differ from those employed in the Soviet Union in a phase of socialist consolidation.[34]

In the course of the debate in the pages of *Das Wort* in 1937 and 1938 it was the philosopher Ernst Bloch in particular who appeared, publicly at least, to be Lukács's main opponent; it was towards Bloch in particular that Lukács explicitly directed his argument in his single contribution. In "*Diskussionen über Expressionismus*" (Discussions on Realism), his June 1938 contribution to *Das Wort*, Bloch countered Kurella's claim of an affinity between expressionism and fascism, and furthermore rebuked Lukács for his 1934 essay "*'Größe und Verfall' des Expressionismus*" ('Greatness and Decline' of Expressionism).[35] In *Die neue Weltbühne* a year earlier Bloch and Hanns Eisler together published, in the form of a dialogue, a plea for the recognition of a positive and productive relationship between the Popular Front and the artistic avantgarde. Implicitly rejecting Lukács's renowned disdain for the avantgarde, Bloch and Eisler maintained that "the Popular Front needs the progressive artists, the progressive artists need the Popular Front."[36] Anna Seghers also took issue with Lukács in correspondence with the latter during the second half of 1938 and early 1939. Seghers accused Lukács of attacking the wrong enemy, of denouncing decadence when in fact the real enemy was fascism.[37] She wrote to Lukács: "But what you see as decadence seems to me to be rather a stocktaking [i.e., of contemporaneous literature]; what you regard as a form experiment [seems to me to be] a vehement attempt at a new content, an unavoidable attempt."[38]

In retrospect, though, Lukács's main opponent was Bertolt Brecht, theoretically at least one of the editors of the journal in which the debate was carried out. Brecht's own contributions were not made public until 1966, twenty-eight years after the debate in *Das Wort* had been declared closed. If Brecht had had his way, the debate would not have taken place at all. Apart from considering Lukács's position untenable, he feared that such a theoretical dispute could only hinder literary production.[39] Brecht, whose antipathy towards the theoretician Lukács existed long before the debate of 1937-38 and continued long after, attempted unsuccessfully to prevent the publication of Lukács's article "*Es geht um den Realismus*" in the June 1938 issue of *Das Wort*.[40] A few weeks later Brecht promised in a letter to Kurella (then acting as editor of *Das Wort*) to send a response to Lukács's article for publication in the journal. Neither this response, entitled "*Volkstümlichkeit und Realismus*" (Volkstümlichkeit and Realism), nor another article also written for *Das Wort*,

*"Weite und Vielfalt der realistischen Schreibweise"* (Breadth and Diversity of the Realist Style), appeared in the journal. Whether Brecht ever sent these two items to Moscow remains uncertain.[41]

That Brecht and Lukács held conflicting views on literary aesthetics at the time of the expressionism debate is attributable to their widely varying interpretation of Marxist philosophy. In particular, Lukács and Brecht represented irreconcilable viewpoints regarding the nature of the relationship between art and reality. As Klaus-Detlef Müller has argued, "The central question of the realism problem is the relationship between art and reality."[42] For Lukács the work of art was essentially a passive reflection of a total, objective reality, "a stepping out of reality into an aesthetic reality of its own kind."[43] Art presented a totality, at the same time offering insights into the true nature of the relationship between all components of the real world. For Brecht, in contrast, the work of art is not a reflection of reality which is removed from reality; rather, it is a part of reality, entering into a dialectical relationship with it in the hope of changing it for the better. Art is "oriented towards reality in that it wants to provide impulses to change it."[44] Where Lukács sought the harmony of "appearance" and "essence," Brecht deliberately searched for contradictions within reality. Art for him had not only to reflect and reveal the shortcomings of reality but also to contribute to the correction of those shortcomings.

For Brecht there could be no correct "form" of realism. Realism was not the depiction of, but rather an attitude to, reality. Literary form was not the result of a permanent and universally valid set of aesthetic principles, but of the historical circumstances to which literature reacted. "Realism" therefore was not a term used by Brecht to identify a particular literary form or epoch. On the contrary, it was an attitude or approach to reality which could manifest itself in any epoch and in a range of forms. For Brecht realism resulted primarily from the questioning of reality, not of aesthetics. It was therefore "not a matter of describing the empirical world, the real objects, but of describing how things *really were*. The selection of the literary forms and the technical means remained for him secondary to the demands of the class struggle."[45]

Brecht turned Lukács's accusations of formalism back against Lukács himself, claiming that it was Lukács who insisted on a specific "form" of realism (the novels of Balzac, Tolstoy, Scott and so on). Brecht vigorously proclaimed: "Realism is not a matter of form. One cannot take the form of a single realist (or a limited number of realists) and call it *the* realist form. That is unrealistic."[46] What for Brecht was decisive was whether or not the author adopted a critical and progressive attitude towards the reality as it was presented. Consequently Brecht's canon of realist literature was much broader than that of Lukács and included authors whom the latter accused of formalism: Joyce, Alfred Döblin, Dos Passos and Kafka. Precisely these authors had, in Brecht's estimation, developed techniques which were suited to a "realist" presentation of twentieth-century reality. It was not a question of *which* techniques or forms were employed, but of whether they were employed realistically. "Naturally there can be interior monologues which are to be labelled formalist, but there are also those which are realist, and with montage one can . . . present the world in a distorted way and also in a correct way, there is no doubt about that."[47] Similarly

Brecht judged that techniques of the nineteenth-century novel, as praised so strongly by Lukács and as employed in the twentieth century by Thomas Mann, for example, did not necessarily present the whole truth. [48]

The condemnation of expressionism as "decadent" and as a precursor of fascism was for Brecht untenable, even reactionary, since the expressionist movement was a response to a particular historical reality, namely that of the final phase of capitalism, of a decaying bourgeois world order, but also of a progressive proletariat. The application of new techniques was not problematical, but the use to which they were put. Brecht's favourable judgment of expressionism was that here (i.e., amongst the expressionists) "there was a lot to learn for the realists, who after all are so interested in learning and who seek the practical side of things. From Kaiser, from Sternheim, from Toller, from Göring much was to be gained for the realists."[49]

Brecht's opposition to, or to be more precise his disgust with, the doctrine of socialist realism as propounded by Lukács, is especially evident in his private *Arbeitsjournal* (Work Journal). There he complains bitterly of the *Moskauer Clique* (Moscow clique)[50] and the *Murxisten* (murxists).[51] Directing his venom explicitly at Lukács, he laments, "this lukács is magically attracted by the problem of ideological decline. that is sua res. the Marxist categories are being taken ad absurdum here by a kantianer, in that they are not refuted but applied, there the *class struggle* is a hollowed out, prostituted, plundered term, burnt out to the point that it cannot be recognised, but it is there and it appears."[52] Brecht wonders that Lukács should praise his (Brecht's) scene *Der Spitzel* (The Informer),[53] especially as it was part of the montage of twenty-seven scenes *Furcht und Elend des Dritten Reiches* (in English usually translated as *Private Life of the Master Race*).[54] What was probably an attempt by Lukács to extend the olive branch to Brecht, to count him amongst the modern realists after his phase of formalist aberration, failed miserably.


## SPAIN AND SOCIALIST REALISM


Although the expressionism debate was carried out for the most part in the pages of *Das Wort* at the time of the Spanish Civil War, and although *Das Wort* published numerous contributions on the war, the participants in the debate curiously made no explicit reference to the literature of the war. Despite this paradox, the expressionism debate is of considerable significance for the Marxist literature of the Spanish Civil War. As the East German scholar Werner Mittenzwei points out, Brecht and Lukács "must be regarded as representatives of contrary positions within Marxism."[55] At the time of the Spanish Civil War, the widely varying aesthetic positions of Lukács and Brecht mark the extremes in the gamut of Marxist aesthetics in the period 1936-39.[56] At one extreme was the semi-official position of the Moscow resident Lukács, that is, a "socialist realism" adopting the formal models of the literature of an ascendant bourgeoisie, approved and promoted in Moscow as a valuable accompaniment to the political strategy of the Popular Front; at the other extreme stood the "non-

Muscovite" Brecht, who recommended the employment of new techniques and forms under the proviso that they be used "realistically," that is, with the aim of changing rather than merely reflecting reality, and who only grudgingly approved of the Popular Front. That approval, though, was without substantial aesthetic implications and without the abandonment of a commitment to class struggle.

*Das Wort* was just one of several media via which the doctrine of socialist realism was propagated in Western European literary circles, including in Spain.[57] The literary congresses staged by anti-fascists such as those in Paris in June 1935 and in Spain in July 1937 also played a role; important also were the efforts of particular individuals in promoting the Moscow line. One of the key figures outside the Soviet Union was unquestionably Louis Aragon, the former surrealist. Aragon's relationship to Lukács was problematical, and yet it was Aragon who more than any other imported the doctrine of socialist realism from Moscow to France.[58] He proved himself to be "the most ardent of French apologists for socialist realism, elaborating on the close social and political ties which writers like Fadeyev, Gorky and Alexis Tolstoy were forging with the masses and lauding, with little regard for the possible sensitivities of his French readers, the most outrageous declarations of the Soviet writers."[59]

Despite these efforts, the doctrine of socialist realism as formulated in the Soviet Union could make little impact in the West. With the exception of Aragon and a small number of communists (such as Léon Moussinac and Paul Nizan), the Western intellectual response to the doctrine was notably cold. This applies to Marxists and also to those who at the time were ideologically closely aligned with Marxism. The negative response of German émigrés, from Wolf and Bredel in 1934 through to Seghers in 1939, has already been mentioned; the outstanding French example of an unfavourable response to the doctrine was that of André Malraux, who from the very beginning refused to embrace a *réalisme socialiste*. Malraux was never a member of the Communist Party, but as from about the year 1932, in which he became a member of the Association des Ecrivains et Artistes Révolutionnaires (AEAR, Association of Revolutionary Writers and Artists), Malraux can certainly be regarded as a communist sympathiser.[60] Political sympathy, however, did not entail aesthetic alignment. "Never did Malraux dissociate himself from the anti-naturalist, symbolist, subjective tradition of French art theories, which for Aragon was certainly the pre-condition for all revolutionary literature."[61]

In the case of Britain, the response to developments in Marxist aesthetic discourse in the Soviet Union seems primarily to have been one of relative ignorance rather than rejection or affirmation. The first issue of *Left Review* was published in October of 1934, the year of the First Soviet Writers' Congress. A report on the congress by Amabel Williams Ellis appeared in the second issue, but according to H. Gustav Klaus the author "neither mentioned the concept of Socialist Realism nor gave much space to the other leading theme, the taking-over and critical revaluation of the bourgeois literary tradition, and one cannot help wondering whether she fully understood what was on the agenda."[62] Although the writings of Christopher Caudwell, Ralph Fox and Alick West establish the 1930s as the first important period in British Marxist literary theory, it is noteworthy that these theorists did not become engaged in the realism debate which was of such overriding importance for Central and Eastern European theorists.[63]

The reason for the failure of socialist realism to make a major impact on aesthetic discourse in the West had been hinted at by Friedrich Wolf as early as 1934: the theory behind the doctrine was too far removed from Western political reality. As David Pike puts it, "seldom have literary discussions been more meaningless than in 1936 in the Soviet Union. . . . Between theory and practice there was no connection."[64] In distant Moscow the particular demands of countries where the struggle between pro-fascist and anti-fascist forces was part of everyday life were overlooked. What was urgently needed was an aesthetic which would guide literary production in a Soviet Union which was in a phase of internal consolidation, but which was also appropriate for a Western Europe which found itself in a phase of open or at least latent warfare. To borrow the German terminology, Western Europe required a *Kunstform* which was simultaneously a *Kampfform*. Instead, Lukács and the Muscovites came up with a doctrine which seemed to promise tolerance in its recognition of the validity of bourgeois literary forms, but which in fact displayed a censorious intolerance towards what it regarded as a "formalist" aesthetic. Lukács and his collaborators, in formulating a doctrine which would supposedly supersede the dogmatic narrowmindedness of the RAPP programme and would serve the political interests of the Popular Front, had paradoxically arrived at an aesthetic position which was at least as limited in scope as that of the RAPP, and which writers in Western Europe tacitly rejected as irrelevant and unworkable. Implicitly and intuitively they followed the line of Brecht, not of Lukács, and sought a literature which was both an art form *and* an instrument in the struggle against fascism.

The inappropriateness of the Soviet theory of socialist realism for literary practice in the West is apparent in the literature of the Spanish Civil War. The literature produced by Marxists and sympathisers was not written *in accordance with* the doctrine of socialist realism; it is more accurate to say that it was written *despite* socialist realism.

Precisely the genres which Lukács refused to recognise as art forms are dominant in Spanish Civil War literature: reportage, essay, documentation, autobiography and diary. As Helmut Kreuzer has identified, the literature of the war "in this respect continues the documentary-political tendencies of the '20s and radicalises them."[65] Moreover, the mixed forms which Lukács especially loathed came to prominence, so that the fiction of the war is often characterised by elements and combinations of reportage and autobiography. One thinks for example of Malraux's *L'Espoir* and Gustav Regler's *The Great Crusade*.[66] Works by Ilya Ehrenburg and Willi Bredel, which the authors themselves categorise as novels, are notable for their elements of reportage.[67] Even the works which *in retrospect* have been branded by East European scholars as shining examples of socialist realism clearly contravene Lukács's formal requirements. The outstanding novels for them (those of Malraux and Regler being *ideologically* unacceptable) are those of Eduard Claudius and Bodo Uhse.[68] The central figure of Claudius's novel *Grüne Oliven und nackte Berge* is

Jak Rohde, who bears obvious similarities to the author.[69] Like Regler, Claudius was a war commissar in Spain; his hero Rohde is a similarly devoted and disciplined member of the Party. "I joined the Party because one cannot fight a battle without formation. I have come out of the war, but the war still goes on. Yesterday I was at the front, now I am behind enemy lines. I am a partisan, a part of the spectre, and wherever the Party sends me, I shall go."[70] Unlike Regler and many others, Claudius's experiences in Spain "did not make him lose faith in communism and as a result he is still acclaimed in the East as the exemplary worker-poet and trusty fighter for the party and for the cause of the proletariat in its struggle against oppression".[71] Bodo Uhse's novel *Leutnant Bertram* is less directly autobiographical than Claudius's novel, but nevertheless follows a scheme of character development obviously borrowed from the author's own life.[72] The hero is a pilot in Nazi Germany who fights in Spain as a member of the Condor Legion, sees the error of his ways and defects to the republican camp shortly after the bombing of Guernica. He pleads: "No-one will believe me and yet – and yet I would like to convince you that I have nothing more to do with those up there."[73]

One of the most interesting illustrations of this tendency towards mixed forms is the book *Spanien zwischen Tod und Geburt* (in English as *Spain between Death and Birth*) by the Yugoslavian author Oto Bihalji-Merin.[74] Adopting a montage technique (which Lukács would also of course have condemned), the author combines impressions of Spanish people and cities, descriptions of the war and historical interludes. This tendency towards mixed forms extends also to other media, that is, there is a definite trend towards combining literary and nonliterary forms. An example is Arthur Koestler's little-known work *Menschenopfer unerhört, ein Schwarzbuch über Spanien* (Incredible Human Sacrifice, a Black Book on Spain), which combines reportage with photography.[75] Indeed, this combination of literature and photography is common across the range of the political spectrum. Perhaps the best example, however, of the trend towards a synthesis of forms and media, is Malraux, who directed the filming of his own novel.[76]

Lukács's aesthetic doctrine was not equipped to deal with such trends. In fact, Lukács's doctrine was inadequate even for dealing with much more traditional, non-epic forms. With some justification Brecht complained: "What about realism in verse, what about it in drama?"[77]

In republican Spain the war led to a burgeoning of theatrical activity, but across the political spectrum the drama is poorly represented in the non-Spanish literature of the war.[78] This applies also to Marxist literature, but in the small quantity that does exist there is an obvious preference for "agitprop" pieces as they had been developed in the 1920s and early 1930s. One thinks of Ludwig Renn's sketch *Mein Maultier, meine Frau und meine Ziege* (My Mule, My Wife and My Goat), and of Friedrich Wolf's *Die "Newa" kommt* (The "Neva" is Coming).[79] Brecht's *Gewehre der Frau Carrar* (Frau Carrar's Rifles) is a special case which will be considered in more detail below.

In the Marxist lyric contribution to the literature of the war an enormous variety of forms is to be found. German poets, just as the German dramatists, showed a predilection for lyric *Kampfformen*, for proletarian poetry and revolutionary songs as developed during the years of the Weimar Republic. At the same time there were produced much more "private" literary forms, elegies which record despair and tragedy, poetry characterised by a "metaphorical language resembling that of expressionistic poetry."[80] Whether they wrote in a public, proletarian form or in a more private, "neo-expressionist" form, it is significant that German poets at least refused to heed Lukács's advice to abandon the literary heritage of the immediate past.

Spanish poets preferred the *romancero*, a popular lyric genre with origins dating back to the middle ages, when the *romancero* celebrated the advance of the *reconquista*. As has already been mentioned, the Spanish Civil War *romanceros* generally adopt the form of their medieval predecessors, that is, they contain eight-syllable lines and employ assonance rather than full rhyme in every second line.

Two Spanish poets-cum-editors in particular, namely Rafael Alberti and Antonio Machado, were responsible for the promotion of the *romancero* in republican Spain. In late 1932 Alberti undertook a journey to Berlin (where he took up contact with the editors of the journal *Linkskurve*) and then to the Soviet Union. He returned to Spain as a "convinced and not uncommonly dogmatic communist,"[81] and along with María Teresa León founded his own short-lived journal *Octubre*.[82] In August 1936, motivated by the attempted military putsch of the previous month, Alberti's second journal came to fruition. Entitled *El Mono Azul* (The Blue Monkey or The Blue Overalls[83]), it published large numbers of *romanceros* during the war, including many by Alberti himself.[84] Antonio Machado, who, like Alberti, became famous during the 1930s for his commitment to the political Left, albeit in a less dogmatic form, also founded an influential journal. *Hora de España* was published from January 1937 to October 1938 and in that time published copious quantities of *romanceros*.[85]

The *romancero* proved popular in left-wing circles outside Spain as well. *Left Review* in England published a number of them in translation. As a former editor of *New Writing*, John Lehmann recalls the enthusiasm with which British writers offered their services as translators of Spanish *romanceros*.[86] In its May 1938 issue, *Das Wort* published a series of four *romanceros*, also in translation, but not from the Spanish. As an indication of the internationalisation of the genre, one is in translation from Italian, one from Polish, one from English and one from French. The translator in each case was the ubiquitous Alfred Kurella.[87]

The widespread and evidently enthusiastic adoption of the *romancero* form both within and outside Spain did provoke some minor controversy in left-wing intellectual circles. At least one voice of dissent can be registered. The *romancero* was the topic of an informal discussion during the Writers' Congress in Spain. The "dissident" was the Argentinian Raúl González Tuñón; the other participants were the Spaniard Miguel Hernández, the North American Langston Hughes, the Cuban Nicolás Guillén and the Mexican Octavio Paz. Whereas Paz praised the *romancero* as the form best suited to expressing the sentiments of the people, González Tuñón, who under the influence of Russian literature in the pre-socialist realism days had devoted himself to the proletarian cause in his novels, countered that the *romancero* could offer little as a revolutionary lyric form. Possessing such a long traditon, it suffered from over-use. Hernández agreed with Paz and added that it was the personal technique of the poet that was the decisive factor. Langston Hughes suggested: "I believe we cannot forget the traditional forms for now. They are recognised by the people. . . . Furthermore they aimed at the assimilation of two elements, namely of form and content. It is good to speak to the people with one voice which does not unsettle them."[88]

Despite the efforts of Alberti and Machado in Spain, and of the editors of such publications as *Left Review*, *New Writing* and *Das Wort* outside Spain, the *romancero* can hardly be considered a specifically Marxist or even left-wing contribution to the literature of the war. The genre was generally approved by left-wing intellectuals at the time and it has been retrospectively accepted into the canon of socialist realism,[89] but it cannot be considered the product of any specific contemporaneous aesthetic, Marxist or otherwise. The repopularisation of the *romancero* in Spain had begun with García Lorca in the 1920s, some ten years before the outbreak of the war. During the war, the *romancero* exercised an ideologically universal appeal. Poetry produced in the nationalist zone is quantitively vastly inferior to that produced in the republican zone; nevertheless it is apparent that the *romancero* was the preferred lyric genre amongst nationalist and fascist poets, as well as for those of the Left, including the anarchists. Serge Salaün estimates that a mere 3 percent of the total number of *romanceros* produced during the war are "strictly communist," whilst just eight percent are more generally "Marxist."[90]

Whether or not they were clearly in a minority, this tendency of Marxist writers to make use of traditional forms such as the *romancero* cannot be overlooked. At the same time, there is ample evidence to illustrate the Brecht-Bloch-Eisler thesis that *new* literary forms could be developed to serve the proletarian cause.

One of the most convincing pieces of evidence is Jack Lindsay's work "On Guard for Spain," which generically occupies the middle ground between poetry and theatre. It is generally known as a "mass declamation," a form which achieved remarkable popularity in British left-wing circles during the time of the Spanish Civil War.

The idea to convert a poem into a theatrical production appears not to have come from Lindsay himself. The Australian-born Lindsay, at that time recently converted to Marxism (but not a member of the Communist Party and not a participant in the Spanish Civil War), wrote a lengthy declamatory poem entitled "Who are the English?" in early 1936, which was published in *Left Review*. Subsequently it was performed by the Unity Theatre "as a kind of dance-mime with spoken verse."[91] When the war broke out in Spain, *Left Review* editor Edgell Rickword asked Lindsay to do a similar sort of poem on the theme of the war.[92] Lindsay agreed and wrote "On Guard for Spain! A Poem for Mass Recitation," which was published in the March 1937 issue of *Left Review*.[93] More importantly, the poem was "performed" all over Britain by the Unity Theatre and groups connected with the Left Book Club.[94]

There appears to exist no direct evidence of a borrowing of ideas on Lindsay's part, and yet distinct similarities between Lindsay's mass declamation and certain forms of German proletarian theatre of the 1920s and early 1930s can be observed. If a conscious adoption of German models did take place, then it is more likely to have been by those who first staged mass declamations in Britain, namely the Unity Theatre. When the latter opened its premises in London on 19 February 1936, its program included the poem *Requiem* by the radical left-wing German poet and dramatist Ernst Toller.[95] *Requiem*, dating from 1920 and Toller's expressionist phase, deals with the murders of Karl Liebknecht and Rosa Luxemburg and is classified as a *Chorwerk* (Chorus Work). In London it was "performed as a massed chant with stylised movements."[96] Jack Lindsay himself prefers to distinguish between his mass declamation on the one hand and German or American models on the other. "On Guard for Spain," he claims, was "a distinctive type of mass-declamation which I think I am correct in saying was quite different from the forms developed by Brecht in the early thirties of Germany, and in the U.S.A. during the New Deal."[97]

To distinguish between Lindsay's mass declamations and the theatrical techniques of Bertolt Brecht is indeed a useful starting point. Whereas Brecht through his alienation effects sought to avoid the audience's direct emotional participation in events on stage with the aim of provoking an intellectual response, Lindsay goes all out for emotional identification and impact. Lindsay recalls that after one performance Harry Pollitt, the secretary general of the British Communist Party, wrote to him "that he had never in all his life seen an audience so powerfully affected as by the declamation."[98] Similarly Jerry Dawson, a member of the Merseyside Unity Theatre, remembers: "I saw people in tears even at the mention of the name of certain Spanish towns, even just the list of names could achieve that, because they knew what had happened there. These audiences didn't see declamations as something arty, as poetry being recited to them, but as an emotional expression of things they'd come across politically in their newspapers."[99]

As a performance of the poem would last just under thirty minutes, it was often staged as a component of a political rally or meeting. The typical meeting in support of the Spanish Republic "consisted of speeches by Victor Gollancz, Harry Pollitt and the Duchess of Atholl, with a performance of 'On Guard.'"[100] Although the text that appears in *Left Review* does not indicate it, the poem was divided into sections to be spoken by one or more voices. "One voice would take up a line, two more strengthen it, and then more moving on to the climaxes, preserving the rhythmic qualities of the verse within its free form."[101] The group would simultaneously make use of movement, in some instances even of props (such as uniforms and a republican flag); indoor performances achieved additional effects through lighting and silhouettes.[102]

Although the strategies employed here are quite different, the *function* of the mass declamation was similar to that of the *romancero*. That function specifically was the breaking down of the barrier between poetry and the "people." The simplicity of language and the directness of the appeal to the emotions were means of bridging this gap. More important, however, was the fact that the poem was performed, and that in being performed it allowed the players, but also the audience, to *participate* in it. This specific intention of the mass declamation was set out by Lindsay in a programmatic manner. In an article in *Left Review* he made a

plea for Declamation, Mass-Recitation, as the initial and primary form of our new poetry. For there we get the most direct contact with the new audience. Not that every poem can or ought to be written for mass-recitation; we must set as our goal the creation of a poetry that resumes and transmutes all the socially valid forms of the past with a new content, and seeks to go beyond them all with an enriched drama and lyric. . . . For the peculiar nature of the social struggle of our day, as we near the terrible death-agonies and convulsions of imperialism, demands of the poet that the core of his expression, his sense of the human whole, should be overwhelmingly political. He seeks contact with his audience in conditions of increasing danger; and his methods must be based on this fact. Mass declamation becomes the form of contact from which endless new developments can stem. [103]

This linking of poetry and people which the declamation form was designed to achieve is reinforced by the content of the poem, which places enormous value on the role of the people in the war. The first line informs the listener: "What you shall hear is the tale of the Spanish people."[104] Lindsay quickly establishes a simple scheme which sees the "Spanish people" opposed to the "fascists." Without disregarding the peasantry, it is clear that by "people" he means primarily the "workers," that is, the urban industrial workers, who are the anonymous heroes of the poem. Many of the fascists, in contrast, are identified and demonised individually: "Franco the Butcher," "Mussolini the gangster" "Hitler the gambler" and others.[105] In an orthodox Marxist manner, though, fascism is not interpreted as the achievement of evil individuals; rather, it is the outcome of a corrupt capitalist system:

Gold was silently spilt
to grease the wheels of counter-revolution.
Those dumps of reaction, the arsenal churches,
bared their armouries of oppression.
The fascist monster, slimed from the night,
roared out over Spain. [106]

The poem contains a *public* voice which chronicles the course of events in Spain before and during the war.[107] Referring to specific events and places, it tells of the 1934 Asturias uprising, the February 1936 elections, the July 1936 military uprising, the responding workers' assault on the Montaña barracks in Madrid, the siege of Toledo, the massacre at Badajoz, and so on. This public voice reminds the audience of the concrete politicomilitary background to the war; it praises the collective heroism of the workers, and, finally, it openly appeals to the audience to support actively the antifascist cause:

Workers,
drive off the fascist vultures gathering
to pick the bones of Spanish cities,
to leave the Spanish fields
dunged with peasant dead

that greed may reap the fattened crops.
Fuse your unity in the furnace of our pain.
Enter this compact of steel,
and then we shall not complain.108

But the poem also contains a *private* voice, a voice which tells of individual anguish and commitment. Some highly emotional sections of narrative, such as the following, are related in the first person:

I rose from the bed of my wife's young body
at the call of Liberty.
O feed with my blood our flag's red flame.
Comrades, remember me.

The fascists shot my children first,
they made me stand and see.
O dip the flag in my heart's blood.
Comrades, remember me. 109

For the Marxist Lindsay, this dialectic of the public and the private in the poem formed an aesthetically and politically viable synthesis. For the non-Marxist Stephen Spender,110 the dialectic simply did not work; to generalise the particular experience of the individual, to regard that experience as typical, was unacceptable. Referring quite specifically to the lines quoted above ("I rose from the bed of my wife's young body"), Spender protested:

Writing such as this may be effective recruiting propaganda, but it is supremely untruthful as poetry. These lines are not bad because there are no conceivable conditions in which one man might experience the sensations they record, but because this man's case is represented as typical, so that the lines have the air of a generalisation. Such writing is simply a record of the hysteria which the poet shares with his audience and himself and does not see at all from the outside. 111

With this comment by Spender begins a whole tradition of unfavourable criticism of the poem. Hugh Ford in 1965 claimed, "If 'On Guard' had any value at all, it was the somewhat negative value of supporting the work of propagandists."112 A decade later, A. T. Tolley regarded it as "an object lesson in how inanity of feeling goes along with inanity of rhetoric."113

Lindsay naturally rejected Spender's criticism. The words, he later insisted, had not been put into the mouth of a young militia lad in Barcelona but were "the voice of a dead man, and they expressed, not a wish to be killed, but the gratitude of the living, the sense of the terrible waste and cruelty of the war forced on the people by the fascists." 114 Lindsay assumed that the hysteria was not in the poem but in Spender himself, and that "he reacted with this sort of blind revulsion from any expression in which he felt a whole-hearted partisanship with the people's cause."115

There is no need to attempt to resolve this dispute in favour of Lindsay or Spender. It is important to note, though, that the Marxist Lindsay's understanding of the function of poetry differed irreconcilably from that of Spender in the late 1930s. Whereas Spender insisted on conveying the "truth" of the individual circumstance as the poet had experienced it (even if this entailed the depiction of an anti-heroic sensibility), Lindsay saw no anomaly in "collectivising" individual experience, in proclaiming the unity of the public and the private world. Whereas Spender distinguishes between the individual and the cause, Lindsay finds the two in harmony.

"On Guard for Spain" is not an example of socialist realism; on the contrary, it furnishes evidence for the inadequacy or even irrelevance of the doctrine of socialist realism as it was being propounded at the time. It indicates that contemporaneous Marxist aesthetics must be understood in broader, non-formalist, *Brechtian* terms. At the same time it indicates that it *is* possible to establish points of discrepancy between Marxist aesthetics and the "liberal" aesthetics of Stephen Spender.

## PARADOX BRECHT

Like Jack Lindsay, Bertolt Brecht observed events in Spain from a safe distance. Living for the most part in Skovbostrand in Denmark, he relied heavily on the media, in particular on the Danish liberal newspaper *Politiken* for information on events on the Iberian peninsula. [116] His second source would have been personal friends who did have the courage to go to Spain and so were in a position to judge the situation for themselves. Most notably Brecht's companion Ruth Berlau, on Mikhail Koltsov's suggestion (but against Brecht's express wishes), travelled to Spain, where she joined Egon Erwin Kisch, Nordahl Grieg and Ernst Busch at the front. In Spain she "received letters from Brecht in verse and prose, begging her not to take risks." [117] Instead of returning to Brecht in Denmark, she went on to Sweden with a Swede who had fought in Spain. [118]

Brecht was invited to attend the International Writers' Congress in Spain in 1937 but elected to avoid the dangers of entering a country at war. He did, however, write an address which was read to the delegates. It is an address which recalls the acts of barbarism committed by fascist governments throughout Europe. Furthermore, at a congress which promoted the theme "In Defence of Culture," it reminds the audience of the material basis of culture and of the consequent necessity to restore and protect that basis: "If this is so, if culture is something inseparable from the overall productivity of the peoples, if just one intrusion can deny the peoples their butter *and* their sonnet, if therefore culture is something so material, what has to be done to defend it?" [119] Brecht's answer to his own question was quite simple. He contended that fascist violence had to be answered with physical force: "Culture, for a long time, for much too long, defended only with intellectual weapons, attacked though with material weapons, being itself not just an intellectual but also, and even especially, a material entity, has to be defended with material weapons." [120]

This July 1937 address belongs to a small body of works by Brecht dealing with the Spanish Civil War. To this body belong also the poem "Mein Bruder war ein Flieger" (My Brother Was a Pilot) and two of the twenty-four scenes of the cycle *Furcht und Elend des Dritten Reiches* (*The Private Life of the Master Race*), namely "*Arbeitsbeschaffung*" (Work Creation) and "*In den Kasernen wird die Beschießung von Almeria bekannt*" (In the Barracks the Shooting of Almería is Made Known). Klaus Völker suggests that Brecht also outlined for Erwin Piscator a plot for a film which used the blockade of Bilbao as its backdrop.[121] By far the best known of Brecht's works on the Spanish Civil War is, however, his one-act play *Die Gewehre der Frau Carrar* (*Señora Carrar's Rifles*). Written by a man who lacked the courage to attend the Writers' Congress in Madrid and Valencia, it is a plea for physical resistance to fascism.

Although it has attracted relatively little critical attention, *Die Gewehre der Frau Carrar* is in fact, after the *Dreigroschenoper* (*Threepenny Opera*), Brecht's most-performed theatrical work.[122] During the time of the Spanish Civil War it was staged in Paris, Copenhagen, Prague, Stockholm, New York, London (twice, both times by the Unity Theatre, the group which had put on Jack Lindsay's "On Guard for Spain"), Västeras (in Sweden), Odessa, San Francisco and Sydney.[123] It was the first play by Brecht to be performed in the Soviet occupation zone of Germany after World War II (at Frankfurt an der Oder in 1947), and by 1970 there had been 366 recorded stagings.[124]

Critical opinion on the play is divided. Rolf Geißler describes it as one of Brecht's weakest plays,[125] and Henri Plard agrees that it is by no means Brecht's best work.[126] Helmut Kreuzer on the other hand insists on seeing the play in terms of the aesthetic doctrines of the day. He names it as an example of the unity of aesthetic form and political purpose.[127]

The genesis of the play needs to be sketched briefly. The director Slatan Dudow (with whom Brecht had collaborated in the making of the 1932 film *Kuhle Wampe*) in a letter to Brecht in September 1936 requested a play about the Spanish Civil War. Thereafter Brecht and Margarete Steffin worked on altogether nine versions of a play which originally bore the title *Generäle über Bilbao* (Generals over Bilbao).[128] The first of these versions is dated March 1937; the last, which is not substantially different from the first, is dated 24 August 1937. The changing of the title can be attributed to military developments in Spain. The Basque capital of Bilbao had fallen to nationalist forces in June of 1937. It was a development which also persuaded Brecht to shift his setting from a Basque to an Andalusian fishing village. The play was first staged by Dudow and his amateur theatre company of emigrés in Paris on 16 October 1937. The poster announcing this first production proclaimed: "Brecht's new work is dedicated to the Spanish people's heroic battle for freedom."[129] The text of the play was published by Wieland Herzfelde's Malik Verlag in London in December of 1937.

Under the title of the published version of the play are the words: "With the use of an idea by J. M. Synge." This is a reference to Synge's one-act play *Riders to the Sea*, though it is a reference which Brecht could have omitted with a clear conscience, since the links between his play and Synge's play are very tenuous. In Synge's play a mother warns her sons not to go to sea or they would drown. In Brecht's play a mother prefers to send her son to sea rather than to the battlefront.

Just as in his earlier plays *Die heilige Johanna der Schlachthöfe* (*St. Joan of the Stockyards*) and *Die Mutter* (*The Mother*), Brecht centers his play on a female protagonist, the mother and widow Teresa Carrar. Her husband was killed in the 1934 Asturian uprising, fighting for the rights of the oppressed. Not wishing the same fate to befall her two sons after the outbreak of war in Spain, she does not allow them to fight against the Generals. She is an ardent proponent of neutrality, hoping in this way to preserve her sons' lives. In her opposition to violence she is supported by one other character, the Padre. Other characters, most notably her brother Pedro Jaqúeras, who returns from the front in order to retrieve a quantity of rifles hidden in the Carrar household, point out the folly of a neutralist stance. Their anti-pacifism is vindicated finally. When the body of her elder son Juan, murdered in his fishing boat by the fascists, is delivered to Carrar, she is convinced of the necessity of the fight. She herself retrieves the rifles she had hidden and sets off to the front with her younger son José.

The play is provided with a quite specific geopolitical setting. The action takes place in a house in an Andalusian village, east of Almería and some four hours west of Motril. Reference is made in the play to the August 1936 "massacre of Badajoz," to the presence of the International Brigades, and specifically to the German Thälmann Brigade, to such figures as Generals Franco and Mola, and also, as mentioned, to the 1934 uprising in the Asturias. Inserted into the play are extracts from the Seville radio addresses of General Quiepo de Llano, widely known as the "Radio General."[130]

For the most part Brecht, relying entirely as he did on information filtering to him in Denmark, created a plausible historical background to his play, in which only minor inaccuracies can be detected. A statement by General Mola that he would destroy the capital city of a perverse people is wrongly attributed to Quiepo de Llano.[131] The late shifting of the setting from a Basque to an Andalusian fishing village caused only a few minor problems. The English blockade mentioned early in the play is in fact a reference to the blockade of Bilbao.[132] Teresa Carrar's husband's participation in the 1934 Asturian uprising means that he had to travel from the very south of Spain to the very north, to Oviedo, and then back.[133] It is not an impossible but a rather unlikely scenario. The Padre gives precise details on the extent of clerical support for the Republic in Bilbao, a detail which similarly was a leftover from earlier versions.[134]

These minor inaccuracies aside, this attention to the creation of a precise historical setting is the first sign that in *Die Gewehre der Frau Carrar* we are not dealing with a typically Brechtian play, but with an example of what Brecht would call theatre of illusion. The realistic setting recalls the traditional theatre of pre-Brechtian plays. There is a good deal of other evidence which reinforces this viewpoint. For example, the structure of the play corresponds closely to that of traditional tragedy: exposition is followed by a buildup to a point of crisis which in turn is succeeded by the dénouement. There is also an uncommonly strict observance of the three unities. The entire action takes place in a single house in the time that it takes Carrar's loaf of bread to bake, some forty-five minutes. Indeed, one critic has suggested that "it is not easy to find, in the European literature of the twentieth century, a play more condensed, more conforming with the need for concentration which dramatic art poses traditionally."135 The praying of the women which accompanies the arrival of the corpse near the end of the play is reminiscent of the chorus of ancient Greek tragedy.

But the most telling feature of this play which identifies it as a non-Brechtian play is the role of empathy. Unlike earlier and later plays, Brecht here does not discourage the audience from empathising with the protagonist. Like Jack Lindsay, Brecht seeks to use the audience's *emotional* response to events on the stage to his advantage. As a propaganda play, which it undoubtedly is, the play could not work unless the audience *did* emotionally identify with Carrar's dilemma and *did* emotionally reconstruct her conversion. As Carrar is persuaded of the necessity to take up arms against the fascists, so too the audience is to be brought to the realisation that a position of neutrality is untenable.136

Brecht himself was fully aware that the play must be regarded as a recourse to older models. Although in the realism debate he adopted the view that the artistic avant-garde could be employed in a politically progressive manner, he chose not to apply avantgarde dramatic techniques when the Spanish Civil War was on the agenda. In his work journal he describes *Die Gewehre der Frau Carrar* as "all too opportunistic."137 At the end of the published version of the play Brecht inserted a note which openly stated that the play is "Aristotelian (empathy) drama." He went on to add, however, that the "disadvantages of this technique can to a certain degree be compensated if the play is staged in combination with a documentary film which shows what is occurring in Spain, or with some sort of propagandistic event."138

Although the presence of Aristotelian elements, at least as Brecht understood them, cannot be overlooked, *Frau Carrar* cannot be regarded as a purely Aristotelian play. Fate does not play a role here, as it does in a play such as *Riders to the Sea*. The murder of the son at sea in Brecht's play does not occur because anonymous fate intervenes; rather, it has quite specific social origins. He was shot by the fascists because of the shabby cap he was wearing, a cap which identified him unambiguously as a member of the working class.139

This episode suggests that Brecht in *Frau Carrar* is primarily interested in types, not in individuals, as is the case in Aristotelian drama. Teresa Carrar is therefore "THE MOTHER," José Jaqúeras is "THE WORKER," and so on. The conclusion is also decidedly un-Aristotelian. Fear and pity unquestionably play a role, but catharsis immediately gives way to commitment. Neither the protagonist nor the empathising audience is left paralysed by events; both are persuaded to take part in the struggle against fascism. Finally, apart from his suggestion that the play be performed in association with other propagandistic events, Brecht made additions to the play which could be seen as alienation devices. For the first Swedish performance of the play he added a prologue and an epilogue, both of which are set in a concentration camp in Perpignan, and which served to create a degree of objectifying distance from the play proper.140

In pointing out that *Die Gewehre der Frau Carrar* is not a characteristically Brechtian play, that despite some Brechtian elements it is largely, and by Brecht's own admission, Aristotelian empathy drama, the question must be raised whether Brecht in his theatrical practice was not abrogating some of the principles he was defending in the context of the realism debate. The answer is that there is no such abrogation involved. Brecht had never rejected Aristotelian drama per se. His objection to it was not based on an outright rejection of the strategy of empathy, but of "its social function: the coming to terms with unperceived forces, the suffering of which [the audience] relates to emotionally, without the possibility of intervention being recognised."[141] In the realism debate, it will be recalled, Brecht argued that realist literature was literature which uncovered the social forces at work and which set about destroying those forces in an historically progressive manner. Furthermore, he argued that the form a literary work took would depend upon the particular set of historical circumstances which prevailed at any particular time. Under certain circumstances he considered the application of Aristotelian techniques justified. He argued that if a certain social situation had reached a very ripe stage then Aristotelian works could be employed to trigger a practical response.[142] Brecht clearly felt that the Spanish Civil War provided just such a set of circumstances in which an Aristotelian play could help to trigger off a popularly based political action. To the set of historical circumstances which prevailed in 1937 should be added those which surrounded the production of the play. It was written specifically for an amateur theatre troupe operating in Parisian exile. To have expected such a troupe to perform a play which entailed the intensive use of alienation effects would have been extremely risky.

*Die Gewehre der Frau Carrar* is not a Brechtian play, but neither is it a contravention of Brecht's conception of realism. Rather, it is a legitimate illustration of that conception. Like Ludwig Renn's *Mein Maultier, meine Frau und meine Ziege*, it is an example of a form of agitprop drama which sets out to achieve specific, unashamedly political goals. Like Jack Lindsay's "On Guard for Spain," it is a recognition of the efficacy of a direct appeal to the emotions in the encouragement of practical action.

In considering the ideological content of the play, it is important to note the broadness of its appeal. The play was written not specifically to promote the communist cause, but more generally to persuade its audience of the untenability of neutrality, of the necessity to become actively involved in the struggle against fascist oppression.

Despite this broadness of appeal, it is nonetheless possible to provide the play with a fairly precise ideological location. It is implicitly anti-liberal, anti-humanist and therefore, if one recalls how important the "Humanism" slogan was for the Popular Front, anti-Popular Front. Brecht's anti-humanist line was detected very early on by Martin Andersen-Nexö, who in a 1938 review of the play in *Das Wort* described it as showing "the entire misery of democracy in the battle against reaction: its softened up humanism."[143] In the play itself it is particularly evident in the treatment of the obvious representative of humanism, namely the Padre. The Padre is the one character in the play who consistently supports the doctrine of pacifism and neutrality. He makes it clear that he is no supporter of the Generals; on the other hand he can never condone the bearing of arms. The self-contradictory nature of his position is exposed by the worker José Jaqúeras, who defeats him intellectually in argument, finally forcing the Padre into silence.[144]

In his insistence on the necessity of applying violence in resisting oppression and bringing about historical progress, Brecht can be seen to be promoting an orthodox Marxist-Leninist line. It is in this area that one can detect a difference between the Marxism of Brecht and the "liberal humanism" of writers like Auden and Spender, for whom, as we have seen, the condoning of violence, even as a response to violence committed by others, was problematical. In contrast to Brecht and Lindsay, Auden and Spender at least had the dubious advantage of experiencing the results of that violence at first hand.

The play is at no point explicitly pro-communist. In fact, no political affiliations of any denomination are revealed. It is known that Teresas Carrar's husband fought in the 1934 Asturian uprising, in which communists and socialists played a major role, but it is not revealed whether or not he was a Party member. The colour or colours of the flag which is a relic from that uprising are not revealed. However, the colour symbolism accompanying the death of Carrar's son cannot be overlooked: the body is carried into the house on a sail which is stained red with blood, and Carrar adopts it as her new flag.[145]

Whether Brecht would have approved the tactics employed by the Communist Party during the war is impossible to know. Given that reports which were dispatched from republican Spain were subject to a system of censorship which within months of the outbreak of war was controlled by communists or by sympathisers, it is probable that Brecht was largely unaware of the extent to which the communists were using violence to suppress rather than promote revolution. One can only speculate on whether Brecht, in full awareness of the circumstances, would have transferred his allegiance to a more radical Marxist grouping such as the POUM. In a letter to his mentor Karl Korsch dated November 1937, Brecht mentions that in Paris he had met his friend Paul Partos, who had just come from Spain and returned there in a great hurry.[146] Partos was a Hungarian Marxist who had been associated with left-wing communist circles around Karl Korsch in the 1920s. Brecht neglects to mention in his letter that in Spain Partos had opted to join the anarchists.[147]

## NOTES

1. The exact reasons for the dissolution of the journal are to my knowledge unclear but are likely to be associated specifically with the arrest of Koltsov in December of 1938, and more generally with the Soviet abandonment of the Popular Front strategy.

2. For a history of the journal see especially Hans-Albert Walter. "Die Exilzeitschrift *Das Wort*". *Basis. Jahrbuch für deutsche Gegenwartsliteratur* 3 (1972): pp. 7-60.

3. See David Pike. *German Writers in Soviet Exile, 1933-1945*. Chapel Hill: University of North Carolina Press, 1982. p. 205. Alfred Kantorowicz suggests that Ludwig Marcuse was almost appointed editor. Alfred Kantorowicz. *Politik und Literatur im Exil. Deutschsprachige Schriftsteller im Kampf gegen den Nationalsozialismus*. Munich: dtv, 1983. p. 25.

4. It remains controversial whether Brecht perhaps did at one stage join the Party. Ruth Fischer, the sister of Brecht's close friend Hans Eisler, states that he joined the Party in 1930. Ruth Fischer. *Stalin and German Communism*. Cambridge, MA: Harvard

University Press, 1948. p. 615. If this is the case, it is nevertheless true that Brecht made no effort to pronounce publicly his attachment to the organisation.

5. Hans-Albert Walter. *op. cit.* p. 22.

6. *Ibid.* p. 79.

7. Extracts from Koltsov's diary appeared in the June 1938 issue, a chapter from Kesten's novel in the November 1938 issue.

8. "*Volkstümlichkeit*" is best left untranslated. It means something like "folk character". It is noteworthy that in the mid-1930s such vocabulary was becoming widely used in left-wing circles.

9. Walter. *op. cit.* p. 54.

10. Herman Ermolaev. *Soviet Literary Theories, 1917-1934. The Genesis of Socialist Realism.* Berkeley, Los Angeles: University of California Press, 1963. p. 144. Ermolaev provides here a detailed account of the emergence of the doctrine of socialist realism.

11. Pike. *op. cit.* p. 259.

12. Hans-Jürgen Schmitt and Günter Schramm (eds.). *Sozialistische Realismus-konzeptionen. Dokumente zum 1. Allunionskongreß der Sowjetschriftsteller.* Frankfurt a.M.: Suhrkamp, 1974. p. 47.

13. See Pike. *op. cit.* pp. 262-71.

14. "Plebeianism" is Pike's (questionable) translation of "*Volkstümlichkeit.*" *Ibid.* p. 265.

15. Most important of a wealth of literature on the topic are Klaus L. Berghahn. "'Volkstümlichkeit und Realismus.' Nochmals zur Brecht-Lukács-Debatte."*Basis* 4 (1973): pp. 7-37; Werner Mittenzwei. "Die Brecht-Lukács-Debatte." *Sinn und Form* 19 (1967) 235-69, also in *Das Argument* 10, 46 (1968): pp. 12-43; Hans-Jürgen Schmitt (ed.). *Die Expressionismus-Debatte. Materialien zu einer marxistischen Realismus-konzeption.* Frankfurt a.M.: Suhrkamp, 1973; Klaus Völker. "Brecht und Lukács. Analyse einer Meinungsverschiedenheit." *Kursbuch* 7 (1966): pp. 80-101. Also in *alternative* 12, 67/8 (1969): pp. 134-47.

16. Bernhard Ziegler (that is Alfred Kurella). "Nun ist dies Erbe zuende . . ." In Schmitt. *op. cit.* p. 50.

17. "*Volksnähe*" is also difficult to translate. It means something like "closeness to the people." Ziegler. *op. cit.* p. 60.

18. Kantorowicz. *op. cit.* p. 219.

19. Walter. *op. cit.* p. 32.

20. Ernst Bloch to the editors of *Das Wort* 8 October 1937. TsGALI (Central Archive for Literature and Art): 631/12/141/145. Quoted in Pike. *op. cit.* p. 388.

21. Fritz Erpenbeck to Ernst Bloch, 15 October 1937. TsGALI: 631/12/141/144. In Pike. *op. cit.* p. 388.

22. Alexander Stephan. *Die deutsche Exilliteratur 1933-1945. Eine Einführung.* Munich: Beck, 1979. p. 158.

23. Pike. *op. cit.* p. 280.

24. *Ibid.* p. 306.

25. *Ibid.* p. 289.

26. *Ibid.* p. 294.

27. Georg Lukács. "Es geht um den Realismus." In Schmitt. *op. cit.* p. 205.

28. Mittenzwei. *op. cit.* p. 266.

29. Georg Lukács. "Reportage oder Gestaltung? Kritische Bemerkungen anläßlich eines Romans von Ottwalt." In Georg Lukács, 35-55. *Essays über Realismus. Probleme des Realismus I.* Neuwied and Berlin: Luchterhand, 1971 (1932). p. 44.

30. *Ibid.* p. 39.

31. The *Reportageroman* by Ernst Ottwalt which Lukács criticises is *Denn sie wissen, was sie tun. Ein deutscher Justiz-Roman.* Berlin: Malik, 1931.

32. Lukács. "Es geht um den Realismus." p. 194.

33. *Ibid.* p. 217.

34. Schmitt and Schramm. *op. cit.* pp. 222, 224.

35. Ernst Bloch. "Diskussionen über Expressionismus." In Schmitt. *op. cit.* 180-91.

36. Ernst Bloch and Hanns Eisler. "Avantgarde-Kunst und Volksfront." Originally in *Die neue Weltbühne* 50 (1937), reproduced in *Zur Tradition der deutschen sozialistischen Literatur. Eine Auswahl von Dokumenten 1935-1941*. Ed. Friedrich Albrecht, 401-9. Berlin and Weimar: Aufbau, 1979. p. 401.

37. The correspondence was published in 1939 in *Internationale Literatur*. Reproduced in full in Schmitt, 264-301. *op. cit.* p. 301.

38. *Ibid.* p. 274.

39. Bertolt Brecht. *Arbeitsjournal. Erster Band 1938 bis 1942*. Ed. Werner Hecht. Frankfurt a.M.: Suhrkamp, 1973. p. 20 (dated 18 August 1938).

40. David Pike. Transl. Lore Brüggemann. *Lukács und Brecht*. Tübingen: Max Niemeyer, 1986. p. 218.

41. *Ibid.* p. 219.

42. Klaus-Detlef Müller. *Die Funktion der Geschichte im Werk Bertolt Brechts. Studien zum Verhältnis vom Marxismus und Ästhetik*. 2nd. ed. Tübingen: Max Niemeyer, 1972. p. 172.

43. *Ibid.* p. 172.

44. *Ibid.*

45. Mittenzwei. *op. cit.* p. 267.

46. Bertolt Brecht. "Praktisches zur Expressionismusdebatte." In *Bertolt Brecht. Gesammelte Werke. Band 19*. Frankfurt a.M.: Suhrkamp, 1967 (1938): p. 296.

47. Bertolt Brecht. "Glossen zu einer formalistischen Realismustheorie." In Bertolt Brecht. *op. cit.* pp. 312-13.

48. Brecht. "Praktisches zur Expressionismusdebatte." p. 293.

49. Bertolt Brecht. "Über den formalistischen Charakter der Realismus Theorie." (1938) In Brecht. *op. cit.* 298-307. p. 305.

50. Brecht. *Arbeitsjournal.* p. 14. By "Moscow clique" he no doubt was referring to, apart from Lukács, such people as Kurella, Andor Gabor and Julius Hay.

51. *Ibid.* p. 30.

52. *Ibid.* p. 12.

53 .Brecht had published the scene in *Das Wort;* Lukács praised it in his *Wort*-contribution "Es geht um den Realismus." *op. cit.* p. 229.

54. Brecht. *Arbeitsjournal.* p. 18.

55. Werner Mittenzwei. "Die Brecht-Lukács-Debatte." (1967, new version 1975) In *Wer war Brecht. Wandlung und Entwicklung der Aussichten über Brecht. Sinn und Form*. Ed. Werner Mittenzwei, 361-402. West Berlin: verlag das europäische buch, 1977. p. 367.

56. Although Brecht's position was not published at the time, it was adequately represented by others: Bloch, Eisler, Seghers and so on.

57. On the availability of the journal in Spain, even allegedly on the battlefront, see Werner Rieck. "*Das Wort* als literarische Chronik des Freiheitskampfes der Spanischen Republik." *Weimarer Beiträge* 25, 6 (1979): pp. 58-59.

58. Aragon praised late nineteenth-century French literature, especially Zola – a position which was inimical to Lukács. In the latter's work Aragon appears "only in insignificant footnotes." Heinrich Balz. *Aragon – Malraux – Camus. Korrektur am literarischen Engagement*. Stuttgart: Kohlhammer, 1970. p. 65.

59. David Caute. *Communism and the French Intellectuals, 1914-1960*. London: André Deutsch, 1964. pp. 322-23.

60. Günther Schmigalle. *André Malraux und der spanische Bürgerkrieg. Zur Genese, Funktion und Bedeutung von "L'Espoir" (1937)*. Bonn: Bouvier Verlag Herbert Grundmann, 1980. p. 47.

61. Balz. *op. cit.* p. 86.

62. H. Gustav Klaus. "Socialist Fiction in the 1930s: Some Preliminary Observations." In *The 1930s: A Challenge to Orthodoxy*. Ed. John Lucas, 13-41. Sussex: Harvester Press; New York: Barnes and Noble, 1978. p. 17.

63. For a discussion of the discrepancies between British and German-Soviet literary discourses, see especially *ibid.* pp. 16-21.

64. Pike. *Deutsche Schriftsteller im sowjetischen Exil 1933-1945*. p. 368.

65. Helmut Kreuzer. "Zum Spanienkrieg. Prosa deutscher Exilautoren." *LiLi. Zeitschrift für Literaturwissenschaft und Linguistik* 15, 60 (1985): p. 19.

66. André Malraux. *L'Espoir*. Paris: Gallimard, 1937; Gustav Regler. *The Great Crusade*. New York, Toronto: Longman's Green, 1940. It is worth noting that J. M. Ritchie's comment that the narratives of the war were "on the whole too documentary and rooted in Socialist Realism" contains an inner contradiction. The official line on socialist realism at the time recommended precisely the *avoidance* of documentary tendencies. See J. M. Ritchie. *German Literature under National Socialism*. London, Canberra: Croom Helm; New Jersey: Barnes and Noble, 1983. p. 186.

67. Willi Bredel. *Begegnung am Ebro. Roman*. Paris: Ed. 10. Mai, 1939; Ilya Ehrenburg. Transl. Ricardo Marín. *¿Qué más queréis? Novela*. Barcelona: Publicaciones Antifeixistas de Catalunya, 1938.

68. See especially *Bodo Uhse. Eduard Claudius. Abriß der Spanienliteratur*. Ed. by the Kollektiv für Literaturgeschichte im Verlag Volk und Wissen. East Berlin: Volk und Wissen, 1961. passim.

69. Eduard Claudius. *Grüne Oliven und nackte Berge*. Zürich: Steinberg, 1945. The author's real name is Eduard Schmidt; the novel was written in a Swiss prison and in various internment camps between 1939 and 1943.

70. *Ibid.* new edition. Halle a.d.S.: Mitteldeutscher Verlag, 1976. p. 300.

71. Ritchie. *op. cit.* p. 183.

72. Bodo Uhse. *Leutnant Bertram*. Mexiko: El Libro Libre, 1943.

73. *Ibid.* p. 614.

74. Peter Merin (that is Oto Bihalji-Merin). *Spanien zwischen Tod und Geburt*. Zürich: 1937; in English as *Spain Between Death and Birth*. New York: Dodge, 1938. Alfred Kantorowicz assumes on the basis of conversations Bihalji-Merin carried out with POUM leader Nin and with Gorkin (both condemned by the Stalinists) that the author had already broken with the Communist Party at the time of writing the book. Alfred Kantorowicz. *Politik und Literatur im Exil. Deutschsprachige Schriftsteller im Kampf gegen den Nationalsozialismus*. Munich: dtv, 1983 (1978). p. 183.

75. Arthur Koestler. *Menschenopfer unerhört, ein Schwarzbuch über Spanien*. Paris: Editions du Carrefour, 1937.

76. That Hemingway wrote the script for the Joris Ivens film *Spanish Earth* is also worth mentioning; my examples here are intentionally limited, though, to communists and fellow travellers.

77. Bertolt Brecht. "Über den formalistischen Charakter der Realismustheorie." In Bertolt Brecht. *Gesammelte Werke*. Vol. 19. p. 299.

78. On the theatre during the war see especially Robert Marrast. *El teatre durant la guerra espanyola: Assaig d'història i documents*. Barcelona: Inst. del Teatre, 1978; also

Robert Marrast. "Le théâtre à Madrid pendant la guerre civile." In *Les écrivains et la guerre d'Espagne*. Ed. Marc Hanrez, 173-87. Paris: Pantheon Press France, 1975.

79. Renn's play appeared in the September 1938 issue of *Das Wort*, Wolf's in the November 1937 issue. Both are published in *Adelante! Pasaremos! Wir werden durchkommen! Erzählungen, Reportagen und Dokumente aus dem spanischen Bürgerkrieg*. Cologne: Verlag Internationale Solidarität, 1976. pp. 245-51, 141-48.

80. Elke Bleier-Staudt. "Die deutschsprachige Lyrik des Spanischen Bürgerkriegs." *LiLi. Zeitschrift für Literaturwissenschaft und Linguistik* 15, 60 (1985): p. 66.

81. Hans-Ulrich Gumbrecht. *Geschichte der spanischen Literatur*. Unpublished manuscript 1988. p. 291.

82. The first edition of *Octubre* appeared in June 1933, the final edition in April 1934.

83. The ambiguity of the title was no doubt intentional. The journal was adorned with blue monkeys, figures which connoted a cheeky, even defiant, attitude to tradition and convention. The one-piece worker's overalls, on the other hand, were a symbol of the working class, whose interests the journal claimed to represent.

84. For more information on the journal see especially Michel García. "El mono azul." In *Les écrivains et la guerre d'Espagne*. Ed. Marc Hanrez, 189-200. Paris: Pantheon Press France, 1975.

85. For more information on *Hora de España*, see especially Monique Roumette. "*Hora de España*." In *Les écrivains et la guerre d'Espagne*. op. cit. 201-14; Angel Sánchez-Gijón. "Le reviste letterarie nella guerra civile spagnola: *Hora de España*." *Carte Segrete* 1 (1967): pp. 121-38; Kessel Schwartz. "*Hora de España* and the Poetry of Hope." *Romance Notes* 15 (1973): pp. 25-29; Kessel Schwartz. "The Past as Prologue in *Hora de España*." *Romance Notes* 10 (1969): pp. 15-19; Villar Dégano. "Ideología y cultura en *Hora de España* (1937-1938)." *Letras de Deusto* 16, 35 (1986): pp. 171-200.

86. John Lehmann. *The Whispering Gallery*. London, New York, Toronto: Longman's, Green and Co., 1955. p. 279.

87. *Das Wort* 5 (May 1938): pp. 92-96.

88. Quoted in A. Augier. *Nicolás Guillén. Notas para un estudio biográfico-crítico. Volumen II*. Universidad Central de Las Villas, 1964. p. 71. See also Christel Schnelle and Kurt Schnelle. "Der antifaschistische Schriftstellerkongreß von 1937 in Spanien und die Herausbildung und Entwicklung progressiver und sozialistischer Tendenzen in der spanischen und lateinamerikanischen Literatur." In *Internationale Literatur des sozialistischen Realismus 1917-1945*. Ed. Georgi Dimow et al., 445-97. East Berlin and Weimar: Aufbau, 1978. p. 474.

89. See especially Lidija M. Jurjewa. Transl. Astrid Maaß. "Die weltliterarische Bedeutung des Spanienthemas." In *Internationale Literatur des sozialistischen Realismus 1917-1945*. Ed. Georgi Dimow et al., 617-43. East Berlin, Weimar: Aufbau, 1978. p. 626.

90. Serge Salaün. *La poesía de la guerra de España*. Madrid: Castalia, 1985. pp. 331, 326.

91. Jack Lindsay. *Fanfrolico and After*. London: Bodley Head, 1962. p. 263.

92. *Ibid*. p. 263.

93. Jack Lindsay. "On Guard for Spain! A Poem for Mass Recitation." *Left Review* 3, 2 (March 1937): pp. 79-86. A slightly longer version is available in *The Penguin Book of Spanish Civil War Verse*. Ed. Valentine Cunningham, 253-63. Harmondsworth: Penguin, 1980.

94. Lindsay. *Fanfrolico and After*. p. 264.

95. The full German title was *Requiem den gemordeten Brüdern* (Requiem to the Murdered Brothers).

96. Letter from Bram Bootman (who was one of the chanters on the night), *Listener* 12 April 1973. p. 483. Quoted in Valentine Cunningham. "Introduction," 25-94. In *The Penguin Book of Spanish Civil War Verse*. *op. cit.* p. 44.

97. Jack Lindsay in a letter to Valentine Cunningham. Quoted in Cunningham. *op. cit.* p. 45.

98. Lindsay. *Fanfrolico and After*. p. 264.

99. Interview with Don Watson. In Don Watson. "Jack Lindsay: Poetry and the Spanish Civil War." In Jack Lindsay. *The Thirties and Forties*. Ed. Robert Mackie, 61-73. London: University of London Institute of Commonwealth Studies Australian Studies Centre, 1984. p. 69.

100. Publisher Gollancz was head of the Left Book Club, which had set out to publish one book per month against "Fascism and War." Katherine, Duchess of Atholl, was a fervent opponent of the British government's non-intervention policy. According to Hugh Thomas, her book *Searchlight on Spain*. Harmondsworth: Penguin, 1938, was "the most successful of all the propaganda books on the Spanish war." Hugh Thomas. *The Spanish Civil War*. 3rd. ed. Harmondsworth: Penguin, 1986 (1961). p. 609. For "On Guard for Spain" see Lindsay. *Fanfrolico and After*. p. 264.

101. Watson. *op. cit.* p. 67.

102. *Ibid.* pp. 67-68.

103. Jack Lindsay. "A Plea for Mass Declamations." *Left Review* 3, 9 (Oct. 1937): pp. 516-17.

104. Lindsay. "On Guard for Spain." p. 79.

105. *Ibid.* pp. 80, 84. The association of fascism with gangsterism foreshadows Brecht's 1941 play *Der aufhaltsame Aufstieg des Arturo Ui* (*The Resistible Rise of Arturo Ui*).

106. *Ibid.* p. 81.

107. Neither of the published versions of the poem indicates how the speaking roles were allotted. Jack Lindsay possesses an actor's copy which was broken down into speaking parts, and which Don Watson makes use of. *op. cit.* pp. 64-67. It shows that one of the speaking roles was indeed assigned to a "Chronicle;" others were "Choir," "A Man," "A Woman," "Men," "Women".

108. Lindsay. "On Guard for Spain." p. 86.

109. *Ibid.* p. 83.

110. Labelling Lindsay a "Marxist" and Spender a "non-Marxist" is hardly controversial. Nevertheless, it is ironic that it was Spender who, for a short time at least, had joined the Communist Party; Lindsay had not.

111. Quoted (source unnamed) in Jack Lindsay. *After the 'Thirties. The Novel in Britain, and Its Future*. London: Lawrence & Wishart, 1956. p. 56.

112. Hugh Ford. *A Poets' War: British Poets and the Spanish Civil War*. Philadelphia: University of Pennsylvania Press; London: Oxford Univ. Press, 1965. p. 142.

113. A. T. Tolley. *The Poetry of the Thirties*. London: Victor Gollancz, 1975. p. 320.

114. Lindsay. *After the 'Thirties*. p. 56.

115. *Ibid.* p. 57.

116. For the importance of this newspaper see especially Klaus Bohnen. "Produktions-prozeß bei Brecht. Zur Entstehung der *Gewehre der Frau Carrar*." In *Brechts "Gewehre der Frau Carrar"*. Ed. Klaus Bohnen, 167-94. Frankfurt a.M.: Suhrkamp, 1982. pp. 173-84.

117. Ronald Hayman. *Brecht. A Biography*. New York: Oxford University Press, 1983. p. 202.

118. *Ibid.* p. 202.

119. Bertolt Brecht. "Rede zum II. Internationalen Schriftstellerkongreß zur Verteidigung der Kultur." In Bertolt Brecht. *Schriften zur Literatur und Kunst 2, 1934-1941*, 45-48. Frankfurt a.M.: Suhrkamp, 1967. p. 47.

120. *Ibid.* p. 48.

121. Klaus Völker. *Bertolt Brecht. Eine Biographie*. Munich, Vienna: Hanser, 1976. p. 258.

122. Jan Knopf. *Brecht-Handbuch. Theater. Eine Ästhetik der Widersprüche*. Stuttgart: J. B. Metzlersche Verlagsbuchhandlung, 1980. p. 155.

123. Details from Bohnen. *Brechts "Die Gewehre der Frau Carrar." op. cit.* pp. 202-3. For the staging in Sydney, only the year is given (1939), not the exact dates.

124. Knopf. *op. cit.* p. 155.

125. Rolf Geißler. "Der Spanische Bürgerkrieg im Spiegel der deutschen Literatur. Report und Reflexion." *Literatur für Leser. Zeitschrift für Interpretationspraxis und geschichtliche Texterkenntnis* 3 (1979): p. 184.

126. Henri Plard. "Les écrivains allemands." In *Les écrivains et la Guerre d'Espagne*. Ed. Marc Hanrez, 21-35. Paris: Pantheon Press France, 1975. p. 21.

127. Helmut Kreuzer. "Zum Spanienkrieg. Prosa deutscher Exilautoren." *LiLi. Zeitschrift für Literaturwissenschaft und Linguistik*. 15, 60 (1985): p. 19.

128. For the nine versions see Klaus Bohnen. "Produktionsprozeß bei Brecht. Zur Entstehung der *Gewehre der Frau Carrar*." pp. 169-73.

129. Quoted by Hayman. *op. cit.* p. 203.

130. Bertolt Brecht. *Die Gewehre der Frau Carrar*. In Bertolt Brecht. *Stücke VII. Stücke aus dem Exil*. 5-60. Frankfurt a.M.: Suhrkamp, 1957. pp. 9-10, 30-31. According to the play, Quiepo de Llano made an address every evening at nine o'clock. Hugh Thomas insists that they were always at ten o'clock. Of his radio broadcasts Thomas writes: "Quiepo de Llano's successful use of the microphone with his graphic language was symbolic of how old Spain triumphed, with new weapons." Hugh Thomas. *op. cit.* pp. 753, 938.

131. Brecht. *Die Gewehre der Frau Carrar*. p. 10. The statement was made by General Mola at the commencement of the war in the north. See Bohnen. "Produktionsprozeß bei Brecht." p. 183.

132. Brecht. *Die Gewehre der Frau Carrar*. p. 45.

133. *Ibid.* pp. 14-15.

134. *Ibid.* p. 32.

135. Michel Vanhelleputte. "Bertolt Brecht et la Guerre d'Espagne." *Revue Belge de Philologie et d'Histoire* 65, 3 (1987): p. 519.

136. The credibility of Carrar's conversion is a bone of contention and a problem which concerned Brecht himself. The case against neutrality is built gradually through dialogue; when it finally comes, however, the conversion is sudden. Impressed by Helene Weigel's interpretation of the role, Brecht argued that it should be played in such a way that Carrar is seen to become outwardly more obstinate in her pacifism, until she collapses from the final blow, the death of her son. See Bertolt Brecht. "Die Dialektik auf dem Theater." In Bertolt Brecht. *Versuche 15*. Berlin: Suhrkamp, 1957. pp. 96-97. For the problematics of the conclusion see especially Werner Mittenzwei. "*Die Gewehre der Frau Carrar*." pp. 159-61.

137. Bertolt Brecht. *Arbeitsjournal. Erster Band 1938 bis 1942*. Ed. Werner Hecht. Frankfurt a. M.: Suhrkamp, 1973. p. 41.

138. Brecht. *Die Gewehre der Frau Carrar*. p. 60.

139. *Ibid.* p. 58.

140. See Bohnen. *Brechts "Die Gewehre der Frau Carrar."* pp. 89-91.

141. Jörg-Wilhelm Joost; Klaus-Detlef Müller and Michael Voges. *Bertolt Brecht. Epoche, Werk, Wirkung*. Munich: Beck, 1985. p. 271.

142. Bertolt Brecht. *Gesammelte Werke. Band 15*. p. 249.

143. Martin Andersen-Nexö. "*Die Gewehre der Frau Carrar*. Ein deutscher Emigrantendichter über den spanischen Volkskampf." *Das Wort* 6 (June 1938): p. 141.

144. Brecht. *Die Gewehre der Frau Carrar*. See especially pp. 40-41.

145. *Ibid*. p. 59.

146. In Bertolt Brecht. *Briefe*. Ed. Günter Glaeser, 348-49. Frankfurt a.M.: Suhrkamp, 1981. p. 349.

147. Patrik von zur Mühlen. *Spanien war ihre Hoffnung. Die deutsche Linke im Spanischen Bürgerkrieg 1936 bis 1939*. Berlin, Bonn: Dietz, 1985. p. 100.

# 6. Heresies of the Left

## THE AESTHETICS OF REPORTAGE IN THE 1930s

If Stephen Spender describes the Spanish Civil War as a "poet's war",[1] there is just as much justification in labelling it a reporters' war. In the very first year of the war Jean-Richard Bloch noted: "The time is for war correspondents, not writers."[2] Although the reporters had to contend with strict censorship procedures in nationalist and republican territories, generally speaking access to Spain for suitably credentialled reporters was not highly problematical. The Spanish Civil War was more widely reported than any previous war, and this breadth of coverage was reinforced by the presence of photographers and cameramen. Newspapers all over the world sent their best reporters to Spain: the *New York Times* sent Herbert Matthews, the *Daily Express* Sefton Delmer and the *Chicago Tribune* Jay Allen. *Pravda* was represented by Mikhail Koltsov, *Izvestia* by the ubiquitous Ilya Ehrenburg. Antoine de Saint-Exupéry travelled to republican Spain to report for *Paris-Soir*, which was the most popular of the French dailies and had probably the largest number of reporters in Spain, namely six on each side.[3] The *Völkischer Beobachter* sent Roland Strunk, who was already known for his reports on the Abyssinian war, as was the *London Times* correspondent in the Basque territories, George Lowther Steer. Arthur Koestler went to Spain under the pretext of being a reporter for the *News Chronicle*; George Orwell went there, as he himself put it, "with some notion of writing newspaper articles."[4] Ernest Hemingway, the most famous of them all, first arrived in war-torn Spain in March 1937 as a correspondent for the North American Newspaper Alliance, an organisation which served over sixty newspapers. Using the Hotel Florida in Madrid as his base, he remained in Spain on and off for the next two years.[5]

Although works by these and countless other reporters of the Spanish Civil War unquestionably found large readerships, the reportage genre has not received the commensurate attention of literary scholars and theorists.

"Reportage," originally a French term and still rarely encountered in English, is generally understood to refer to nonfictional prose accounts of events or circumstances, usually, but not always, narratives. Usually, but again not always, they were written by eyewitnesses. It is apparent that in the 1930s the term was applied to a great variety of literary forms – to newspaper articles, to magazine and journal articles, as well as to books. The content of the works which received the title "reportage" covered a similarly broad range. The Yugoslav writer Theodor Balk (real name Dragatin Fodor) suggested in 1935:

Let us compare all that is today denoted as "reportage." Someone writes a biography of Madame Duberry and he calls it *grand reportage historique*. Someone makes a trip around the world and publishes his diary: "A Reportage from All the World." Someone collects the reports of an Arctic expedition – it is reportage. I shall never forget how someone proposed that I write a "reportage" on the Spanish uprising although I myself was hundreds of kilometres from the scene of the struggle and had never visited Spain. Diary, biography, reports – everything is reportage.[6]

Balk, a member of the German Communist Party, went on to fight for the Republic in the Spanish Civil War.[7] That an exponent of reportage, as Balk himself was, should have such political affiliations or sympathies was by no means unusual in the 1920s and 1930s. The outstanding example of the revolutionary commitment of many of the exponents of the genre was the American reporter John Reed, who, in his famous book *Ten Days That Shook the World*, provided an account of the 1917 Russian revolution.[8] Of this event Balk wrote: "The time was ripe for putting the naked and sober report into gripping form. The time for a writer to report freshly-warm about a world in which today and tomorrow changed the face of the world with cinema speed. The time for reportage."[9] In his list of the great contemporaneous writers of reportage, Balk names, apart from Reed, a number of other supporters of the political Left: Egon Erwin Kisch, Upton Sinclair, Larissa Reissner, Ilya Ehrenburg and Sergei Tretyakov. He names only one practitioner from the bourgeois sphere, namely Albert Londres.[10] Balk's reduction of bourgeois reportage to just one representative is arguably inequitable; nevertheless it is true that the political Left and the Communist Party in particular placed great importance on the genre. In the Soviet Union and in Germany it had set up a system of worker-correspondents, whose task it was to report on conditions in the factories, in the lives of the workers, and in the bourgeois state.[11]

It is possible to detect a widespread unwillingness to acknowledge reportage as a valid literary form or art form in the 1920s and 1930s. This reluctance cannot, however, be interpreted merely as a symptom of bourgeois distrust of a genre which was increasingly being adopted by the proletariat as a weapon in the class struggle. To be sure, many of the critics of the genre can be regarded as representatives of the bourgeois camp. One of the harshest attacks on reportage, for example, came from the Austrian novelist Hermann Broch.[12] But it as also apparent that some of the opponents of the genre were to be found within the Marxist camp. By far the most prominent of these was Georg Lukács.

Lukács's thoughts on the topic of reportage are set out in his already discussed (see Chapter 5) 1932 *Linkskurve* essay on a proletarian novel by Ernst Ottwalt.[13] In a subsection entitled *"Was ist Reportage?"* (What is Reportage?), Lukács insists that reportage was "an absolutely justified, necessary form of journalism [*Publizistik*]."[14] Good reportage, in Lukács's estimation, established a connection between the general and the particular, the necessary and the coincidental. It did not merely present facts; rather, it also pointed out causes and consequences.[15] Reportage appealed to our emotions but did so through persuading us intellectually. In this respect it operated predominantly with the methods of science, and precisely this adoption of a scientific methodology, according to Lukács, disqualified reportage as an art form.[16] The individual instance presented in the reportage was merely an example, an illustration for the general context. The quality of the reportage was determined by the clarity of the examples, and these examples became interchangeable with an entire arsenal of facts, examples and illustrations that the writer of reportage had observed, collected and systematised. In order to highlight the general context, they would of course have to be typical examples, and the writer would have to apply abstractions in order to establish the links between the typical and the general. For this reason, Lukács contends that the typical in reportage was different in principle from the typical in literature [*das Gestaltet-Typische*, *das Dichterisch-Typische*], which required no such application of abstractions:

The concrete totality of literary portrayal deals only with individuals and individual fates, who in their living interaction illuminate, complete, complement one another, make one another comprehensible, whose individual links with each other constitute the typical. In contrast, the individual case in reportage only receives its really typical character, the full realisation of its typical character, in the conceptual summary and explanation of the context which it is called upon to illustrate, regardless of whether this conceptual summary is necessarily or deliberately kept to a minimum. The concreteness of reportage, like that of every conceptual (scientific) reproduction of reality, is completed only in the conceptual disclosure and explanation of the causes and context.[17]

Lukács was not criticising the genre of reportage per se, in fact, as mentioned above, he specifically praised the work of the American reporter Herbert Knickerbocker.[18] Rather, he was refusing to attribute to it the status of art. He was much harsher in his treatment of the *Reportageroman* (reportage novel, such as the work of Ernst Ottwalt discussed here by Lukács), a genre which in his opinion was an intolerable hybrid, an illegitimate combination of fiction and reportage. Important here is Lukács's very clear distinction between three genres: the novel, the reportage novel and the reportage.

In the debate in Marxist circles concerning the status of reportage, Lukács's great opponent also happened to be one of the great practitioners of the genre, namely the Prague-born reporter Egon Erwin Kisch. The development of Kisch's theory of reportage can be broken into three main phases.[19]

The first phase covers the period 1918 to 1925. In a 1918 essay *"Wesen des Reporters"* (Nature of the Reporter), Kisch claims that "every milieu-study is reportage" and points out that every writer (and he names as examples Zola and

Gustave Flaubert) required the study of milieu.[20] For Kisch, the reporter was always dependent on objectivity (*Sachlichkeit*); the results of his research were necessarily from firsthand experience, from life.[21] At the same time, the reporter required what Kisch called a "logical imagination" (*logische Phantasie*) in order to construct a complete picture of the situation, which facts alone could not provide.[22] Regarding the reporter's ability to reconstruct experience, Kisch uses the analogy of a photographic plate, a device which the artist did not require and which the average person did not possess.[23] This concept of the impartial reporter is reinforced in Kisch's foreword to his own 1924 book *Der rasende Reporter* (The Mad Reporter). There Kisch writes: "The reporter has no partiality [*Tendenz*], has nothing to justify and has no standpoint. He has to be an unbiased witness and to give unbiased testimony, as reliable as a testimony can be."[24] The world which the reporter described did not need to be far removed from everyday reality. "Nothing is more baffling than the simple truth, nothing is more exotic than our environment, nothing is more imaginative than objectivity. And there is nothing more sensational in the world than the time in which one lives."[25]

Kisch's journey to the Soviet Union in late 1925 and early 1926 marks the beginning of a second phase in his conception of reportage. Kisch returned from that journey a much more committed advocate of the communist cause.[26] The impact of this change of understanding of reportage is expressed in his response to the work of John Reed. In his foreword to the German edition of *Ten Days That Shook the World*, Kisch described Reed's work as "classical journalism."[27] Whereas Zola had defined art as a piece of truth seen through a temperament, Reed had expanded that definition to the formula "through a revolutionary temperament."[28] Reed's technique was regarded as exemplary by Kisch, as the ideal way to present truth, the highest goal of reportage and of art in general. Reed had observed the Russian revolution as a "passionate chronicler."[29] With this it was apparent that Kisch's earlier insistence on the reporter's impartiality had been abandoned. He now demanded from the reporter "extreme subjectivity and the highest objectivity at the same time."[30]

It was during this second phase also that Kisch took up the attack against prevailing aesthetic doctrines, which refused to acknowledge the artistic qualities of reportage. In response to the 1928 survey on the topic "Is there a proletarian art?", Kisch answered that all real art was opposition, rebellion or revolution, that it had to be truthful and that it had to combat the lies of diversionary, "timeless" art.[31] In the same year in an article for the Czech journal *Čin* (Action) Kisch went so far as to pronounce the end of the age of the novel and the beginning of the age of reportage. The war had made all novels trivial. People had experienced their own novel, with the result that fiction had become superfluous. Its successor was a quite particular form of reportage which Kisch called "pure reportage."[32]

Kisch's third phase began in 1933, the year in which he was forced to leave Germany as a result of political circumstances there. During his exile years Kisch was unquestionably a leading figure in the European anti-fascist movement, and yet it was a period in which he expressed scepticism at the capacity of reportage to influence decisively the course of political events.[33]

Although no complete manuscript is extant, a key document of Kisch's theoretical position of the exile years was his address at the 1935 Paris International Congress for the Defence of Culture, entitled *"Reportage als Kunstform und Kampfform"* (Reportage as Form of Art and Form of Struggle). As the title alone suggests, Kisch was continuing to argue that reportage possessed the status of an art form. Ideologically, Kisch in Paris fully accepted the wisdom of a Popular Front of communist and non-communist elements, which for writers and intellectuals would entail a commitment to a form of internationalist humanism. In contrast to Lukács, however, the ramification of this adherence to the Popular Front tactic for Kisch in the area of aesthetics was *not* an adoption of the bourgeois cultural heritage. Kisch continued to argue against bourgeois aesthetics and for the artistic status of reportage.

There is not just "high literature." Not only in the first period of socialist society will there be literary forms which address hurried, still untrained, still undeveloped readers, but these literary forms must have a character which is precisely the opposite of that which they now have in five-sixths of the world. Let me use reportage as an example, a particular literary art-form which has been discredited by the bourgeois aestheticians and indeed was disparaged by writers who wrote of their own world, so that even they looked down on it with disdain.

The reporter was despised as the lowest species of journalist before the works of a John Reed and a Larissa Reissner (who were joined by the Russians Tretyakov and Koltsov, the German Holitischer, the American Spivak, the Frenchman Londres and many others) taught that the factual report [*Tatsachenbericht*] too could be made independently and artistically. And whoever was not taught that would have been able to be taught that from the hostile, spiteful attitude of the critical old-guard [*kritische Tempelhüter*].34

This outline of the development of Kisch's theory of reportage over two decades is useful for two reasons. Firstly, it indicates that despite strong opposition from within both bourgeois and Marxist circles, an attempt was being made during the 1920s and 1930s to press for the recognition of reportage as a valid literary and art form, to break down the theoretical barriers between reportage and fictional forms. Secondly, Kisch's earlier and later theoretical positions demarcate the spectrum of forms of literary reportage in this period. At one extreme reportage is the product of a neutral, impartial reporter, who records events much as a camera records detail. At the other extreme, reportage is the work of the biased, passionate observer, whose revolutionary temperament is deliberately injected into the reportage. Kisch's own development suggests that in 1936, the time of the beginning of the conflict in Spain, the trend was towards the latter, that is, towards a version of the genre which combined objectivity with subjectivity.

Kisch himself spent some time in Spain during the war. He first went there in May 1937 and attended the Writers' Congress in Valencia and Madrid in July of that year. He visited the front on a number of occasions, was in Teruel in December of 1937 and in Barcelona in March of 1938.35 An anecdote, recounted by the German communist writer Willi Bredel, suggests that Kisch was requested by an American newspaper to write something about the aerial bombardment of Madrid which would evoke an emotional response from American readers. Kisch told Bredel that he would report on the animals in the Madrid zoo, which "at the howling of the approaching bombs crawled whimpering like children into the farthest corners of their cages."[36] Kisch explained that no American would be interested in the mortal agony of the people of Madrid, but dead animals might mobilise animal protection societies, and the human population of the city might gain some benefit from that.[37] Amongst several published pieces by Kisch on the Spanish Civil War, no such reportage is to be found; Kisch was at most half-serious and certainly sarcastic. Nevertheless, the recognition of the need for reportage to appeal to the reader's emotions is significant.

One of the most convincing attempts to justify and legitimate the use of reportage in the literature of the Spanish Civil War came not from Kisch but from a similarly renowned fellow reporter by the name of Ernest Hemingway. Hemingway wrote the foreword to *The Great Crusade*, a book by the German writer Gustav Regler, who was a personal friend of Hemingway. At the end of his foreword, Hemingway wrote: "The greatest novels are made up. Everything in them is created by the author. . . . But there are events which are so great that if a writer has participated in them his obligation is to try to write them truly rather than assume the presumption of altering them with intention. It is events of this importance that have produced Regler's book."[38]

An interesting detail about *The Great Crusade* is that, although Hemingway stresses that it is the truthful retelling of Regler's experiences of the war, it is generally classified as a novel rather than as reportage.[39] Hemingway's own novel *For Whom the Bell Tolls* contains elements of fact, as does Malraux's *L'Espoir*. On the other hand, works which are sometimes categorised as reportage, such as Orwell's *Homage to Catalonia* or Koestler's *Spanish Testament*, contain elements which are often associated with prose fiction.

In short, in dealing with the literature of the Spanish Civil War it is exceedingly difficult to apply the Lukácsian system of a strict distinction between the novel, the reportage novel and the reportage. We are much better served in adopting the scheme of Kisch, which recognises no such clear distinctions, and whilst demanding objectivity in reportage, also permits and even recommends the insertion into the account of the persona of the passionate, biased reporter. The observer of action is at times also a participant in the action.

Much of the literature of the Spanish Civil War insists on its own objectivity, that is, it insists that the events, the people and the scenes it describes correspond precisely to events, people and scenes of "real life." The analogy which Kisch had formulated many years earlier, that is, of the reporter and a photographic plate, which is comparable also with Christopher Isherwood's formula "I am a Camera,"[40] is adopted explicitly by a number of writers on the Spanish Civil War. This is true of Stephen Spender's poem "War Photograph" and also of George Barker's poem "Elegy on Spain," which is dedicated to the photograph of a child killed in an air raid on Barcelona. It begins with the lines:

O ecstatic is this head of five-year joy –
Captured its butterfly rapture on a paper:

And not the rapture of the right eye may
Make any less this prettier than a picture,
O now, my minor moon, dead as meat
Slapped on a negative plate, I hold
The crime of the bloody time in my hand.[41]

Similarly, John Sommerfield concludes a gruesome description of a scene of war with a photographic analogy:

And we stood there wailing, steel-helmeted, hung about with arms and ammunition, gas-masks dangling on our chests, a hundred and forty soldiers, the machine-gun company of the Marty Batallion of the International Brigade; and the rain came down, the broken water-main gushed continuously, the tall buildings gaped their wounds, and from the corpse in the gutter the blood and brains washed slowly away, mingling with those of the dead dog.
    It was as good a war picture as I could think of. [42]

Passages such as this lend weight to David Mellor's contention that the "photographic imagination of the war, which structured the media imagination of the war, was dominant, becoming the primary point of reference and departure for all other accounts of the Spanish Civil War."[43]

Other writers stress the objectivity of their work by drawing an analogy with another visual medium, namely painting. Most notably comparisons are drawn with the great Spanish painter Francisco Goya. During the Napoleonic wars in Spain, Goya had painted a series of paintings under the title "*Desastres de guerra*" (Disasters of War, or Horrors of War). The German writer Rudolf Leonhard uses the title of one of the paintings of this series, namely "*Yo lo vi*" (This I Saw) as the motto for a collection of stories on the Spanish Civil War. [44] Implicit of course is the claim that, as in Goya's painting, that which is depicted is empirically verifiable. The Spanish novelist and journalist Ramón Sender in his reportage *Contraataque* [45] similarly compares the Spain he described with paintings by Goya which depicted the horrors of the war against the French more than one hundred years earlier:

Most of [Goya's] *Horrors of the War* came from there [i.e., the meadow of San Isidio and the Casa de Campo]; and there they returned a century later. Don "Paco the Deaf," as his neighbours called him (peasants and workers), kept these scenes in the depths of his weary eyes, and when he got back to his house drew them. Sometimes there was a man hanging from a tree with his legs cut off and nailed to branches alongside, which filled the paper with a revolting human horror, and gave the victim a monstrous grandeur which in its bitterness approaches caricature. At the foot he had written, simply, "I saw this." Another time he drew a wounded man, bandaged and on crutches on sentry duty in his white sleeves, on one of those dark windy nights he loved so much, and put under it, "Still useful." Goya came from my part of Spain, and his dry words, full to overflowing with a condensed emotion, are familiar to us of Aragón, shock us less than they shock those of other provinces, because they express our own land, dry but fertile. [46]

It is important to note that Goya's (and Sender's) "dry," unadorned presentation of what he saw does not preclude emotion. On the contrary, the dryness, the restraint, is an indicator of condensed and powerful emotion. In recalling the murders of his wife and of his brother, for example, Sender writes: "I shall use the fewest possible words; I shall give only the bare facts. I shall silence, extinguish, the voices which rise clamorously and imperatively in my heart. I have written always with a kind of indefinite need to reveal myself completely and impartially to the world, and not to conceal myself."[47] To put it in Kisch's terms, the analogy to painting applied by Sender demonstrates the compatibility and even the desirability of objectivity *and* subjectivity. Goya and Sender portray the horrible reality of war, but neither Goya nor Sender attempts to disguise the fact that the events depicted are seen through the medium of a particular temperament.

Although photography is arguably the most objective of media, the photographic analogy similarly supports the validity of Kisch's notion of the compatibility of extreme subjectivity and objectivity in reportage. The most famous photograph of the Spanish Civil War, perhaps indeed of all wars, is Robert Capa's controversial photograph "Death of a Loyalist Soldier."[48] It depicts a militia soldier as he is being shot. Arms outstretched and leaning backwards, he is on the point of releasing his rifle. Most of the photography of the war is characterised by the distanced position adopted by the photographer.[49] Capa, however, is an exception, and it is clear in this photograph that the photographer, the observer, was in the immediate vicinity of the action depicted, that he himself was in danger of suffering the same fate as the militia soldier. Much of the impact of the photograph lies in the realisation that the photographer was not a distanced observer but a participant. The poor focus, the scratches and the failure to centre the action all testify to this. As Phillip Knightley puts it, the suggestion it makes is that it was "taken by someone who must have put himself at great risk, someone who was, perhaps, nearly killed as well."[50] Capa summed up his philosophy of war photography with the words: "If a picture is bad, you were not close enough."[51] Coming from one of the most famous exponents of photographic reportage, these words could have served as the motto for many of the practitioners of literary reportage, who similarly depict themselves not merely as disinterested observers of the war but as participants in it.

## HERETICAL REPORTAGE

Reportage was practiced by writers across the whole range of the political spectrum, many of whom unwittingly followed Capa's advice of getting as close to the action as possible. Reportage, in other words, transcends political boundaries: Hannes Trautloft's *Als Jagdflieger in Spanien* may be categorised as reportage, just as may Sender's *Contraataque*.

Apart from being works of reportage, these two books have another feature in common, and that is that they both deal with war, with specifically military events, albeit from different sides. That Spanish Civil War reportage should deal at length with military events is by no means surprising. On the contrary, in most cases it is a more or less accurate reflection of the author's particular experiences on Spanish soil. Trautloft and Sender, for example, deal extensively with their combat experiences. This applies to much of the literature produced by combatants, whether they were fighting for the Republic or for Franco.

Some Spanish Civil War literature, though, deals not solely with war but with the concomitant phenomenon of revolution. Given that there was no social revolution in nationalist territory, it does not surprise that the pro-franquist literature of the war does not deal with the revolution, except to allege that revolutionary developments in republican territory had led to terror and atrocities on an unrivalled scale. Similarly, and perhaps less predictably, the communist literature of the war generally does not report or examine the social revolution. To some extent this can be explained by the fact that many of the members of the International Brigades had little or no knowledge of what was occurring behind the lines. This would be true, for example, of John Sommerfield's above-mentioned book *Volunteer in Spain*, also of such books as Ludwig Renn's *Im Spanischen Krieg* (In the Spanish War), Alfred Kantorowicz's collective effort *Tschapajew* or Willi Bredel's *Begegnung am Ebro* (Encounter at the Ebro).[52] At the same time it is apparent that many communist authors *did* know of the social revolution, but for more sinister, ideologically motivated reasons chose not to report it. They deliberately maintained silence on the subject of the revolution because of the official communist policy towards the revolution. As the Communist Party set out to suppress the revolution or at best to promote a "bourgeois-democratic" revolution at the expense of a proletarian revolution (see Chapter 1), one of the functions communist writers received was to create the impression in the world outside Spain that no radical and widespread social revolution was taking place.

Among Party members, the only hint of aberration from the official Party line, the only suggestion of "heresy," appears to be the Soviet author Mikhail Koltsov. Koltsov was in Spain from 8 August 1936 until 2 April 1937, then again from 24 May 1937 until the beginning of November of that year. Officially he was a correspondent for *Pravda*, but unofficially he was much more than that. Hugh Thomas suggests that he was "probably Stalin's personal agent in Spain, with on occasion a direct line to the Kremlin."[53] He appears in *For Whom the Bell Tolls* in the figure of Karkov. Reports by Koltsov appeared in *Pravda*, as well as in other Moscow publications (including *Das Wort* and *International Literature*). These reports provide the basis for his incomplete *Ispanskij dn'evnik* (Spanish Diary), which was not published until 1957.[54]

Lukács could not have approved of Koltsov's diary as good reportage or as an example of socialist realism.[55] Like so much of the reportage of the war, it contains a mixture of forms, including travel report, satire, dialogue and political polemic. Most importantly, next to the central figure of the narrator-protagonist, Koltsov introduces into the narrative a character by the name of Miguel Martínez, a Mexican communist who actively takes part in the defense of Madrid. Michel Heim claims that Martínez is "none other than Koltsov the commissar, the alter ego of Koltsov the reporter."[56] To support his claim, he points out that Koltsov's brother Boris Efimov described the creation of Martínez in the following way:

The Christian name was taken from the author himself: Miguel (Mikhail). Koltsov first thought of the surname d'Anillo ('ring' in Spanish, and a literary translation of 'koltso,' the word from which the surname Koltsov is derived). But he later abandoned this pseudonym as too transparent and his choice fell on a name which is very simple and very widespread amongst the Spaniards and the Mexicans: Martínez.[57]

The reasons for the invention of Martínez are clear enough. There is, as Reinhold Görling has pointed out, a kind of division of labour: Martínez is the soldier, officer and political commissar, while the narrator is the journalist and writer. In this way Koltsov is able to capture some of the complexity of his involvement in the war. [58]

It was not this aesthetic heresy of introducing fictional elements into a documentary work which would have been the primary concern of communist officialdom. Both Martínez and the narrator are witnesses to the war at the front, but also to the revolutionary activity behind the front, and Koltsov does not disguise the existence and extent of the revolution. With passionate sympathy the narrator describes the revolutionary atmosphere in Barcelona in the early days of the war:

Even I am infected by this passion in the air, I feel the dull beating of my heart. With difficulty I push my way forward in this jammed mass, surrounded by young people with rifles, by women with flowers in their hair and bright sabres in their hands, by old men with revolutionary scarves over their shoulders, by portraits of Bakunin, Lenin and Jaurès, in the midst of songs, orchestra music and the cries of newspaper vendors.[59]

As a communist, Koltsov saw the need for discipline in the anti-fascist camp, but he was far from advocating the suppression of revolutionary energies. Revolutionary energy for Koltsov was something which could be placed in service of the revolution. For Koltsov "there was no question of organising revolutionary change without revolutionising social organisation."[60]

It has been suggested that, by supporting genuinely revolutionary activity in Spain, Koltsov and other "heretics" were hoping to bring about change in the Soviet Union itself, where the revolutionary fervour of twenty years before had been extinguished. The American communist Louis Fischer, for example, wrote: "The cause of Spain aroused intense enthusiasm throughout Russia. Many communists and non-communists hoped that events in Spain might lend new life to the dying flame of the Russian revolution."[61] History shows though that the Stalinist policy during the Spanish Civil War remained rigidly anti-revolutionary, that Koltsov and others within the Party were not able to revolutionise Soviet policy in Spain, and certainly not in the Soviet Union. History also shows that Koltsov's reservations concerning Stalinist practices both within and outside the Soviet Union did not go unnoticed in Moscow. Koltsov was arrested in December 1938. The *Great Soviet Encyclopedia*, without stating the cause, gives as his date of death 4 April 1942.[62] His longtime German companion Maria Osten (real name Maria Greshöner), who edited a collection of reportage in Russian and wrote articles on Spain for the *Deutsche-Zentral-Zeitung* in Moscow, seems to have suffered a similar fate.

For members of the Communist Party, to commit ideological heresy, that is, to challenge the Stalinist line, was fraught with danger and in many cases besides those of Koltsov and Osten was paid for with the ultimate price. It was somewhat safer, but certainly not without its hazards, to criticise the Party from without rather than within.

One man who managed to report on the social revolution in Spain, to criticise Stalinist policy and practices, and to get away with it, was Franz Borkenau. Borkenau was an Austrian sociologist and ex-communist. He was born in Vienna in 1900, and although he was of jewish descent, he received a Catholic upbringing. In 1921, as a student at the University of Leipzig, he joined the Communist Party. Three years later, having achieved his doctorate, Borkenau took up a position in the Comintern in Berlin. His conflict with the Party began as early as 1928; by the end of 1929 his open rejection of Communist Party policy had led to exclusion from the Party. With the assistance of a scholarship from the renowned Frankfurt Institute for Social Research, Borkenau applied his unorthodox Marxist sociological approach in an ambitious book project on the development of bourgeois ideology, which was finally published in Paris in 1934.[63] It was in Paris that Borkenau had landed after being forced into exile from Germany in 1933, but financial circumstances persuaded him to accept a professorship for one year in Panama.[64]

Borkenau had returned to Europe by the time of the outbreak of the Spanish Civil War. Rather than inspiring him to overtly political action, the war triggered Borkenau's passionate interest in political analysis, in particular the analysis of revolution. The tangible outcome of that passionate interest is his book *The Spanish Cockpit*, which was first published in London in 1937.[65]

*The Spanish Cockpit* reports on two journeys Borkenau made to republican Spain during the war, the first of which began on 5 August 1936 and lasted until 15 September of the same year. The second journey began in mid-January 1937 and lasted until 25 February. An attempt to travel to nationalist Spain was unsuccessful.[66] Apart from reports on these two journeys, the book contains a lengthy opening chapter which details the historical background to the war, a shorter chapter on the Battle of Guadalajara, and a chapter of conclusions.

It is in the chapter on his first journey into republican territory, suitably titled "A Diary in Revolution, 1936," that Borkenau places his personal experience of and response to revolutionary events in the centre of attention. As the title suggests, to do this he preserves the form of the diary but explains that it is the reworking of an original diary, "the transcription, into comparatively readable English, of German catchword notes taken during my first journey in revolutionary Spain, and scribbled into various note-books."[67] This preservation of the diary form, as opposed to a continuous account of the journey, a book of travels, was not the result of aesthetic considerations. On the contrary, Borkenau contends that from the point of view of "literary attractiveness" a continuous account would have been preferable.[68] His arguments for the diary form sound very much like Hemingway's defence of Regler's documentary novel:

There was only one consideration which argued in favour of the method here adopted, but this one decisive: in a matter so controversial as the Spanish Civil War every presentation that departed from the observed facts themselves, to however slight a degree, would open the door to doubt. The form of a diary, giving my day-to-day observations, was the one which offered the best chance to stick close to the actual facts. Nothing has been done, for this reason, to smooth out contradictions. When I have observed contrasting facts I have presented them as I saw them.[69]

As in so much of the reportage of the Spanish Civil War, the author deliberately cultivates the persona of the narrator as the reliable guarantor of veracity. The diary traces Borkenau's journey to Barcelona and the Aragón front, through Valencia and Madrid and on to southern Spain. He visited the front on a number of occasions but was never involved in combat. His primary interest is in the politics of republican Spain and in the attempts to implement a social revolution there. The resulting report on the revolution is the result of his own experiences and to a certain extent of hearsay evidence, whereby he is always careful to reveal his sources. Nevertheless, Borkenau himself confesses that in this process of collecting facts and then interpreting them, a certain bias is inevitable:

Nobody in an event such as the Spanish Civil War would simply collect facts without drawing inferences as to the probable course of events, the strong and the weak points of the contending parties and similar things. But in forming opinions, the observer inevitably takes sides, in however detached a way. To remove the marks of these opinions would mean to pretend an objectivity which nobody can attain, and to mislead the reader, instead of putting him into a position to judge for himself. The latter aim is best achieved by clearly separating the presentation of the facts from the presentation of the author's opinions.[70]

Furthermore, in a manner which recalls Kisch's demand for a combination of subjectivity and objectivity, Borkenau insists that in reporting such a thing as a revolution, the dry facts are simply not sufficient, since

half of its significance lies in the general ambience and atmosphere in which it moves. This atmosphere, unless reproduced with the creative power of an artist – which, unfortunately, involves an artist's subjectiveness – can best be conveyed through the medium of those impressions, hopes, mistakes, and disappointments it creates in the sympathetic observer. I would go so far as to say that the rising, transformation, and decay of these illusions is half of the history of the revolution itself.[71]

Borkenau's role as a "sympathetic observer" needs to be defined more clearly. It is generally true that Borkenau's sympathies rested with the Left, but it is also apparent that he did not unreservedly lend his support to any particular party or political grouping of the Left. He reveals that he entered Spain with a letter of recommendation from "a fairly well-known Spanish socialist,"[72] but he is critical of broad sections of the Left, including the socialists. He accuses all political groups, for example, of a lack of realism.[73] Similarly, in noting marked discrepancies between political theory and practice, Borkenau observes: "It seems that socialism and anarchism have that in common with catholicism that, whatever their change of attitude in practice, the dogma is never allowed to change."[74]

The account of Borkenau's second journey differs formally from that of the first. Rather than recording observations in a strict diary form, the second account is given to a more extensive analysis and discussion of political problems. There were, as Borkenau explains, quite practical reasons for this change of form. By January 1937 the freedom to travel throughout republican Spain "had become a privilege granted only to journalists with a definite party allegiance."[75] As a consequence, the range of day-to-day observations Borkenau was now able to report was relatively limited; at the same time, he felt that his knowledge of the situation was sufficient to allow more generalisations.[76] In the report of the second journey, the balance of subjectivity and objectivity tilts more towards the latter.

Clearly the set of circumstances which hindered Borkenau's mode of operation on the second journey possessed sinister undertones for him. In the short time that he was out of Spain, political changes had taken place in republican territory. It was apparent to Borkenau that a period of "totalitarian tendencies" had begun,[77] a fact which immediately manifested itself in the outward appearance of Barcelona:

Barcelona came as a shock, as in August, but in the opposite sense. Then it had overwhelmed me by the suddenness with which it revealed the real character of a workers' dictatorship. This time it struck the observer by the clean sweep of all signs of this same dictatorship. No more barricades in the streets; no more cars covered with revolutionary initials and filled with men in red neckties rushing through the town; no more workers in civilian clothes, but rifles on their shoulders; as a matter of fact, very few armed men at all, and those mostly asaltos and guardias in brilliant uniforms; no more seething life around the party centres and no large car-parks before their entries; and the red banners and inscriptions, so shiny in August, had failed. There was still no definitely "bourgeois" element visible in the streets. Certainly the really rich people, if there are any, did not appear in public. But the Ramblas, the chief artery of popular life in Barcelona, were far less clearly working-class now than then. In August it was dangerous to wear a hat: nobody minded doing so now, and the girls no longer hesitated to wear their prettiest clothes. A few of the more fashionable restaurants and dance-halls have reopened, and find customers. To sum it up, what one calls the petty-bourgeois element, merchants, shop-keepers, professional men, and the like, have not only made their appearance, but make a strong impress upon the general atmosphere.[78]

This initial impression of the decline of revolutionary fervour in Barcelona is reinforced by Borkenau's impressions of the fate of the revolution in rural Spain. He concludes that the social revolution had failed, that the vital question of land ownership had not been resolved, and that *all* the major political groupings in republican Spain were to blame:

The Spanish revolution set out to give the peasant the land of the grandee, individually or collectively. Instead of doing so it had landed itself in the *impasse* of discussing whether the peasants' *own* land ought to be owned individually or collectively. And the blindness as to this central problem is the same among communists, socialists, and anarchists, not to mention the POUM, which prefers to remain in the lofty realm of Marxist abstractions.[79]

The trend away from the revolutionary spontaneity evident in the first months of the war and towards what Borkenau identified as totalitarianism impinged heavily on the conduct of Borkenau's work. In contrast to the first journey, during the second one he was "continually molested and hampered in my work by being shadowed and repeatedly denounced."[80] Borkenau accuses the communists of striving to establish a bureaucratic tyranny in Spain as had already been done in the Soviet Union, and in referring to the manner in which the Spanish communists treated those suspected of cooperating with Trotskyists, Borkenau goes so far as to compare them with the Nazis.[81] The freedom with which Borkenau had been allowed to express critical opinion of *all* parties during his first journey had evaporated by early 1937 to the point of placing him at considerable personal risk. Borkenau was ultimately put in jail in Valencia, having been denounced by his English secretary, a communist.[82] He was released after two days when a British friend pledged for his good behaviour.[83] He had narrowly avoided falling victim to a terrorism which was no longer an instrument of the masses, as in the early stages of the war, but of a ruthless ruling group.

Typically, Borkenau's final chapter, "Conclusions," is critical of both revolutionary and non-revolutionary elements in republican Spain. The anarchist trust in a military victory won by the spontaneous resistance of the masses was ill founded. In the era of modern warfare, the guerrilla tactics which had been employed successfully in 1707 and 1808 were no longer applicable.[84] Similarly, Borkenau's estimation of the overall extent, success and implications of the revolution is sober. A widespread expropriation of industrial property had taken place, but "the attempt at thorough socialisation was likely to lead to conflict between Spain and the great democratic powers."[85] As for the villages, there the revolution had been very slow. To win the war, the republican government in Borkenau's opinion "must not play with 'socialist' industry in town, but make every effort to bring about a broad peasant movement and submerge Franco in the waves of revolting villages."[86]

None of the major political sections of the Left had advocated or pursued this formula for victory. Following orders from Moscow, the communists "had dropped every ideal, not only of a proletarian, but even of a village revolution after the example of the French Revolution."[87] Many of the measures introduced by the communists were "reasonable and inevitable,"[88] but the overall impact of communist intervention in the war was inimical to the revolutionary cause, because the communists acted "not with the aim of transforming chaotic enthusiasm into disciplined enthusiasm but with the aim of substituting disciplined military and administrative action for the action of the masses and getting rid of the latter entirely."[89] The overall impact of communist intervention in the Spanish Civil War had been antipathetic to the interests and claims of the Spanish people. The Trotskyists though were no better, since they were "repeating senseless formulae such as 'constitutional assembly,' taken out of the books about the Russian revolutions of 1905 and 1917."[90] The anarchists "played about with the creation of the kingdom of heaven in the form of the abolition of money and complete collectivisation in the individual villages."[91] "But no party was able to organise resistance against even the small amount of foreign intervention with which they were faced, and none had any constructive idea whatsoever in politics. The creative political power in which both the French and Russian revolution had been so rich was conspicuously absent in Spain."[92]

In *The Spanish Cockpit*, Borkenau demonstrates that it is possible to write an explicitly political book without being partisan. The author's sympathies lie with the Spanish Republic, and yet he is openly critical of anarchists, Trotskyists, socialists *and* communists. Written by a former member of the Communist Party, it can be regarded as a work of heresy, but one which commanded enormous respect amongst the many supporters of the Left who, during the Spanish Civil War and many years later than Borkenau, were losing their political innocence.

## ORWELL'S *BILDUNGSREPORTAGE*

One of Borkenau's greatest admirers was George Orwell. In *Time and Tide* on 31 July 1937 Orwell reviewed *The Spanish Cockpit* and John Sommerfield's *Volunteer in Spain*. While dismissing the work of the communist Sommerfield as "sentimental tripe,"[93] Orwell was generous in his praise of Borkenau's work:

Dr. Borkenau has performed a feat which is very difficult at this moment for anyone who knows what is going on in Spain; he has written a book about the Spanish war without losing his temper. Perhaps I am rash in saying that it is the best book yet written on the subject, but I believe that anyone who has recently come from Spain will agree with me. After that horrible atmosphere of espionage and political hatred it is a relief to come upon a book which sums the situation up as calmly and lucidly as this.[94]

This was Orwell's first encounter with the work of Borkenau, but it was by no means the last time that Orwell was to express a positive appraisal of Borkenau's writing. In *Homage to Catalonia* itself, published in April 1938, Orwell in a footnote recommends *The Spanish Cockpit* as "by a long way the ablest book that has yet appeared on the Spanish war."[95] In September 1938 Orwell reviewed Borkenau's book *The Communist International*, describing it as "a profoundly interesting book."[96] Two years later he reviewed Borkenau's *The Totalitarian Enemy*. In this instance he asserted that it was "not one of Dr. Borkenau's best books," but that it "contains a study of the nature of totalitarianism which deserves and in fact needs to be widely read at this moment."[97] Finally, in his essay "Wells, Hitler and the World State," Orwell names Borkenau amongst the most accomplished exponents of what he labels the "political book":

One development of the last ten years has been the appearance of the "political book," a sort of enlarged pamphlet combining history with political criticism, as an important literary form. But the best writers in this line – Borkenau, Koestler and others – have none of them been Englishmen, and nearly all of them have been renegades from one or other extremist party, who have seen totalitarianism at close quarters and known the meaning of exile and persecution. [98]

It appears that Orwell's admiration for Borkenau was returned. After the publication of his review of *The Spanish Cockpit*, Borkenau wrote to Orwell to inform him that he was "the only reviewer who had mentioned the essential point of the book, i.e. that the Communist Party is now the chief anti-revolutionary party."[99] After the publication of *Homage to Catalonia* in April 1938, Borkenau wrote to Orwell: "To me your book is a further confirmation of my conviction that it is possible to be perfectly honest with one's facts quite irrespective of one's political convictions."[100] Borkenau's 1953 book *European Communism* is dedicated to the memory of George Orwell.[101]

That such a genuine and lasting relationship of mutual admiration should be established in the political climate of the 1930s was a rare thing. Orwell was very sparing in his praise of authors who had written on the Spanish Civil War. He almost went out of his way to present to the British public works which had a pro-POUM or a pro-anarchist line (thus he reviewed *Red Spanish Notebook* by Mary Low and Juan Brea, as well as Mairin Mitchell's *Storm over Spain*). Interestingly, he praises Auden's *Spain* as "one of the few decent things that have been written about the Spanish war."[102] In general, though, Orwell's estimation of the literature of the war was a damning one:

The immediately striking thing about the Spanish war books, at any rate those written in English, is their shocking dullness and badness. But what is more significant is that almost all of them, right-wing or left-wing, are written from a political angle, by cocksure partisans telling you what to think, whereas the books about the Great War were by common soldiers or junior officers who did not even pretend to understand what the whole thing was about. Books like *All Quiet on the Western Front*, *Le Feu*, *A Farewell to Arms*, *Death of a Hero*, *Good-Bye to All That*, *Memoirs of an Infantry Officer* and *A Subaltern on the Somme* were written not by propagandists but by victims. They were saying in effect, "What the hell is all this about? God knows. All we can do is to endure."[103]

Just as Orwell was critical of the bulk of the literature of the war, so many critics were critical of Orwell's own contribution, *Homage to Catalonia*. Because of its explicitly anti-communist content, the reception in communist circles was limited. It is a testimony to the influence of communism on the British literary scene that when Orwell died only 900 of the 1,500 copies of *Homage to Catalonia* had been sold.[104] The relatively small number of reviews which were published were mainly hostile. John Langdon-Davies wrote in the *Daily Worker*: "The value of the book is that it gives an honest picture of the sort of mentality that toys with revolutionary romanticism but shies violently at revolutionary discipline. It should be read as a warning."[105] He and other reviewers continually presented it as "a defence of 'Trotskyites and anarchists' who betrayed the Republican cause."[106] Only two reviews, those by Philip Mairet in *The New English Weekly* and Geoffrey Gorer in *Time and Tide*, were entirely favourable.[107]

The "elective affinity" between Borkenau and Orwell came about because their respective experiences of Spain were similar, and because their heterodox ideological positions were similar (without being identical). Both were deeply affected by the Spanish experience, both produced works of reportage in response to it, and both occupied ideological positions located somewhere between communism and anarchism.

Like Borkenau, Orwell went to Spain as a curious observer of revolutionary events there. In *Homage to Catalonia* he declares that he went to Spain "with some notion of writing newspaper articles, but I had joined the militia almost immediately because at that time and in that atmosphere it seemed the only conceivable thing to do."[108] Whether the taking up of arms had perhaps even been the primary motive for going to Spain remains a point of some contention. Biographer Bernard Crick insists that at the time writing was "a quite secondary motive for coming to Spain."[109] Orwell's own apparent vagueness about the order of his priorities is, however, supported by a comment he makes in his "Notes on the Spanish Militias," where he claims that he "had intended going to Spain to gather materials for newspaper articles etc., and had also some vague idea of fighting if it seemed worth while, but was doubtful about this owing to my poor health and comparatively small military experience."[110]

What is less controversial is the process by which Orwell gained access to republican Spain. Under the impression that he would require some form of political credentials, Orwell first of all consulted Harry Pollitt, the secretary general of the British Communist Party. The meeting with Pollitt proved unsatisfactory, perhaps because Orwell refused to guarantee that he would join the communist-organised International Brigades,[111] perhaps because he admitted a sympathy for the anarchists,[112] and perhaps also because Pollitt was aware that Orwell had just written (but not yet published) a book which was critical of Communist Party policy.[113] Orwell then contacted the Independent Labour Party (ILP), a comparatively small and uninfluential force in British politics which had disaffiliated itself from the Labour Party. The ILP accredited Orwell as a correspondent for its newspaper the *New Leader*, and it furnished him with a letter of introduction to John McNair, the ILP representative in Barcelona. Orwell took up contact with McNair in Barcelona on 30 December 1936. Judging from McNair's recollection of this first meeting, Orwell had by that time firmly resolved to fight:

I asked him what I could do to help him and he replied, "I have come to Spain to join the militia to fight against Franco." I asked him if he had ever been a soldier and he mentioned that he had been a police officer in Burma. I had read *Burmese Days* and remembered this. I then told him about the three militia forces actually in Barcelona. He then mentioned that he wanted to write about the situation. I suggested that the best thing he could do would be to use my office as his headquarters, get the atmosphere by going to Madrid, Valencia and the Aragon Front and then get down to the writing of his book. He then said this was quite secondary and his principal reason for coming was to "fight against fascism."[114]

Orwell did indeed join the fight against fascism. As *Homage to Catalonia* records, he joined a militia of the POUM, the Spanish affiliate of the ILP. The question of the order of his priorities in going to Spain is of little importance here. What this process of enlistment *does* show is that the choice of militia was largely one of circumstance and chance. Orwell had first of all approached the Communist Party; only as a second resort did he consult the ILP and consequently become involved with the POUM.

The fact that Orwell did fight in Spain makes *Homage to Catalonia* substantively different from *The Spanish Cockpit*. The former is more genuinely a piece of war literature in that it describes in detail the author's experience at the front. It belongs firmly in the tradition of war literature which Orwell so much admired, because its narrator and protagonist is cast in the mould of the common soldier and victim. In the spirit of Remarque, *Homage to Catalonia* faithfully records the horror of life and death in the trenches. In his essay "Looking Back on the Spanish War" Orwell confirms the accuracy of Remarque's portrayal: "The picture of war set forth in books like *All Quiet on the Western Front* is substantially true. Bullets hurt, corpses stink, men under fire are often so frightened that they wet their trousers."[115]

More than being war literature, *Homage to Catalonia* is also a book about the Spanish revolution. Significantly, its title informs the reader that it is a homage to the part of Spain in which the social revolution achieved its greatest heights. Orwell might not have travelled nearly as extensively in revolutionary Spain as did Borkenau, but his experience of the revolution was no less intense. His descriptions of revolutionary Barcelona are just as enthusiastic as those found in the works of Koltsov, Borkenau and other pro-revolutionary writers, in whose works scenes of Barcelona achieve the status of a topos:

The revolutionary posters were everywhere, flaming from the walls in clean reds and blues that made the few remaining advertisements look like daubs of mud. Down the Ramblas, the wide central artery of the town where crowds of people streamed constantly to and fro, the loudspeakers were bellowing revolutionary songs all day and far into the night. And it was this aspect of the crowds that was the queerest thing of all. In outward appearance it was a town in which the wealthy classes had practically ceased to exist. Except for a small number of women and foreigners there were no "well-dressed" people at all. Practically everyone wore rough working-class clothes, or blue overalls, or some variant of the militia uniform. All this was queer and moving. There was much in it that I did not understand, in some ways I did not even like it, but I recognised it immediately as a state of affairs worth fighting for. [116]

Even the time Orwell spent at the front was not a period removed from revolution, since the POUM militia to which Orwell was attached was itself a revolutionary organisation. As he himself puts it, the Spanish militias "were a sort of microcosm of a classless society."[117] Just as traditional class hierarchies had apparently been abolished in Barcelona, so in the POUM militia traditional structures of military hierarchy were abandoned. It was a system in which everyone "drew the same pay, ate the same food, wore the same clothes, and mingled on terms of complete equality. If you wanted to slap the general commanding the division on the back and ask him for a cigarette, you could do so, and no one thought it curious."[118]

As a work on the revolution *Homage to Catalonia*, like Borkenau's book, also deals with the decline and defeat of the revolution. In Orwell's case, this entails an account of the replacement of the militia system by a communist-inspired system which promoted discipline and encouraged hierarchical structures. In a way which is uncannily reminiscent of Borkenau, Orwell expresses the fate of the revolution by describing the dramatically changed atmosphere of the city during his second visit there:

Everyone who has made two visits, at intervals of months, to Barcelona during the war has remarked upon the extraordinary changes that took place in it. And curiously enough, whether they went there first in August and again in January, or, like myself, first in December and again in April, the thing they said was always the same: that the revolutionary atmosphere had vanished. No doubt to anyone who had been there in August, when the blood was still scarcely dry in the streets and militia were quartered in the smart hotels, Barcelona in December would have seemed bourgeois; to me, fresh from England, it was liker to a workers' city than anything I had conceived possible. Now the tide had rolled back. Once again it was an ordinary city, a little pinched and chipped by war, but with no outward sign of working-class predominance.

The change in the atmosphere of the crowds was startling. The militia uniform and the blue overalls had almost disappeared; everyone seemed to be wearing the smart summer suits in which Spanish tailors specialise. Fat prosperous men, elegant women, and sleek cars were everywhere. [119]

Like Borkenau, Orwell devotes much effort to describing the change of political circumstances which accompanied the decline of the revolution. He also notes the rising fortunes of the Communist Party, the trend towards totalitarianism, and the dangers implicit in these changed circumstances. And like Borkenau, Orwell almost fell victim to the Stalinist terror, as those who supported the revolutionary parties were subjected to a ruthless campaign of harassment and suppression.

Although one can point to a number of substantive similarities between the books of Orwell and Borkenau, as literary texts they differ in several ways. Both are examples of reportage, but in Orwell's book the elements of subjectivity are much more pervasive. In *The Spanish Cockpit* it is really only in the (albeit lengthy) chapter on Borkenau's first journey that the narrator consistently injects himself into the narrative. In Orwell's book the proportions of subjectivity and objectivity are roughly reversed. Only two of the fourteen chapters (the relatively lengthy chapters five and eleven) are devoted to a discussion of political abstractions, in which the persona of the narrator is not entirely withheld but plays a strictly limited role. In the other twelve chapters, however, the narrator liberally injects his personal experiences, feelings and opinions into the narrative.

The degree of subjectivity in the text, the extent to which the narrator not only presents but also *thematicises* his feelings, can be seen by comparing two descriptions of a single event. In May 1937 Orwell was shot through the throat. His friend Georges Kopp described what occurred in the following manner:

Eric was wounded on the 20th May at 5 a.m. The bullet entered the neck just under the larynx, slightly on the left side of its vertical axis and went out at the dorsal right side of the neck's base. It was a normal 7mm bore, copper-plated, Spanish Mauser bullet, shot from a distance of some 175 yards. At this range, it has a velocity of some 600 feet per second and a cauterising temperature. Under the impact, Eric fell on his back. The hemorrhaging was significant.[120]

In contrast, the narrator of *Homage to Catalonia* characteristically describes the event in such a way as to place himself literally in the centre of attention:

Roughly speaking it was the sensation of being *at the centre* of an explosion. There seemed to be a loud bang and a blinding flash of light all round me, and I felt a tremendous shock – no pain, only a violent shock, such as you get from an electric terminal; with it a sense of utter weakness, a feeling of being stricken and shrivelled up to nothing. The sand-bags in front of me receded into immense distance. I fancy you would feel much the same if you were struck by lightning. I knew immediately that I was hit, but because of the seeming bang and flash I thought it was a rifle nearby that had gone off accidentally and shot me. All this happened in a space of much less than a second. The next moment my knees crumpled up and I was falling, my head hitting the ground with a violent bang which, to my relief, did not hurt. I had a numb, dazed feeling, a consciousness of being very badly hurt, but no pain in the ordinary sense.[121]

Given this high level of subjectivity, Orwell's major task was to convince the reader of the narrator's reliability as a source of information and as a political commentator. As Robert Stradling points out, Orwell "carried honesty as a badge, more self-consciously and prominently than almost any other English writer."[122] To achieve this impression of impeccable honesty, Orwell adopts a number of textual strategies, some of which had been used by Borkenau, but which Orwell employed much more extensively.

Firstly, Orwell's narrator stresses that what he reports is the outcome of his own experience, something which he has witnessed with his own eyes. The guarantee of the veracity of the events depicted is therefore that of the eye-witness. At the same time, the narrator warns of his fallibility when reporting events that he himself has not seen and when offering interpretations of political circumstances. The narrator even warns of his own bias, asking the reader to "beware of my partisanship, my mistakes of fact, and the distortion inevitably caused by my having seen only one corner of events."[123] To admit that he *might* be wrong was of course an effective way of persuading the reader that he was *probably* right.[124]

Secondly, and again in a manner comparable with that of Borkenau, Orwell's narrator creates the impression of reliability by attributing both positive and negative qualities to all sections of the Left in Spain. Certainly, the book may be regarded as an indictment of Stalinist policies in Spain, but, like Borkenau, the narrator of *Homage to Catalonia* admits to recognising the reasonableness of some aspects of Communist Party policy. In fact, he confesses that at one time he "preferred the Communist viewpoint to that of the P.O.U.M.,"[125] and that he contemplated transferring to the International Brigades, which in effect would have meant placing himself under communist command.[126] On the other hand, although ultimately attracted to the POUM viewpoint, he observes that "the day-to-day policy of the P.O.U.M., their propaganda and so forth, was unspeakably bad."[127] Even more damningly, he judges the "revolutionary purism" of the POUM to be "rather futile".[128] He respects the revolutionary intentions of the anarchists, estimates that they had saved the situation in the first two months of the war, and at one point even suggests that he would have liked to join them.[129] But he also considers that "they were incapable of organising resistance beyond a certain point."[130]

Orwell's narrator establishes his credibility as a reporter by recording scenes and events in minute detail. In many cases the details are apparently trivial, but they serve nonetheless to vouch for authenticity. Describing life in the trenches, for example, he compiles a precise list of the clothing he was wearing: "It is of some interest as showing the amount of clothes the human body can carry. I was wearing a thick vest and pants, a flannel shirt, two pull-overs, a woollen jacket, a pigskin jacket, corduroy breeches, puttees, thick socks, boots, a stout trench-coat, a muffler, lined leather gloves, and a woollen cap. Nevertheless I was shivering like a jelly. But I admit I am unusually sensitive to cold."[131]

Finally, Orwell's narrator establishes his reputation for honesty and reliability by being brutally frank about his own shortcomings and inadequacies. He openly admits to dreading the "mud, lice, hunger, and cold", to being "horribly frightened" under fire, and to being "a very poor shot with a rifle".[132] He confesses that after suffering the privations of trench life for several months, he "wallowed in every luxury that I had money to buy," while at the same time "feeling a vague horror and amazement that money could still be wasted upon such things in a hungry war-stricken country."[133] Perhaps more surprisingly, though, in a book which is (justifiably) regarded as one of the great anti-war books of the twentieth century, he confesses to experiencing an occasional, almost atavistic enthusiasm for military action. In observing a train full of Italian troops he writes: "It was like an allegorical picture of war; the trainload of fresh men gliding proudly up the line, the maimed men sliding slowly down, and all the while the guns on the open trucks making one's heart leap as guns always do, and reviving that pernicious feeling, so difficult to get rid of, that war *is* glorious after all."[134]

Whether the overwhelming impression of honesty achieved in this way is a feature of a historically reliable text is a moot point. Orwell's many detractors claim that the impression is a false one.[135] For the literary historian, however, it is the construction of the character of the narrator-protagonist which is of greater importance. Although this character might be given the name of "Orwell," it cannot be assumed that this Orwell is identical with the author Orwell. On the contrary, it is advisable to attribute separate identities to them. In examining the body of Orwell's works during the 1930s, Raymond Williams suggests: "Instead of dividing them into 'fiction' and 'documentaries' we should see them as sketches towards the creation of his most successful character, 'Orwell'".[136] In *Homage to Catalonia* this successful character from earlier documentary works is reintroduced as the reliable observer-cum-participant. Unfortunately, in the case of *Homage to Catalonia*, there is no way of tracing the process by which the author Orwell has shaped and organised his actual experiences of the Spanish Civil War to produce his "Orwell" character. Williams has demonstrated that by comparing Orwell's previous book, *The Road to Wigan Pier*, with the original diary notes on which it is based, it is possible to observe the literary process at work: "There is the expected and necessary development of a scene, in the published version: as fuller and more fluent description, details recollected from memory. But there is also a saturation of the scene with feeling."[137] One can only assume that a very similar, if not identical, process occurred in the writing of *Homage to Catalonia*, but it cannot be illustrated, because Orwell's diaries and letters were stolen in Barcelona. [138]

There is no imputation here that in writing the book and creating the Orwell character, the author deliberately distorted historical facts. However, it is clear that he organized and reported his experiences in such a way as to perform a particular function, and that function was a predominantly political one. Orwell wished to rebuff claims that were being made in the British press and to present a more favourable picture of the much-maligned POUM. The best clue to this organizing of experience in the literary process so as to favour a particular political viewpoint comes in a letter Orwell wrote to the *Manchester Guardian* correspondent Frank Jellinek. In it, Orwell confesses: "Actually I've given a more sympathetic account of the POUM line than I actually felt, because I always told them they were wrong and refused to join the party. But I had to put it as sympathetically as possible, because it has had no hearing in the capitalist press and nothing but libels in the left-wing press." [139]

As a piece of political polemic in favour of the POUM, *Homage to Catalonia* is effective because it charts the development to commitment of its protagonist. In this respect it works in much the same way as *Die Gewehre der Frau Carrar*, whose central character also is transformed in the course of the play to a state of political commitment. *Homage to Catalonia* could perhaps be labelled *Bildungsreportage*, that is, a factual report in which, just as in the fictional genre of the *Bildungsroman*, the protagonist undergoes a process of personal development. With a detachment provided by the elapse of time, he critically considers the course of his own development.

In the case of *Homage to Catalonia* it is a development from political innocence to maturity. The starting point of this tale of development is a frank admission of political naiveté: "When I came to Spain, and for some time afterwards, I was not only uninterested in the political situation but unaware of it. I knew there was a war on, but I had no notion what kind of war. If you had asked me why I had joined the militia I should have answered: ' To fight against Fascism,' and if you had asked me what I was fighting *for*, I should have answered: 'Common decency.'"[140] At another point the narrator confesses being "bored" with the political side of the war.[141]

It can on course be argued that the original naiveté depicted here corresponds closely to Orwell's own initial naiveté. The process by which Orwell sought his political credentials to enter Spain as described above (that is, approaching first the Communist Party, then the ILP) suggests a degree of naiveté or at least uncertainty on his part. To reinforce this view, it can be noted that in his "Notes on the Spanish Militias" Orwell confesses that he "was only rather dimly aware of the differences between the political parties, which had been covered up in the English left-wing press."[142]

At the same time, there is some evidence to support the claim that the appearance of naiveté was not entirely genuine but was cultivated by Orwell in order to accentuate his protagonist's development. Malcolm Cowley, for example, proposes that Orwell "was a lot less of a political innocent than he presents himself as being,"[143] and Emanuel Edrich similarly speaks of "the exploitation of naiveté."[144] There are no empirical standards with which to measure the extent to which the narrator's naiveté is contrived. However, there are at least two areas in which a degree of contrivance may at least be suspected. Firstly, the narrator of *Homage of Catalonia* flirts with Communist Party policy, only to finally reject it vehemently. Orwell himself confesses in a letter to Stephen Spender that he had been "very hostile to the Communist Party since about 1935."[145] Secondly, given Orwell's practical knowledge of the British press, it can be argued that it is unlikely that he would have been as surprised at the politically motivated distortions in the reporting of the Spanish Civil War as his narrator plainly is.[146]

The first step in the erosion of the narrator's political innocence comes with the fall of Málaga. Being on the Aragón front at the time, Orwell had no involvement in the fall of the town; rather, it was the manner in which the story was leaked out that unsettled him: "The news sent a sort of chill all along the line, for, whatever the truth may have been, every man in the militia believed that the loss of Málaga was due to treachery. It was the first talk I had heard of treachery or divided aims. It set up in my mind the first vague doubts about this war in which, hitherto, the rights and wrongs had seemed so beautifully simple."[147] Referring explicitly to the theme of personal development, the narrator assesses the significance of the time spent at the front:

I wish, indeed, that I could have served the Spanish Government a little more effectively; but from a personal point of view – from the point of view of my own development – those first three of four months that I spent in the line were less futile than I thought. They formed a kind of interregnum in my life, quite different from anything that had gone before and perhaps from anything that is to come, and they taught me things that I could not have learned in any other way.[148]

The climax and turning point of his development were the so-called May events of May 1937 in Barcelona. For him they were the final proof that treachery and divided aims did indeed prevail in republican Spain. Orwell describes his participation in the Barcelona street fighting on behalf of the POUM in some detail. When he returned to Barcelona from the front on April 26 (coincidentally the day of the bombing of Guernica), he was allegedly contemplating joining the International Brigades, partly with the intention of being transferred to Madrid.[149] Participation in the Barcelona fighting in defence of the POUM changed all that:

The next three days and nights I spent continuously on the roof of the Poliorama, except for brief intervals when I slipped across to the hotel for meals. I was in no danger, I suffered from nothing worse than hunger and boredom, yet it was one of the most unbearable periods in my whole life. I think few experiences could be more sickening, more disillusioning, or, finally, more nerve-racking than those evil days of street warfare. 150

In his own eyes, but also in the eyes of others, he had definitively thrown in his lot with the POUM and become an intransigent opponent of the communists. This expression of commitment to the POUM almost cost him his life. Orwell and his wife "escaped" from Spain with the Stalinist secret police on their heels. With that his innocence had been finally destroyed.

This state of political maturity reached by the protagonist needs to be described in some detail because of its complexity and apparently paradoxical nature. It comprises a rejection of communist policies as inappropriate, counterproductive and even morally reprehensible. But this disillusionment with communist doctrine is not symptomatic of a disillusionment with political ideology in general. On the contrary, as has been shown, Orwell presented a more favourable picture of the POUM than he felt justified. It is worth noting that Orwell joined the ILP *after* his return from Spain.[151] Similarly, it is apparent that Orwell did not abandon his belief in the revolutionary power of anarchism. He was later to state that if he had had "a complete understanding of the situation I should probably have joined the [anarchist] C.N.T."[152] The Spanish Civil War, if anything, helped to strengthen and advance Orwell's faith in "socialism," however difficult it might be to define the Orwellian brand of socialism. The experience of the community of the front was for him "a crude forecast of what the opening stages of Socialism might be like. And, after all, instead of disillusioning me it deeply attracted me. The effect was to make my desire to see Socialism established much more actual than it had been before."[153] At the end of his account of the suffering and treachery of the war, he concludes that "the result is not necessarily disillusionment and cynicism. Curiously enough the whole experience has left me with not less but more belief in the decency of human beings."[154]

That the final stage of the protagonist's *Bildung* is the affirmation of a belief in a revolutionary brand of socialism is a point which needs to be stressed, since *Homage to Catalonia* is often interpreted as a document of political disillusionment, a forerunner to the cynicism and despair of *Animal Farm* and *1984*. In this respect, Orwell differed from Borkenau who, as has been shown, maintained certain reservations regarding the revolutionary policies of the anarchists and the POUM. As Richard Lowenthal has observed, Borkenau by 1937 had achieved some distance from the revolutionary hopes of his youth.[155] Orwell, in contrast, preserved and even strengthened his faith in revolution. This subtle but important difference in the respective post-Spanish Civil War political beliefs of Orwell and Borkenau is made clear by Orwell himself in his review of Borkenau's book *The Communist International*:

Where I part company from him [i.e., Borkenau] is when he says that for the western democracies the choice lies between Fascism and an orderly reconstruction through the cooperation of all classes. I do not believe in the second possibility, because I do not believe that a man with £50,000 a year and a man with fifteen shillings a week either can, or will, co-operate. The nature of their relationship is quite simply, that the one is robbing the other, and there is no reason to think that the robber will suddenly turn over a new leaf. It would seem, therefore, that if the problems of western capitalism are to be solved, it will have to be through a third alternative, a movement which is genuinely revolutionary, i.e. willing to make drastic changes and to use violence if necessary, but which does not lose touch, as Communism and Fascism have done, with the essential values of democracy. Such a thing is by no means unthinkable. [156]

The claim that *Homage to Catalonia* is a record of *political* disillusionment is one which therefore must be treated with some caution. However, it is true that a form of disillusionment *does* take place, but in a sphere which transcends explicitly political considerations. Hypersensitive to the manner in which the press in particular presented a distorted image of events in Spain, and aware also of the difficulties he himself faced in conveying to his readers the truth of what he had witnessed, Orwell in *Homage to Catalonia* begins to question the possibility of communicating historical truth. Probably more than any other piece of literary reportage emanating from the Spanish Civil War, *Homage to Catalonia* illustrates Kisch's maxim of simultaneous "extreme subjectivity" and "highest objectivity," but it also *problematises* it. Orwell once explained that one of the motives for his writing was a desire "to see things as they are, to find out true facts and store them up for the use of posterity."[157] One of the lessons of the Spanish Civil War, though, was that the "true facts" about the war, the objective truth, were enormously difficult to grasp, if not impossible. To observe and report events from a necessarily limited viewpoint could severely compromise objectivity, could make historical truth elusive. At one point in *Homage to Catalonia* he contends: "I have tried to write objectively about the Barcelona fighting, though, obviously, no one can be completely objective on a question of this kind."[158] In a similar vein he later adds: "And I hope the account I have given is not too misleading. I believe that on such an issue as this no one is or can be completely truthful."[159] Finally, in his essay "Looking Back on the Spanish War," written in 1943, Orwell confesses receiving the feeling "that the very concept of objective truth is fading out of the world."[160] It is in this insight and not in disillusionment with any particular political ideology that the origins of much of Orwell's later work are to be found.

## NOTES

1. Stephen Spender. "Stephen Spender." In *The God That Failed.* Ed. Richard Crossman, 229-73. New York: Harper and Row, 1949. p. 244.

2 Jean-Richard Bloch. "Avant-Propos." In Jean-Richard Bloch. Espagne, Espagne. Paris: Editions Sociales Internationales, 1936. p. 9.

3. John B. Romeiser. "The Limits of War Reporting: Louis Delaprée and Paris-Soir." In *Red Flags/Black Flags. Critical Essays on the Literature of the Spanish Civil War*. Ed. John B. Romeiser, 133-56. Madrid: José Porrúa Turanzas, 1982. p. 137.

4. George Orwell. *Homage to Catalonia* and "Looking Back on the Spanish War." Harmondsworth: Penguin, 1966 (1938). p. 8.

5. Estimations of Hemingway's ability as a war correspondent vary. Anthony Burgess disparagingly argues: "The fact is that Hemingway was never a very good war correspondent. His fiction-writer's talent impelled him to invent, organise reality into aesthetic patterns, cultivate the 'impression' which Ford Madox Ford encouraged writers to carry over from fiction to real life. His temporary masters wanted to know the facts of the Spanish war, and Hemingway dished up a kind of subfiction in which he was the central character." Anthony Burgess. *Ernest Hemingway and His World*. New York: Scribner's, 1978. p. 79.

6. Theodor Balk. "Egon Erwin Kisch and His Reportage. On the 50th Year of a Noted Revolutionary Reporter." *International Literature* 4 (1935): p. 67. Balk is referring here to the 1934 Asturian uprising.

7. Patrik von zur Mühlen. *Spanien war ihre Hoffnung. Die deutsche Linke im Spanischen Bürgerkrieg 1936 bis 1939*. Berlin, Bonn: Dietz, 1985. p. 163.

8. John Reed. *Ten Days That Shook the World*. New York: Boni and Liveright, 1919.

9. Balk. *op. cit.* p. 62.

10. *Ibid.* p. 64.

11. For information on the worker-correspondents, see especially Christian Siegel. *Die Reportage*. Stuttgart: Metzler, 1978. pp. 107-16.

12. *Ibid.* pp. 80-83.

13. Georg Lukács. "Reportage oder Gestaltung?" Kritische Bemerkungen anläßlich eines Romans von Ottwalt." In Georg Lukács. *Schriften zur Literatursoziologie*. Ed. Peter Ludz, 122-42. 2nd. ed. Neuwied, Berlin: Luchterhand, 1963. (Originally in *Die Linkskurve* 6, 7/8 (1932): pp. 22-30, 26-31.)

14. *Ibid.* p. 126.

15. *Ibid.* pp. 126-27.

16. *Ibid.* p. 127.

17. *Ibid.* p. 128.

18. *Ibid.* p. 131.

19. This three-phase scheme for the development of Kisch's theory of reportage is borrowed directly from Christian Siegel. See Christian Siegel. *Egon Erwin Kisch. Reportage und politischer Journalismus*. Bremen: Schünemann Universitätsverlag, 1973. pp. 88-129.

20. Egon Erwin Kisch. "Wesen des Reporters." Appears (abridged) in *Literarische Reportage. Ein Arbeitsbuch*. Ed. Erhard Schütz, 42-43. Frankfurt a.M., Berlin, Munich: Diesterweg, 1979. p. 42.

21. *Ibid.* p. 42.

22. *Ibid.*

23. *Ibid.* p. 43.

24. Egon Erwin Kisch. *Der rasende Reporter*. Berlin: Reiss, 1975. vii f. Also (abridged) in Schütz. *op. cit.* p. 44.

25. *Ibid.* p. 40.

26. Siegel. *Egon Erwin Kisch*. p. 99.

27. Egon Erwin Kisch. "Vorwort" to Reed's *Zehn Tage, die die Welt erschütterten*. Vienna, Berlin: 1927. p. vi. Quoted in Siegel. *Egon Erwin Kisch*. p. 101.

28. *Ibid.* p. 101.

29. *Ibid.*

30. Siegel. *Egon Erwin Kisch*. p. 102.

31. Kisch's reply published in the *Neue Bücherschau*. 11 June 1928. p. 585. Quoted in Siegel. *Die Reportage*. p. 130.

32. Egon Erwin Kisch. "Roman? Nein, Reportage!" *Cin* 6, 1 (1929). Quoted in Siegel. *Die Reportage*. p. 130.

33. Siegel. *Egon Erwin Kisch*. pp. 120-21. As evidence of Kisch's scepticism Siegel cites Kisch's obituary on the death (in a concentration camp) of Erich Mühsam and a 1935 conversation with Ernst Bloch.

34. Egon Erwin Kisch. "Reportage als Kunstform und Kampfform." In Schütz. *op. cit.* p. 45. Originally in *Internationale Literatur 5*, 3/4 (1935): pp. 18f.

35. Siegel. *Egon Erwin Kisch*. p. 244.

36. Willi Bredel. "Kisch wollte die Amerikaner rühren." In *Kisch-Kalender*. Ed. F. C. Weiskopf and Dieter Noll. East Berlin: Aufbau, 1955. p. 192.

37. Siegel. *Egon Erwin Kisch*. p. 243.

38. Ernest Hemingway. "Vorwort." In Gustav Regler. *Das große Beispiel. Roman einer internationalen Brigade*, 11-15. Cologne: Kiepenheuer & Witsch, 1976 (1940).. p. 15.

39. For example, the German title (see previous note) describes it as a *Roman* (novel).

40. Christopher Isherwood. *Goodbye to Berlin*. London: Hogarth Press, 1954 (1939). p. 13.

41. George Barker. "Elegy on Spain." In Cunningham (ed.), 197-201. *op. cit.* p. 197.

42. John Sommerfield. *Volunteer in Spain*. London: Lawrence and Wishart, 1937. Extract *ibid.* 193-94. p. 194.

43. David Mellor. "Death in the Making: Representing the Spanish Civil War." In *No pasaran! Photographs and Posters of the Spanish Civil War*. Ed. Frances Morris, 25-31. Bristol: Arnolfini, 1986. p. 27.

44. Rudolf Leonhard. *Der Tod des Don Quijote. Geschichten aus dem spanischen Bürgerkrieg*. 2 vols. Zürich: Stauffacher, 1938.

45. The book deals with Sender's experiences immediately before and during the first six months of the war: the murder of his wife and brother by the nationalists and Sender's activity on the battlefronts around Madrid. It was first published in English and French translations in 1937 and in Spanish in 1938. Sender had been a supporter of the anarchists during the 1920s, but in the 1930s and in *Contraataque* adopts an unambiguously pro-communist line. Emir Rodríguez Monegal describes it as "a work of very direct propaganda, written with the very explicit aim of raising the morale of the republicans." Emir Rodríguez Monegal. "Tres testigos españoles de la guerra civil." *Revista Nacional de Cultura* 29, 182 (1967): p. 8. It seems, however, that Sender never joined the Communist Party. See Patricia McDermott. "Ramón Sender. 'Un gran recuerdo típico.'" *Romance Studies* 3 (1983): p. 48; Patrick Collard. "La guerre civile dans l'oeuvre de Ramón J. Sender: de la littérature de propagande au récit 'exemplaire.'" *Revue belge de philologie et d'histoire* 65, 3 (1987): pp. 522-23; Marcelino C. Peñuelas. *La obra narrativa de Ramón J. Sender*. Madrid: Editorial Gredos, 1971. p. 28. Marcelino C. Peñuelas. *Conversaciones con Ramón J. Sender*. Madrid: Editorial Magisterio Español, 1970. p. 56. Well before the war ended, Sender had become a bitter opponent of Stalinism.

46. Ramón Sender. Transl. Sir Peter Chalmers Mitchell. *The War in Spain*. London: Faber and Faber, 1937. p. 281.

47. *Ibid.* pp. 302-3.

48. The photograph is controversial primarily because of a statement by the *Daily Express* correspondent O. D. Gallagher that Capa had faked it. The published version states that it was taken from a republican trench in Andalusia. During an attack Capa lifted the camera above his head and shot blindly. He sent the undeveloped film to Paris. See Rainer Fabian and Hans Christian Adam. *Bilder vom Krieg. 130 Jahre Kriegsfotografie*. Hamburg: Stern, 1983. pp. 253-54.

49. Reinhold Görling. *"Dinamita Cerebral." Politischer Prozeß und ästhetische Praxis im Spanischen Bürgerkrieg.* Frankfurt a.M.: Vervuert, 1986. p. 92.

50. Phillip Knightley. *The First Casualty. The War Correspondent as Hero, Propagandist, and Myth Maker from the Crimea to Vietnam.* London: Andre Deutsch, 1975. p. 210.

51. Quoted (unsourced) in Faber and Adam. *op. cit.* p. 253.

52. Ludwig Renn. *Der spanische Krieg.* East Berlin: 1955; Alfred Kantorowicz (ed.). *"Tschapajew," das Bataillon der einundzwanzig Nationen, dargestellt in Aufzeichnungen seiner Mitkämpfer.* Madrid: Editions du Carrefour, 1937; Willi Bredel. *Begegnung am Ebro.* Paris: Ed. 10. Mai, 1939.

53. Hugh Thomas. *The Spanish Civil War.* 3rd.ed. Harmondsworth: Penguin, 1986 (1961). p. 393 n. 5.

54. It appeared in that year in the Soviet Union as the third volume of Koltsov's selected works. In 1960 it appeared in censored form in East Germany, bearing the title *Die rote Schlacht.* A Spanish edition, *Diario de la guerra de España,* was published in Paris in 1963. There is no English version.

55. Reinhold Görling accurately describes Koltsov as being "anything but a representative of socialist realism." Görling. *op. cit.* p. 313.

56. Michel Heim. "La littérature soviétique." In *Les écrivains et la Guerre d'Espagne.* Ed. Marc Hanrez, 89-99. Paris: Pantheon Press France, 1975. p. 91.

57. In G. A. Skorochodov. *Michail Kol'cov.* Moscow: 1959, p. 158. Quoted *ibid.* p. 92.

58. Görling. *op. cit.* pp. 315-16.

59. Mikhail Koltsov. *Die rote Schlacht.* East Berlin: Deutscher Militärverlag, 1965. p. 17.

60. Görling. *op. cit.* p. 320.

61. Louis Fischer. *Russia's Road from Peace to War: Soviet Foreign Relations, 1917-1941.* New York: Harper and Row, 1969. p. 273.

62. *Great Soviet Encyclopedia.* 2nd. ed. Vol. 12. Moscow: Sovetskaia Entsiklopediia Publishing House, 1973. p. 594.

63. Franz Borkenau. *Der Übergang vom feudalen zum bürgerlichen Weltbild: Studien zur Geschichte der Manufakturperiode.* Paris: Alcar, 1934.

64. These biographical details contained in Richard Lowenthal. "Introduction," 1-29. In Franz Borkenau. *End and Beginning. On the Generations of Cultures and the Origins of the West.* New York: Columbia University Press, 1981. pp. 2-5.

65. Franz Borkenau. *The Spanish Cockpit. An Eye-Witness Account of the Political and Social Conflicts of the Spanish Civil War.* Ann Arbor: University of Michigan Press, 1963. (Originally London: Faber and Faber, 1937.) Surprisingly, a German edition did not appear until 1986 (*Kampfplatz Spanien. Politische und soziale Konflikte im spanischen Bürgerkrieg.* Stuttgart: Klett-Cotta, 1986).

66. *Ibid.* p. x.

67. *Ibid.* p. 64.

68. *Ibid.*

69. *Ibid.*

70. *Ibid.* p. 65.

71. *Ibid.* p. 66.

72. *Ibid.* p. 67. Presumably Borkenau had good reasons for not revealing the identity of the person in question.

73. *Ibid.* p. 109.

74. *Ibid.* pp. 86-87.

75. *Ibid.* p. 171.

76. *Ibid.*

77. *Ibid*. p. 173. This is a good indication of Borkenau's sensitivity to internal political developments in republican Spain. He is describing Barcelona some five months *before* the so-called "May events," and yet he is acutely aware of underlying tensions in the city.

78. *Ibid*. p. 175. It is interesting to contrast this description of Barcelona in January 1937 with the infinitely more enthusiastic one provided by Orwell, who plainly was ignorant of political tensions at that time. Orwell's response is discussed below.

79. *Ibid*. p. 205.

80. *Ibid*. p. 236.

81. *Ibid*. pp. 241, 240. The use of the term "Trotskyists" is problematical, but it is without doubt a reference to members and supporters of the POUM.

82. *Ibid*. p. 249. The identity of the secretary is not revealed.

83. *Ibid*. p. 250. In this instance also, the identity of the person concerned is not revealed.

84 . *Ibid*. p. 282.

85 . *Ibid*. p. 284.

86 . *Ibid*. p. 284.

87. *Ibid*. p. 285.

88. *Ibid*. p. 290.

89. *Ibid*. p. 292.

90. *Ibid*. p. 285. It is apparent that the general problematics of political revolution greatly concerned Borkenau at this time. He compares the Spanish revolution with both French and Russian models, as indeed he does in an essay published in the same year as *The Spanish Cockpit*. See Franz Borkenau. "State and Revolution in the Paris Commune, the Russian Revolution and the Spanish Civil War." *Sociological Review* 29, 41 (1937): pp. 41-75.

91. *Ibid*. p. 285.

92. *Ibid*.

93. George Orwell. "Review of *The Spanish Cockpit* by Franz Borkenau, *Volunteer in Spain* by John Sommerfield." In *The Collected Essays, Journalism and Letters of George Orwell. Volume 1. An Age Like This 1920-1940*. Ed. Sonia Orwell and Ian Angus, 309-11. Harmondsworth: Penguin, 1970. p. 311. (Originally *Time and Tide*. 31 July 1937.)

94. *Ibid*. p. 309. The story behind the publication of the review is interesting. An article Orwell had written on Spain had been turned down by the *New Statesman* because of Orwell's explicitly pro-POUM line. According to Orwell, to "sugar the pill" the *New Statesman* sent him *The Spanish Cockpit* to review but then refused to print the review on the grounds that it was "against editorial policy." However they offered to pay Orwell for it, "practically hush-money." See George Orwell. "Letter to Rayner Heppenstall." 31 July 1937. *Ibid*. 311-13, esp. p. 312. The publication of *Homage to Catalonia* is similarly revealing about the degree of communist influence in publishing. The manuscript was rejected sight unseen by Victor Gollancz and eventually published by Secker and Warburg who, as Orwell noted, were "coming to be known rather inaccurately as 'the Trotskyist publishers.'" See Orwell. "Letter to the Editor of *Time and Tide*." *Ibid*. 330-32, esp. p. 331.

95. Orwell. *Homage to Catalonia*. p. 57.

96. Franz Borkenau. *The Communist International*. London: Faber & Faber, 1938. Reprinted with an introduction by Raymond Aron as *World Communism: A History of the Communist International*. Ann Arbor: University of Michigan Press, 1962; George Orwell. "Review of *The Communist International* by Franz Borkenau." In Orwell and Angus (eds.), 385-88. *op. cit*. p. 388. (Originally in *New English Weekly* 22 September 1938)

97. Franz Borkenau. *The Totalitarian Enemy*. London: Faber & Faber, 1940; George Orwell. "Review of *The Totalitarian Enemy* by Franz Borkenau." In *The Collected Essays, Journalism and Letters of George Orwell. Volume 2. My Country Right or Left 1940-1943*. Ed. Sonia Orwell and Ian Angus, 40-42. Harmondsworth: Penguin, 1970. 40-2. p. 40. (Originally in *Time and Tide*. 4 May 1940.)

98. George Orwell. "Wells, Hitler and the World State." *Ibid*. p. 169. (Originally in *Horizon* August 1941.) Orwell lists Borkenau in similarly distinguished company in his 1944 essay on Koestler. See George Orwell. "Arthur Koestler." In *The Collected Essays, Journalism and Letters of George Orwell. Volume 3. As I Please 1943-1945*. Ed. Sonia Orwell and Ian Angus, 270-82. Harmondsworth: Penguin, 1970. p. 271.

99. This is how Orwell summarizes the contents of Borkenau's letter. George Orwell. "Letter to Geoffrey Gorer." 16 August 1937. In Orwell and Angus (eds.), 313-15. *The Collected Essays, Journalism and Letters of George Orwell. Volume 1. An Age Like This 1920-1940*. p. 314. See also Orwell's letter to the editor of *Time and Tide* dated 5 February 1938. *Ibid*. p. 331.

100. Quoted in Bernard Crick. *George Orwell. A Life*. London: Secker & Warburg, 1980. p. 245. Crick points out that Borkenau visited Orwell shortly after this.

101. Franz Borkenau. *European Communism*. London: Faber & Faber, 1953. (Originally *Der europäische Kommunismus: Seine Geschichte von 1917 bis zur Gegenwart*. Munich: Lehnen, 1952.)

102. George Orwell. "Review of *Red Spanish Notebook* by Mary Low and Juan Brea, *Heroes of the Alcazar* by R. Timmermans." In Orwell and Angus (eds.). *The Collected Essays, Journalism and Letters of George Orwell. Volume 1. An Age Like This 1920-1940*. pp. 320-22. (Originally in *Time and Tide*. 9 October 1937) Low and Brea were, as Orwell points out, working for the POUM; George Orwell. "Review of *Storm over Spain* by Mairin Mitchell, *Spanish Rehearsal* by Arnold Lunn, *Catalonia Infelix* by E. Allison Peers." *Ibid*. pp. 324-25. (Originally in *Time and Tide*. 11 December 1937) Mairin Mitchell sympathised with the anarchists; George Orwell. "Inside the Whale." *Ibid*. 540-78. p. 565. As mentioned in Chapter 4, he does, however, go on to accuse Auden of naiveté and amoralism. *Ibid*. p. 566.

103. *Ibid*. p. 549.

104. Stanley Weintraub. *The Last Great Cause. The Intellectuals and the Spanish Civil War*. London, New York: W. H. Allen, 1968. p. 116.

105. John Langdon-Davies. "Review of *Homage to Catalonia* by George Orwell." *Daily Worker*. 21 May 1938. Supplement p. 4. Quoted in Valentine Cunningham, 25-94. "Introduction." In *The Penguin Book of Spanish Civil War Verse*. Ed. Valentine Cunningham. Harmondsworth: Penguin, 1980. p. 79. Langdon-Davies, who was a correspondent for the *News Chronicle* in Spain and reported the "May events" in Barcelona, is treated disparagingly by Orwell in *Homage to Catalonia*. See Orwell. *Homage to Catalonia*. pp. 160-62.

106. Crick. *op. cit*. p. 245.

107. *Ibid*. p. 245. Borkenau's favourable response was not published. Orwell also received letters praising the book from Herbert Read and Naomi Richardson. *Ibid*. p. 245.

108. Orwell. *Homage to Catalonia*. p. 8.

109. Crick. *op. cit*. p. 211.

110. George Orwell. "Notes on the Spanish Militias." In Orwell and Angus (eds.), 350-64. *The Collected Essays, Journalism and Letters of George Orwell. Volume 1. An Age Like This 1920-1940*. pp. 351-52.

111. Crick. *op. cit*. p. 208.

112. Peter Stansky and William Abrahams. *Orwell: The Transformation*. London: Constable, 1979. p. 188.

113. As suggested by T. R. Fyvel in *George Orwell. A Personal Memoir.* London: Weidenfeld and Nicolson, 1982. p. 69. The book in question was *The Road to Wigan Pier.*

114. John McNair. Unpublished M.A. thesis. p. 37. (Orwell Archive, University College, London.) Quoted in Gordon B. Beadle. "George Orwell and the Spanish Civil War." *Duquesne Review* 16, 1 (1971): p. 3.

115. George Orwell. "Looking Back on the Spanish War." In *Orwell. Homage to Catalonia* and "Looking Back on the Spanish War". p. 226.

116. Orwell. *Homage to Catalonia.* p. 9. This description bears comparision with that of Borkenau cited above. For Borkenau the revolution had already begun to sour by January 1937.

117. *Ibid.* p. 102.

118. *Ibid.* p. 29.

119. *Ibid.* pp. 106-7. It seems certain that when Orwell writes, "Whether they went there first in August and again in January," he has Borkenau in mind. By the time of writing *Homage to Catalonia* he would have read *The Spanish Cockpit* and would have known that Borkenau made two visits to Barcelona, the first in August 1936, the second in January 1937, just a couple of weeks after Orwell's first visit.

120. British Museum Additional MS 49304. Quoted in Jeffrey Meyers. "'An Affirming Flame': Orwell's *Homage to Catalonia*." *Arizona Quarterly* 27, 1 (1971): p. 10. Orwell's real name was Eric Blair.

121. Orwell. *Homage to Catalonia.* p. 177.

122. Robert Stradling. "Orwell and the Spanish Civil War: A Historical Critique." In *Inside the Myth. Orwell: Views from the Left.* Ed. Christopher Norris, 103-25. London: Lawrence and Wishart, 1984. p. 122.

123. *Ibid.* p. 220.

124. Somewhat cynically Robert Stradling points out that the reader should keep in mind that Orwell "may be wrong even where he says he may be wrong." Stradling. *op. cit.* p. 122.

125. Orwell. *Homage to Catalonia.* p. 62.

126. *Ibid.* p. 70.

127. *Ibid.* p. 62.

128. *Ibid.*

129. *Ibid.* p. 113.

130. *Ibid.* p. 67.

131. *Ibid.* p. 31.

132. *Ibid.* pp. 21, 44, 176.

133. *Ibid.* p. 112.

134. *Ibid.* p. 184.

135. For Hugh Thomas, *Homage to Catalonia* is "a better book about war itself than about the Spanish war." Hugh Thomas. *op. cit.* p. 653. Bill Alexander and Robert Stradling claim to have detected a whole range of inaccuracies in the text. Bill Alexander. "George Orwell and Spain." In Norris. *op. cit.* 85-102. *passim.*; Stradling *op. cit. passim.* Alexander, it is worth noting, was and still is a member of the Communist Party. Perhaps the most celebrated of the detractors is Claude Simon (who was a communist and member of the International Brigades), who accuses Orwell of inventing details. See especially Anthony Cheal Pugh. "Interview with Claude Simon: Autobiography, The Novel, Politics." *Review of Contemporary Fiction* 5, 1 (1984): pp. 4-13. In examining the charges levelled by Alexander, Stradling and Simon, Valentine Cunningham concludes that on only two points of fact (concerning the use of explosive bullets and the role of the Civil Guard during the May events) was Orwell definitely wrong. "The alleged mistakes

of fact are either not really mistakes of fact, or they are mistakes that do not really impugn the quality of Orwell as reporter. The explosive bullets and the maligning of the Civil Guard do not make much difference either way to Orwell's narratives." Valentine Cunningham. "*Homage to Catalonia* Revisited: Remembering and Misremembering the Spanish Civil War." *Revue belge de philologie et d'histoire* 65, 3 (1987): p. 506.

136. Raymond Williams. *Orwell*. London: Fontana, 1971. p. 52.

137. *Ibid.* p. 50.

138. Orwell. *Homage to Catalonia*. p. 200

139. George Orwell. "Letter to Frank Jellinek." 20 December 1938. In Orwell and Angus (eds.), 401-5. *The Collected Essays, Journalism and Letters of George Orwell. Volume 1. An Age Like This 1920-1940*. p. 404.

140. Orwell. *Homage to Catalonia*. p. 46

141. *Ibid.* p. 57.

142. Orwell. "Notes on the Spanish Militias." p. 353.

143. Malcolm Cowley. "No Homage to Catalonia: A Memory of the Spanish Civil War." *The Southern Review* 18, 1 (1982): p. 135.

144. Emanuel Edrich. "Naïveté and Simplicity in Orwell's Writing. *Homage to Catalonia*." *University of Kansas City Review* 27 (1961): p. 289.

145. George Orwell. "Letter to Stephen Spender." 2 April 1938. In Orwell and Angus (eds.), 345-47. *The Collected Essays, Journalism and Letters of George Orwell. Volume 1. An Age Like This 1920-1940*. p. 347.

146. Like Borkenau, Orwell analyses the depiction of the war in the press, but in much more detail than Borkenau does. See especially Chapter 11 of *Homage to Catalonia*.

147. Orwell. *Homage to Catalonia*. p. 45.

148. *Ibid.* p. 101.

149. *Ibid.* p. 70.

150. *Ibid.* p. 125.

151. Orwell became a card-carrying member of the ILP on 13 June 1938. Eleven days later a piece by Orwell entitled "Why I Joined the Independent Labour Party" appeared in the *New Leader*. In it, Orwell stated that he had joined the ILP because he had realised that it was "the only party I could join with at least the certainty that I would never be led up the garden path in the name of capitalist democracy." George Orwell. "Why I Joined the Independent Labour Party." In Orwell and Angus (eds.), 373-75. *The Collected Essays, Journalism and Letters of George Orwell. Volume 1. An Age Like This 1920-1940*. p. 375.

152. Orwell. "Notes on the Spanish Militias." p. 523.

153. Orwell. *Homage to Catalonia*. pp. 102-3.

154. *Ibid.* p. 220.

155. Richard Lowenthal. *op. cit.* p. 5. To illustrate this point, see especially Borkenau's previously mentioned 1937 essay, "State and Revolution in the Paris Commune, the Russian Revolution and the Spanish Civil War."

156. George Orwell. "Review of *The Communist International* by Franz Borkenau." In Orwell and Angus (eds.), 385-88. *The Collected Essays, Journalism and Letters of George Orwell. Volume 1. An Age Like This 1920-1940*. p. 388.

157. George Orwell. "Why I Write." In George Orwell. *Collected Essays*. London: Secker and Warburg, 1961 (1947).. p. 425.

158. Orwell. *Homage to Catalonia*. p. 153.

159. *Ibid.* p. 220.

160. Orwell. "Looking Back on the Spanish War." p. 235.

# 7. Literature and Anarchism

## ANARCHIST AESTHETICS

If one looks to the founders of anarchist thought, to such thinkers as William Godwin, Pierre Proudhon, Mikhail Bakunin and Peter Kropotkin, one searches in vain for a coherent body of writings on aesthetics. These people were primarily concerned with social, political and economic issues, with the result that aesthetics was either relegated to the background or ignored altogether. Of course, the same could be said of Marx and Engels, whose writings on art and literature enjoy at best a peripheral status in the context of their complete works, and by no means constitute a systematic theory of aesthetics. But whereas their writings generated a remarkably rich aesthetic discourse whose intensity has grown with time, no such development was sponsored by the writings of their anarchist counterparts. In dealing with anarchist aesthetics it is therefore necessary first of all to abandon any hope of entering an established discourse or of identifying a coherent, universally valid doctrine. It is also worth emphasising that anarchist aesthetics does not entail a facile transference of anarchistic political principles to the aesthetic realm. One must *not* assume that anarchist art or literature is characterised by formal or thematic lawlessness. To deal with anarchist aesthetics means to deal with a range of writings which do not constitute a system but which may be fruitfully compared and contrasted.

In the context of this study it is proposed to examine in particular the writings of three people who can be identified with the anarchist movement and who, in one way or another, were involved in the Spanish Civil War. They are the Russian-American Emma Goldman, the Englishman Herbert Read and the German Carl Einstein.

Emma Goldman's literary activities took several forms. She was the publisher and editor of the anarchist journal *Mother Earth*, which appeared from 1906 to 1917. In it she published poems, stories and essays on literary topics. She also delivered numerous lectures on literary topics, not all of which are extant.[1] Drawing from her lectures she produced her major critical work, *The Social Significance of the Modern Drama*.[2] This strong interest in modern drama manifests itself also in a collection of essays, first published in 1911, which contains a piece entitled "The Modern Drama: A Powerful Disseminator of Radical Thought."[3]

As Martha Solomon points out, whether Goldman was acting as publisher, editor, lecturer or critic, she "invariably selected works for publication and discussion with a clear ideological bias."[4] Goldman believed firmly that literature should be ideologically committed. In particular she believed that literature was linked with revolution and that this link between literature and revolution assumed two forms. Firstly, the creative urge of the writer or artist "was simply one manifestation of the individual's yearning for self-expression, the force that underlay the revolutionary spirit."[5] Secondly, Goldman considered that revolutionary circumstances provided writers and artists with the best raw material for their work: "In addressing the social problems and individual yearnings of the day, the artist reached the highest levels of creative expression."[6]

This insistence on a link between literature and political or social radicalism did not mean that Goldman advocated overtly propagandistic literature. On the contrary, she claimed: "An adequate appreciation of the tremendous spread of the modern, conscious social unrest cannot be gained from merely propagandistic literature. Rather must we become conversant with the larger phases of human expression manifest in art, literature, and, above all, the modern drama – the strongest and most far-reaching interpreter of our deep-felt dissatisfaction."[7] It did mean, however, that Goldman rejected non-committed art and literature, or art and literature which remained aloof from social and political issues. It entailed more specifically a firm rejection of the concept of art for art's sake: "Art for art's sake presupposes an attitude of aloofness on the part of the artist toward the struggle for life: he must rise above the ebb and tide of life. He is to be merely an artistic conjurer of beautiful forms, a creator of pure fancy. This is not the attitude of modern art, which is preeminently the reflex, the mirror of life."[8] In this outright rejection of the doctrine of art for art's sake and plea for a mimetic art, Goldman could conceivably have been influenced by Proudhon, who had written:

Art for art's sake, as it has been called, not having its legitimacy within itself, being based on nothing, is nothing. It is debauchery of the heart and dissolution of the mind. Separated from right and duty, cultivated and pursued as the highest thought of the soul and the supreme manifestation of humanity, art or the ideal, stripped of the greater part of itself, reduced to nothing more than an excitement of fantasy and the senses, is the source of sin, the origin of all servitude, the poisoned spring from which, according to the Bible, flow all the fornications and abominations of the earth. . . . Art for art's sake, I say, verse for verse's sake, style for style's sake, form for form's sake, fantasy for fantasy's sake, all the diseases which like a plague of lice are gnawing away at our epoch, are vice in all its refinement, the quintessence of evil.[9]

Although Goldman assigns art a mimetic function, this does not mean that she insisted on the use of representational rather than nonrepresentational forms. She contended that literature "could reveal social truths indirectly or symbolically."[10] At the same time it is clear that she was strongly attracted to nineteenth-century realism and that she disapproved of the technical innovativeness of writers such as D. H. Lawrence, James Joyce and Gertrude Stein.[11] "What she sought, in essence, was radical ideology in conservative literary form."[12] She did profess an obvious predilection for dramatic literature, and the essay on modern drama indicates that her tastes here were remarkably wide-ranging. She praises the dramatic works of Leo Tolstoy, Anton Chekhov, Maxim Gorky and Leonid Andreiev, because they "closely mirror the life and the struggle, the hopes and aspirations of the Russian people."[13] But her tastes and praise extend also to France (Eugène Brieux, Octave Mirbeau), Germany (Arno Holz, Hermann Sudermann, Gerhart Hauptmann, even Max Halbe and Frank Wedekind), Scandinavia (Henrik Ibsen, the "supreme hater of all social shams"[14]) and England (George Bernard Shaw, John Galsworthy, Rann Kennedy). America she judges to be still in its dramatic infancy, since most of the attempts there to mirror life "have been wretched failures."[15] She singles out Eugene Walter's play *The Easiest Way* as being the "only real drama America has so far produced."[16]

These thoughts on art and literature were first published a quarter of a century before the outbreak of the Spanish Civil War, during which Goldman was to engage in propagandistic activity, both within and outside Spain, on behalf of the anarchists. They also predate by many years Goldman's bitter disillusionment with Soviet communism, which set in during the early 1920s. This is not the case with Herbert Read's key theoretical work *Poetry and Anarchism*, which was published in June 1938, at a time when hostility between anarchists and communists had reached new heights.[17] Read, who had two of his poems published in Spender and Lehmann's *Poems for Spain*, at no time formally belonged to an anarchist organisation, nor indeed to any political organisation. In this respect he was much like George Orwell, whom he admired and respected.[18] In fact Read "hesitated to use the term 'anarchism' to describe his ideal socio-political condition, because it conjured up images of cloaked figures with home-made bombs; but in the end he decided that there was no choice."[19] Disillusioned with communism and with other forms of socialism, Read from about 1935 became "the most passionate spokesman for this cause [i.e., anarchism], giving every appearance of representing an official movement, to which, however, he never belonged."[20]

Despite its title, large sections of *Poetry and Anarchism* are not directly concerned with aesthetic issues at all. Like a lot of anarchist writing dating from that period, particularly that which was acutely aware of the political tensions in Spain, it is an attempt to explain and to justify anarchist ideology and (unlike Emma Goldman in 1911) to highlight the differences between anarchism on one hand and Marxist communism or socialism on the other.

Keeping this in mind, it is nevertheless apparent that, like Goldman, Read envisages for literature a revolutionary function. The poet's role was to assist in breaking down existing social and political forms and in ushering in a society based on anarchist principles. For the anarchist Read writing in the late 1930s, the political forms which had to be resisted and overcome with the aid of literature included not just fascism but also the Marxist, non-libertarian form of communism: "In order to create it is necessary to destroy; and the agent of destruction is the poet. I believe that the poet is necessarily an anarchist, and that he must oppose all organised conceptions of the State, not only those which we inherit from the past, but equally those which are imposed on people in the name of the future. In this sense I make no distinction between fascism and marxism."[21]

Like Goldman, Read also contends that the artist does not have the option of ignoring the social implications of artistic production. Just as Goldman condemned the concept of art for art's sake, Read emphasises that art arises from the interaction of the artist and society:

The work of art, by processes which we have so far failed to understand, is a product of the relationship which exists between an individual and a society, and no great art is possible unless you have as corresponding activities the spontaneous freedom of the individual and the passive coherence of a society. To escape from society (if that were possible) is to escape from the only soil fertile enough to nourish art.[22]

Read cites two attempts made by artists to escape that productive relationship with society. The first is that of Paul Gauguin, who fled the confines of French bourgeois society to Tahiti, only to be disappointed. In effect this had been no escape, because modern man "can never escape from himself. He carries his warped psychology about with him no less inevitably than his bodily diseases. But the worst disease is the one he creates out of his own isolation: uncriticised phantasies, personal symbols, private fetishes."[23] The second attempt at escape was, in a manner, more successful. The Russian poet Vladimir Mayakovsky had committed suicide in April 1930. For Read this presented clear evidence that Marxist Russia had failed to bring about a productive relationship between society and the creative individual. In this respect the Soviet Union was no better than fascist Spain, which had murdered García Lorca in 1936.[24]

This point leads to the third similarity in the aesthetic thought of Read and Goldman. Like the American, Read does not accept that the artist or poet should perform a propaganda function in the service of the state. He explicitly condemns this misappropriation of art for blatantly political ends: "Both fascism and Marxism are fully aware of the power of the poet, and because the poet is powerful, they wish to use him for their own political purposes. The conception of the totalitarian state involves the subordination of all its elements to a central control, and not least among such elements are the aesthetic values of poetry and of the arts in general."[25] Read's condemnation of the propaganda function allegedly assigned to the artist in Soviet Russia was so strong as the suggest that there was "not the slightest difference, in intention, in control and in final product, between the art of Marxist Russia and the art of fascist Germany."[26]

Finally, like Goldman, Read accepted that art performs a mimetic function. The poet, he argues, has two principal duties, namely "to mirror the world as it is, and to imagine the world as it might be."[27] The consequence of this, as with

Goldman, is not the embracing solely of realist or representational art forms. Although Goldman showed a preference for nineteenth-century realism, Read in fact announces his contempt for the doctrine of socialist realism which, as we have seen in the case of Lukács, was largely modelled on nineteenth century realism. Refusing to repeat the "familiar arguments" against socialist realism, he simply states: "Its products are so poor by every standard known to the history of art that such arguments are not really necessary. It is more important to show the positive connection between art and individual freedom."[28]

The best way of illustrating how Read's anarchist line in aesthetics differed from the communist line of the time is to examine the variation in response to a series of etchings by Picasso entitled *Sueño y Mentira de Franco* (Dream and Lie of Franco). Anthony Blunt, whose communist sympathies were not publicly revealed until decades later, wrote a review of the etchings in the *Spectator* in October 1937. The review was damning, accusing Picasso of being removed from the reality of war and of producing art for an élite:

And this is Picasso's contribution to the Spanish Civil War. It is not surprising that his offering should be of this kind. For Picasso has spent the whole of his life in the Holy of Holies of Art, served by the chosen, refining more and more his mystical rites, so that for the initiate they grew in significance, but for the world they became ever more remote and unreal. . . . The etchings cannot reach more than the limited coterie of aesthetes, who have given their life so wholly to the cult of art that they have forgotten about everything else. The rest of the world will at most see and shudder and pass by. For the etchings to perform a more important function two things would have been necessary: that Picasso should have seen more than the mere horror of the civil war, that he should have realised that it is only a tragic part of a great forward movement; and that he should have expressed his optimism in a direct way and not with circumlocution so abstruse that those who are occupied with more serious things will not have time or energy to work out all its implications.[29]

A week later Read wrote a reply to Blunt, in which he came to Picasso's defence, pointing out that Picasso had not been as detached from the Spanish struggle as Blunt had suggested. He noted that the republican government had given Picasso the directorship of the Prado Museum and that Picasso's *Guernica*, exhibited at the Paris Exhibition, had been seen and admired by hundreds and thousands of people. As for the *Sueño y Mentira de Franco* etchings, Read commented that "reproductions of these are to be issued in the form of postcards and will thus become available even to the poorest people."[30]

For Read this was evidence which clearly refuted Blunt's view that modern art was inevitably unpopular. Blunt's opposition to modern art, in Read's opinion, did not reflect popular attitudes at all. In a thinly veiled attack on socialist realism, but at the same time on the brand of realism being pushed by the Nazis in Germany, Read wrote that the source of Blunt's views was to be found in "middle-class doctrinaires who wish to 'use' art for the propagation of their dull ideas. That the drab realism which these philistines have enforced in Russia and Germany should become the art of a country like Spain is happily a contradiction of its innate artistic spirit too improbable to entertain seriously."[31]

Indeed, when it comes to the treatment of war, there is some indication that Read was *opposed* to the representation of objective reality. In *Poetry and Anarchism* he discusses some of his own writings on World War I, in which he had participated as a soldier. He recalls that he had written some realistic poems under the title *Naked Warriors*, which sold very poorly, and that he had also written an account of the "Retreat of March," which he had made "as objective as possible," but which took five years to be published.[32] His conclusion was that from the viewpoint of a pacifist (as Read was) it was in fact counterproductive to present war objectively: "though I have since written one or two other descriptions of war incidents, I feel that this [objective] method is not effective, and that, in short, the more effectively war is represented as *literature*, the more attractive war itself becomes. It is obvious that its horrors fascinate people (even women), and it sometimes seems that if one wants to prevent war, it is better to act as if it had never existed."[33]

In *Poetry and Anarchism* Read makes brief reference to the German critic Carl Einstein, who in 1934 had published a book on Georges Braque, and in it had put forward the theory that cubism in general and Braque in particular were "an inevitable outcome of the transition from individual to collective values in society."[34] This reference to a transition to "collective values" hints at the development of Einstein's political ideas, although Read makes no explicit mention of this. The path by which Carl Einstein reached a faith in anarchism is a long and complex one, which here can be treated only briefly. More important than the course of Einstein's development is the culminating point it achieved in 1936.

Born in Neuwied in Germany in 1885, Carl Einstein's contact with the European avantgarde existed well before the outbreak of World War I.[35] It began with an interest in the work of Stefan George, the *George-Kreis* and the French symbolists. It continued in his encounter with cubism, with whose leading representatives, Braque, Picasso and Juan Gris, Einstein became closely acquainted during his many stays in Paris. This exposure to cubism was so profound that Einstein's early theoretical work has been described as the "only example of an attempt at a cubist theory of literature and fine art in the German-speaking world at the beginning of the twentieth century, roughly comparable with the similarly directed efforts of Gertrude Stein or Guillaume Apollinaire in France."[36] Einstein became one of the leading theorists of expressionism, establishing his reputation through work for a range of expressionist journals and through the successful publication in 1915 of his book *Die Negerplastik* (Negro Sculpture), in which he established affinities between the expressionist art of his contemporaries and primitive African art.[37] Einstein also made a name for himself as a practitioner of literary expressionism or what might even be called a kind of literary cubism. As early as 1906 he began work on an "anti-novel" entitled *Bebuquin oder die Dilettanten des Wunders* (Bebuquin or the Dilettantes of the Miracle), which was completed three years later. It has been described as the "negation and parodistic reversal of all conventional principles of the novel" and as "one of the earliest and most radical documents of the turning-away from representational [*gegenständlich-reproduzierend*] art."[38]

By the end of World War I at the latest Einstein's aesthetic radicalism was matched by a political radicalism, though not yet in the form of a commitment to anarchism. Like Herbert Read, Einstein had fought in the war and, like Read, his experiences of war had converted him to pacifism. In November 1918 he was involved in revolutionary activity in Brussels; by the end of the year he was in Berlin where, apart from working with dadaists and other representatives of the postwar avantgarde, he supported the activities of the communist *Spartakusbund*. In 1920 he broke with the dadaists but may have become affiliated with the independent socialists (USPD).

During the 1920s Einstein maintained his contact with exponents of avantgarde art, including Paul Claudel and his good friend Gottfried Benn, and continued to enhance his reputation as an art critic.[39] That reputation achieved international dimensions with the publication in 1926 of *Die Kunst des 20. Jahrhunderts* (The Art of the Twentieth Century).[40] In 1928 Einstein moved into a kind of voluntary exile in Paris. As from 1933, however, the exile was no longer of a voluntary nature. Because of his Jewishness and his political background a return to Germany had become impossible.

Until the early 1930s Einstein insisted on art's idealist and autonomous status. In other words, he saw art as being entirely disconnected from objective, material reality. He saw no possibility of art engaging in social or political processes; instead he jealously guarded its special, private function, its obedience to a form of subjective logic which was quite distinct from the prevailing objective, causal-empirical logic of the era. As with the French surrealists at about the same time, it is enormously difficult to link Einstein's aesthetic radicalism with his political radicalism. Certainly, both were forms of reaction to a world saturated with bourgeois values, but the very nature of Einstein's nonmaterialist aesthetic radicalism meant that he could not enlist it in the service of a political revolution. This is not to suggest that Einstein's transcendental aesthetics was devoid of revolutionary rhetoric. But as the following 1932 manifesto signed by Einstein and entitled "Poetry Is Vertical" indicates, the revolutionary rhetoric applied not to the material world but to the creation of a mythological realm:

The final disintegration of the "I" in the creative act is made possible by the use of a language which is a mantic instrument, and which does not hesitate to adopt a revolutionary attitude toward word and syntax, going even so far as to invent a hermetic language, if necessary.

Poetry builds a nexus between the "I" and the "you" by leading the emotions of the sunken, telluric depths upward toward the illumination of a collective reality and a totalistic universe.

The synthesis of a true collectivism is made possible by a community of spirits who aim at the construction of a new mythological reality.[41]

Einstein preserved this program of a subjectivist-autonomous art until the 1930s. At that time, and against the background of political and economic crisis in Europe, he began to overhaul his aesthetic theory, to the extent that he became a bitter opponent of modernist, subjectivist art. He developed a theory of art which is essentially materialist, and which contained three important elements: "the historically decisive role of the proletarian masses in the production of the material basis of reality, the re-establishment of the capacity for political action of the socially isolated bourgeois-liberal individual and the element of the collectivity of political action."[42] This new theory is to be found in Einstein's (largely unpublished at the time) critical and theoretical writings from the mid- and late 1930s, in the unfinished rewriting of his novel *Bebuquin*, and, above all, in the book *Die Fabrikation der Fiktionen* (The Fabrication of Fictions), which was not published until 1973.[43] Although Einstein himself opted to omit it, the book at one stage bore the programmatic subtitle *Eine Verteidigung des Wirklichen* (A Defense of the Real).[44]

Einstein in these works essentially contradicted his own earlier position. He dismissed the idea of an autonomous, subjectivist art, and with great acerbity criticised its practitioners. In a manner which is reminiscent of the contributions of Kurella, Lukács and others to the expressionism debate, Einstein suggests Weimar Germany's intellectual and artistic idealists had contributed to the rise of fascism. In *Die Fabrikation der Fiktionen* he writes:

Whenever a bourgeois reaction sets in one appeals to the old idealism. The petty bourgeois reactionaries of today create banal ideological needs and speak with pathetic idealism. This is logical, because despite the radical turn of phrase one does not want to and cannot resolve the actual conflicts. Every bourgeois government casts the idealist slogan against economic materialism in order to support itself with fictions. This idealist reactionary tendency, for example the Nazi, offers a certain attraction for the intellectual brought up on a diet of idealism. Here they see the chance to maintain the desired primacy of fictions, whereby their own influence is guaranteed.[45]

Whereas Einstein earlier had praised autonomous, idealist art, he now suggested that by refusing to refer to objective, social reality, art had contributed to the powerlessness of the proletariat. Moreover, by producing art for a privileged bourgeoisie, artists had contributed to the social and political entrenchment of an élite which "uses this art as a means to block out the proletariat from its privileged reality."[46] Rather than revolting against the bourgeois world, as Einstein had earlier maintained, he now considered that the artistic avantgarde had only served to reinforce existing social divisions.

In a manner reminiscent of Walter Benjamin, Carl Einstein saw that the rise of fascism and the fascist strategy of aestheticising politics had to be countered by the politicisation of aesthetics. Rather than being autonomous, rather than constituting a separate reality, Einstein began to develop a materialist aesthetics in which art would refer to and would influence objective social and political reality to the benefit of the oppressed proletariat. In short, Einstein began to affirm the necessity of a politically committed art, and this is the phase of the development of his aesthetic theory which is of most interest here. This is not to suggest, however, that Einstein now developed a fully coherent system of materialist aesthetics. On the contrary, although he is unambiguous in his rejection of his old system, there was no fully developed system to replace it. Perhaps because of his participation in the Spanish Civil War, perhaps also because of some sizable theoretical stumbling blocks, Einstein's revision of his aesthetic theory remained incomplete and may with some justification even be labelled a failure. [47]

Einstein's new system can best be understood as a series of loosely connected principles. As with Emma Goldman and with Herbert Read, art would directly engage reality with the aim of abolishing existing social inequalities. It would do so by above all addressing the working classes rather than the privileged bourgeoisie and by encouraging the former to strive for an equitable restructuring of society. In doing so, it would abandon the predominantly metaphorical character of autonomous art in preference for a metonymic art, a realist art similar in function to that described by Brecht. [48] As in Brechtian realist theory also, Einstein's aesthetic materialism did *not* entail the adoption of models provided by nineteenth-century bourgeois realism. Although he saw the need for the presentation of socially representative characters or types (as opposed to the special individual cases presented in autonomous art), he could not endorse the mimetic-realistic model that Lukács so favoured. Such representative art or literature for Einstein was unacceptable, because it would only reproduce the existing inequitable social relations.

This uncertainty as to the form that art and literature should take is the point at which Einstein's revised theory encountered its greatest difficulties. On the one hand it was apparent to him that to be able to intervene in the political process it would be necessary to employ broadly accepted realist conventions. Precisely the absence of those conventions had made autonomous art politically impotent. On the other hand, Einstein was convinced that society was no longer capable of providing such universally valid conventions: "In the pluralistic, late-capitalist society, which no longer possesses agreement on a conception of reality, art has also at the same time forfeited its collective applicability to this society." [49]

Einstein's solution to this dilemma was an interesting one, and in a sense it is the most radical of all the politically committed positions of the 1930s. Whereas Brecht, but also the anarchists Emma Goldman and Herbert Read, advocated that the artist through artistic activity could influence and improve reality, Einstein goes so far as to advocate the temporary suspension of artistic activity in order to concentrate all energies on direct political action. The artist, in other words, was to abandon the pen and the easel and to agitate for the political revolution. Solving the problem of artistic realism ingeniously, Einstein claimed that only after the revolution would a completely new and at present unforeseeable style of art emerge:

A new intellectual style is possible only after a revolution which creates changed social circumstances and brings forth other human types. The intellectuals must again gain a sense of useful cooperation and abandon the utopia of aesthetically complete but purposeless action.

Artistic conventions are only secondary results of determining social arrangements. From these they acquire their meaning. Intellectuality only possesses significance when it relates to a large social process and is part of it. [50]

It is now Einstein who is applying causal logic: the revolution would bring the liberal, capitalist era to an end and as a result of that would establish a society with generally acknowledged social conventions upon which art could base itself. The final words of *Die Fabrikation der Fiktionen* are an appeal to intellectuals and artists to commit themselves fully to the revolutionary cause:

Individualising idealism is ended, the productive forces have long ago changed to a collective. It is not a matter, as the intellectuals believed, of rejecting reality, but of reorganising it collectively. Within this task art can again find its place if it modestly contributes to the production of a new reality. For this reason the intellectuals have to renounce their claim to a special status or to artistic superiority. Now it is no longer a case of the reorganisation of a fiction or the imitation of a given condition, but of cooperating in the restructuring of social circumstances. The alienated intellectuals must again play a role in society and renounce their special utopia. Intellect [*Geist*] can in future only be understood as a coordinated power. Monological poetry is finished. The intellectuals have to be healed of their isolated manias and normalised. They must again achieve the sense for real creation. [51]

There is nothing in this revised aesthetic which explicitly identifies it as anarchist. Indeed there is no evidence that Einstein showed any inclination towards specifically anarchist political ideology before 1936. In his last book review, published in early 1936, Einstein disparagingly describes Louis-Ferdinand Céline as a "petty bourgeois anarchist." [52] When the Spanish Civil War broke out, however, Einstein journeyed to Barcelona in August 1936, joined the anarchists and became acquainted with such people as Emma Goldman and Buenaventura Durruti. [53] He joined the latter's column and went to the Aragón front as a militiaman. His wife worked in Barcelona as a nurse.

It is not known definitively whether Einstein's decision to join the anarchists was premeditated and the result of an existing commitment to anarchist ideology or whether it was purely the outcome of a set of circumstances beyond Einstein's control. Christoph Braun notes in Einstein a long-standing but unvoiced inclination towards anarchism, which was similar to the *Bohème-Anarchismus* propagated by Erich Mühsam. He claims that Einstein had been drawn to the *Spartakusbund* by its uncompromising radicalism rather than by a disciplined Marxist party program. [54] Heidemarie Oehm similarly maintains that it was no mere coincidence that Einstein joined the ranks of the anarchists rather than the communists. [55] On the other hand, Helmut Rüdiger, a German anarchist already living in Barcelona when Einstein arrived, suggests that Einstein initially was under the influence of French intellectuals, "who had presented the whole thing as more or less communist inspired anti-fascism." [56] Rüdiger suggests that it was only by chance that shortly after his arrival in Barcelona Einstein came in contact with Spanish anarchists and with Rüdiger himself. [57]

In any case it is clear that, whether the inclination had existed beforehand or not, the experience of the anarchist-inspired revolutionary activity in Barcelona in the early part of the war persuaded him to throw in his lot with the anarchists rather than the communists. There is no doubt that he fully endorsed the anarchist line. A friend recalls that during this time Einstein was "quite different from in Berlin: not sarcastic, no longer embittered but enthusiastic, and as a result much younger. I had never known him like this. He hardly spoke about his own life during the past, difficult years of emigration, but continually began to talk of Spanish syndicalism."[58] Given that the anarchists were genuine revolutionaries, Einstein's decision to support them was in a sense an entirely logical one. By fighting with the anarchists he was practicing what he had been preaching in his revised aesthetic theory. He was abandoning intellectual and artistic activity in favour of promoting the primacy of revolutionary action. "In the anarcho-syndicalist movement and in particular in the Durruti Column Einstein believed that he had come across something akin to a genuinely socialist popular movement, which was not organised along party lines, whose revolutionary actions resulted from a spontaneous drive and not from rational party discipline. From it most of all he hoped to achieve the collective renewal of social reality."[59]

This helps to explain why the failure of the revolution and the loss of the war brought Einstein to the point of despair. Both politically and aesthetically he had reached a hopeless impasse. Having spent some time in a French internment camp after the Spanish Civil War, he committed suicide in southern France in July 1940. Fleeing before German occupying troops he, as a former soldier in Spain, knew that the escape route over the Pyrenees was blocked.

## ANARCHIST PROSE LITERATURE

The greater part of the literature of the Spanish Civil War is not favourably disposed towards the anarchists. This applies to the literature produced by fascists and reactionaries; it also applies to much of the literature of the Left. Whereas the attitudes of Orwell and Borkenau towards the anarchists were ambivalent, communists and communist sympathisers were at their kindest mocking, at their worst viciously disparaging.[60] Again and again the anarchists are depicted as being unruly, undisciplined, unpredictable, violent and childishly naive. Even Hemingway, who is widely reputed to be even-handed in his depiction of the war, is hardly equitable in dealing with anarchism in *For Whom the Bell Tolls*. Anarchists play only a minor role in the novel, but when they are encountered they are described as being "like dangerous children; dirty, foul, undisciplined, kind, loving, silly, and ignorant but always dangerous because they were armed."[61]

Outside Spain support for the anarchist cause was limited, but it sometimes cropped up in surprising places. When Aldous Huxley, for example, replied to Nancy Cunard's *Authors Take Sides* survey he wrote:

My sympathies are, of course, with the Government side, especially the Anarchists; for Anarchism seems to me much more likely to lead to desirable social change than highly centralised, dictatorial Communism. As for "taking sides" – the choice, it seems to me, is no longer between two users of violence, two systems of dictatorship. Violence and dictatorship cannot produce peace and liberty; they can only produce the results of violence and dictatorship, results with which history has made us only too sickeningly familiar.

The choice now is between militarism and pacifism. To me, the necessity of pacifism seems absolutely clear.62

Although the contact with the sheer brutality of war brought about a conversion, it is evident that the French intellectual and politician Simone Weil also expressed an initial inclination towards the anarchist cause. She spent some two months in Spain in 1936 and served with a militia until an injury caused during a cooking accident forced her to return to France.63 In a letter to Georges Bernanos dating from 1938 she openly proclaims her sympathy with the anarchists:

From my childhood onwards I sympathised with those organisations which spring from the lowest and least regarded social strata, until the time when I realised that such organisations are of a kind to discourage all sympathy. The last one in which I felt some confidence was the Spanish C.N.T. I had travelled a little in Spain before the civil war; only a little, but enough to feel the affection which it is hard not to feel for the Spanish people. I had seen the anarchist movement as the natural expression of that people's greatness and of its flaws, of its worthiest aspirations and of its unworthiest. The C.N.T. and F.A.I. were an extraordinary mixture, to which anybody at all was admitted and in which, consequently, one found immorality, cynicism, fanaticism and cruelty, but also love and fraternal spirit and above all, that concern for honour which is so beautiful in the humiliated. It seemed to me that the idealists preponderated over the elements of violence and disorder. 64

The rarity of favourable accounts and the overwhelming prevalence of derisive treatments is easily explained. Firstly, the preexisting interest in anarchism among intellectuals and writers was confined to a few. On an international scale anarchism could not hope to match the intellectual support which communism enjoyed in the 1930s. Even in Spain, where anarchism had a genuine mass basis, the movement could boast only a few intellectuals. 65 Secondly, the anarchists wielded very little power in the realm of literary production and the print media. They had minimal control over the kind of information which was being disseminated widely within Spain and beyond Spain. It was predictable enough that no literature sympathetic to the anarchists would be published in nationalist Spain. But in this respect the situation in republican Spain was not substantially different. Anarchist organisations of course had their own organs, the most famous of which was the anarchist newspaper *Solidaridad Obrera* (Worker Solidarity). But the censorship system fell progressively into the hands of communists and socialists, most notably Julio Alvarez del Vayo,66 who had clearly identifiable political reasons for not releasing news on anarchist activity. They ensured that during the war very little information was available on the anarchists, on their widespread social revolution and on the suppression of that revolution by the communists. As Burnett Bolloten has noted,

Although the outbreak of the Spanish Civil War in July, 1936, was followed by a far-reaching social revolution in the anti-Franco camp — more profound in some respects than the Bolshevik Revolution in its early stages — millions of discerning people outside Spain were kept in ignorance, not only of its depth and range, but even of its existence, by virtue of a policy of duplicity and dissimulation of which there is no parallel in history. Foremost in practicing this deception upon the world, and in misrepresenting in Spain itself the character of the revolution, were the Communists. [67]

In terms of its content and propaganda function, much of the anarchist prose literature dating from the very early part of the war is virtually indistinguishable from the literature written by communists and communist sympathisers. It concentrated heavily on the attempted military putsch and on the support that the military had received from international fascism. In time, however, and with the development of a clear antagonism between revolutionary and anti-revolutionary forces in republican Spain, the anarchist line separated itself from the communist line. Increasingly the anarchists were compelled to justify and explain their actions, to promote their concept of social revolution, and to draw attention, both within and outside Spain, to attempts by the communists to crush that revolution. Against the communist strategy of placing the war before the revolution, they had to argue for the inseparability of war and revolution.

Naturally much of this work, in the form of books and pamphlets, was carried out by the leading intellectual figures in the Spanish anarchist movement, by such people as Diego Abad de Santillán, Juan García Oliver and Federica Montseny.[68] Surprisingly, though, a good deal of it was written by foreigners, some of whom were already resident in Spain when the war began. The Austrian historian of anarchism, Max Nettlau, for example, was already in Spain, as were many Germans. A group of German anarchists who called themselves the Gruppe Deutsche Anarchosyndikalisten (Group of German Anarcho-Syndicalists, hereafter DAS), which had been active primarily in Dutch exile, shifted the bulk of its operations to Barcelona with the outbreak of war.[69] With the cooperation of the CNT, DAS began carrying out propaganda work and providing assistance for German-speaking foreigners wishing to enlist in anarchist militias. It had its own newspaper, *Die Soziale Revolution* (The Social Revolution), which was distributed amongst the Germans in the militias.[70] It also published a book entitled *Das Schwarz-Rot-Buch. Dokumente über den Hitlerimperialismus* (The Black-Red-Book. Documents on Hitler-Imperialism).[71] As the title suggests, this was a collection of documents which attempted to prove the collaboration of Hitler's Germany in the franquist putsch.

While this was a collective effort, individual members of the group also published books or pamphlets on the situation in Spain, but usually not in their native tongue. The most prominent members were Augustin Souchy and the already mentioned Helmut Rüdiger.[72] Rudolf Rocker was also a prominent German anarchist of the time and was similarly engaged in propaganda work on behalf of the Spanish anarchists, but he did not set foot in Spain during the war.[73] His work was largely based on material sent to him in New York by Rüdiger.[74]

Other non-Spanish writers also committed themselves to a defence of the anarchist position. These included the Italian anarchist Camillo Berneri, who, just as the DAS in the early part of the war sought to reveal Hitler's complicity with Franco, threw light on Italian fascist involvement in Spain.[75] Berneri, whom Souchy described as "the intellectual head of the Italian anarchists," edited the Italian language anarchist newspaper *Guerra di classe* (Class War), which adopted a firmly anti-Stalinist line.[76] In one article Berneri wrote, "Today we are fighting Burgos, tomorrow we will have to fight Moscow in order defend our freedoms."[77] As a result of this statement the Soviet consul-general made representations to the Catalonian government and Berneri was blacklisted. During the "May events" in 1937 his house was raided and Berneri and another Italian anarchist, Barbieri, were murdered.[78]

The sixty-seven-year-old Emma Goldman was invited to Barcelona by Souchy and the FAI in August 1936.[79] After the recent death of her husband, the American anarchist Alexander Berkman, Goldman had been slow to respond to events in Spain, but once there in September the first few weeks in Barcelona "filled her with elation."[80] She talked on the anarchist radio station and addressed a rally sponsored by the youth section of the FAI.[81] A good indication of this early enthusiasm is to be found in a statement written just a week after her arrival:

Since I came here a week ago till today I have been in a trance. It seems impossible that the miracle should have happened. That the idea Sasha [i.e., Alexander Berkman] and I have propagated, and so many greater spirits than ours, should actually have attained a chance of expression. No, I am not foolish enough to be carried away by external things. I know that the CNT-FAI has not yet ushered in Anarchism. But to see Anarchist tendencies expressed in the midst of danger and battle, to see our own comrades guiding the economic, social and industrial life, is something I had not thought possible in many years in any country. Yet here it is a fact, a living, throbbing reality. As I said in my first address at a huge meeting, copy of which I enclose, whether the CNT-FAI wins or loses, the roots will remain deep in the Spanish earth and it will sprout again and again until it comes to fruition.[82]

This initial enthusiasm was tempered somewhat by her embroilment in tensions within the anarchist camp, tensions which arose because of the controversial decision by the CNT and FAI to accept ministerial positions in the republican government. Some of the members of the Association Internationale des Travailleurs (AIT, International Workers' Association), most notably its executive secretary, the Russian anarchist Alexander Schapiro, were vehemently opposed to such a move. Goldman herself was "caught in the middle."[83] In a letter dating from early 1937 she wrote:

I would despair utterly if I had not learned to understand the psychology of our Spanish comrades. They are a different breed. . . . Anarchism to them was never a cold and grey theory [as it is] for a lot of misfits who come to us in every country. And because anarchism is such a living force to them I am not so uneasy about their entry into the cabinet as I would be with comrades of any other country. I am certain that if they win the war the government will mean a mere scrap of paper to them and they will tear it to bits.[84]

Despite her reservations concerning participation in government, Goldman was made "an official fund-raiser and propagandist for the Catalan

Generalitat."[85] Later it was decided that her propaganda activity would be more effective if carried on outside Spain. In January 1937 she arrived in London, where she threw herself into propaganda and fund-raising activities on behalf of the Spanish anarchists, notably in cooperation with the ILP, with whom Orwell had taken up contact just a short time earlier.[86] After the disappointment of the May events, in particular the shocking assassination of Berneri, whom Goldman had known personally, she returned to Spain, only to detect a serious deterioration in the relative strength of the anarchist movement. Her continued criticism of CNT cooperation with the government caused the CNT to refuse Goldman permission to speak in its name and to prohibit access to the anarchist collectives. "The whole experience was a nightmare, and when the AIT suddenly called her to Paris in late November, she fled Spain for the last time."[87]

Unlike Emma Goldman, many foreign anarchists were granted ready access to the collectives and wrote generally enthusiastic but not entirely uncritical accounts of what they found there. Amongst these were the French anarchist Gaston Leval and the French historian and Bakunin-biographer Hans Erich Kaminski, who was sympathetic to anarchist ideas.[88] In his report on a collective in the village of Alcora it is nevertheless evident that Kaminski was prepared to adopt a critical perspective on developments there:

There is something moving about the ingenuity [i.e., ingenuousness] of all this organisation. It would be a mistake to see in it anything more than a peasant attempt to establish libertarian communism and unfair to criticise it too seriously. One must not forget that the agricultural workers and even the shopkeepers of the village have lived very poorly up till now. Their needs are hardly differentiated. Before the revolution a piece of meat was a luxury for them: only a few intellectuals living among them wish for things beyond immediate necessities. The anarchist communism of Alcora has taken its nature from the actual state of things. As a proof, one must observe that the family card puts the most oppressed human beings in Spain, the women, under the control of men. [89]

Many of the anarchists who travelled to Spain did so not to observe the revolution or to perform propaganda functions but to fight. The number of contemporaneous accounts of life in the anarchist militias is, however, very limited, since in the political climate of the time the primary focus for the anarchists had to be on the revolution. Not surprisingly, therefore, the literature which does deal with the activities of the militias tends to stress the social revolutionary aspects of life there.

Carl Einstein was one such foreigner who opted for military engagement on behalf of the anarchists. Having joined the Durruti Column, he won such favour there as to be appointed technical director of a nine kilometre section of the Aragón front.[90] One of the two short works produced by Einstein during the war deals with that experience of the front.[91] Significantly, however, it is an account which avoids the personal perspective and reveals nothing about Einstein's own experiences there. Instead, Einstein places the activities of the anarchist militias in the context of the war as a whole. Adopting a characteristically anarchist line he insists on the inseparability of war and revolution:

The columns of the CNT-FAI passed through the fertile fields of Catalonia and soon stood in the arid, stony mountain region of Aragón, where the wind has carved steep gorges. The farmers greeted the *milizianos* as their liberators. The latter, together with the farmers, transformed the villages to syndicalist village communities. This was necessary, especially as the large landowners had abandoned house and home. The advance of the black and red troops caused a social transformation, proof that this war is different from just a military action, that it is and must remain identical with the revolution.[92]

This text dates from a time when tensions between revolutionary and non-revolutionary forces in republican Spain were running high, and it is in this context that it should be seen. Einstein identifies the foreign, fascist enemy in the form of the Italian and German aeroplanes which kill men, women and children.[93] He also criticises the Western democracies and their more subtle practices of imperialism or colonising capitalism. More importantly, however, Einstein here is implicitly addressing the anti-revolutionary forces in republican Spain who were choking not just the social revolution but also the military activity of the anarchists. The accusations underpinning the article, but also present in Orwell's account from the same front at about the same time, concern the deliberate withholding of military supplies to the anarchist and POUM militias. Above all it is the communists, who largely controlled the distribution of supplies, whom Einstein is addressing, but he does not do so explicitly. His intention is not to disparage communism but to persuade its adherents of the wisdom of fully supporting the revolution. Published just days before the May events, the article was an ultimately fruitless appeal for solidarity amongst the anti-franquist forces, ending with a direct appeal to the government to allow the anarchists to take the pressure off Madrid by fighting an effective war on the Aragón front: "The war in Aragón can be fought. One can shorten this war if all fronts are coordinated. One can and must take Saragossa. It is the duty of the government to bring about the victory of the anti-fascist front with all means, to force the decisive victory which excludes a foreign peace negotiation. Friends, allow finally these divisions to fight and to be victorious in Aragón."[94]

The other, earlier piece of writing by Einstein stemming from the war is a eulogy for Buenaventura Durruti, who had been killed on 20 November 1936.[95] Originally it was broadcast by a CNT-FAI radio station in Barcelona. In a letter to Rudolf Rocker, Helmut Rüdiger recalls that when Einstein spoke on the radio "his voice choked with tears as he mentioned Durruti."[96] Even without this information, the text by itself shows the supreme admiration which Einstein felt for Durruti. Above all he admired Durruti for his selflessness, for his anarchist mentality which saw the world from a collective viewpoint. If in *Die Fabrikation der Fiktionen* Einstein anticipates that the revolution will bring with it an entirely new language and literature, there are hints here of what that post-revolutionary language and literature might be like:

Durruti, this extraordinarily practical man, never spoke of himself, of his person. He had banished the prehistorical word "I" from grammar. In the Durruti Column one knows only the collective syntax. The comrades will teach the men of letters how to renew grammar in a collective sense.

Deep down Durruti had recognised the power of anonymous work. Anonymity and communism are one. Comrade Durruti appeared far-removed from all the vanity of the stars of the Left. He lived with his comrades, fought as a compañero.97

This is not an example of the kind of hero worship to be found in fascist literature and in the literature of the reactionary Right, and Einstein himself is eager to make that distinction: "The fetishism of *Führertum*, the fabrication of stars we shall gladly leave to the fascists."98 Rather than concentrate on the figure of Durruti, Einstein focusses on the Durruti Column and the revolutionary social conditions which prevailed there. As in his later article, he stresses the anarchist belief in the unity of war and revolution. In doing so the link with *Die Fabrikation der Fiktionen* becomes even clearer. Just as in that book, Einstein here advocates the primacy of action which had typified the Durruti Column: "This anarchosyndicalist column was born in the revolution. This is its mother. War and revolution are for us a single, inseparable act. Others may discuss selectively or abstractly. The Durruti Column knows only action, and we learn through it. We are simple empiricists and believe that action produces insights more clearly than a step-by-step program, which evaporates in the violence of its implementation."99 More than just the heroic figure of Durruti, Einstein's eulogy praises *all* those who joined the Durruti Column. He extols the revolutionary achievement implicit in the non-bureaucratic organisation of the Column itself but also in its implementation of a revolutionary social program wherever it went. As committed revolutionaries, the war was of secondary importance for them. It was merely a means to an end: "We all hate the war, but we understand it as a revolutionary means. We are no pacifists and fight passionately. The war – this outmoded idiocy – can only be justified by the Social Revolution. We are fighting not as soldiers but as liberators. We are advancing and charging forward, not to capture property but to liberate those oppressed by capitalists and fascists. The Column is a unit of class-conscious idealists."100

As in "*Die Front von Aragon*," Einstein does not set out here to proclaim the superiority of anarchism over Stalinist communism or any other left-wing ideology. In fact, the emphasis on the war being merely a regrettable but unavoidable means to an end is something which Einstein has in common with other sections of the Left. Nevertheless, Einstein implicitly establishes the distinctions between the anarchist position and the positions represented by other sections of the Left, especially that of the communists. At a time when the communists were pushing hard for the creation of a centrally controlled, hierarchically structured republican army, Einstein went to considerable lengths to highlight the virtues of the anarchist militia system. In that system the imposition of discipline through a military hierarchy was superfluous, since all militiamen were fully committed to the revolutionary ideal. Whereas the soldier obeyed his commander out of fear and social inferiority, the militiaman "does not obey, but pursues together with his colleagues the realisation of his ideal, a social necessity."101 Rather than commanding his militiamen, Durruti discussed with them and convinced them of the sense of any particular course of action. Consequently the Durruti Column was disciplined "by an ideal and not by the parade march."102 The militia was "a proletarian factor, its essence, its organisation are proletarian and must stay thus. The militias are the exponents of the class war. The revolution imposes on the Column a stricter discipline than any militarisation could. Each person feels responsible for the success of the Social Revolution."[103]

This last point indicates a further major point of difference between the anarchists and the communists. The latter, as has been shown, placed great emphasis on the international character of the war, that is, on the intervention of the Germans and the Italians on Franco's side, but also on the international or multinational anti-fascist solidarity on the republican side. Einstein and the anarchists, on the other hand, do not hesitate to condemn German and Italian intervention, but they insist on interpreting the war as a class war, as a struggle of Spain's urban and rural proletariat against capitalist oppression. Moreover, even in the case of Einstein and the many other foreigners who fought side by side with the Spanish anarchists, they make nothing of the international composition of their own forces. Although they recognised the presence of foreign troops on Spanish soil, the war for them remained very much a Spanish affair.

## ANARCHIST POETRY

Einstein's advocacy of a suspension of art was not heard and certainly not heeded by the Spanish anarchists. It has already been noted that in republican Spain in general the boost in poetic production sponsored by the war was phenomenal. A good deal of this increase is attributable to the anarchists, who on the basis of their numerical strength were the most significant source of republican poetry.

The interest in literature, despite (or perhaps even partly because of) the high incidence of illiteracy amongst the anarchists, was evident well before the outbreak of war. Often the leaders of the anarchosyndicalist trade unions would express their ideas in fictional form. In poetry, in stories, in the novel and in the theatre these people had seen media for the emancipatory education of the masses which were just as important as the theoretical treatise.[104] Of even greater importance in the prewar anarchist publications were short stories, songs and, above all, countless poems which were written by the (often anonymous) workers themselves. The *romance* already boasted a popular tradition dating back to medieval times, but it had been primarily an oral rather than a strictly literary cultural form. Gerald Brenan notes, however, that the interest developed by the anarchists was specifically for the spoken word, which for them had a distinctly pedagogical value:

An immense desire sprang up to read and learn, so as to have access to this store of knowledge and wisdom provided by the Anarchist press. One met peasants reading everywhere, on mule back, at meal time under the olive trees. Those who could not read, by force of hearing others spell out aloud their favourite passages, would learn whole newspaper articles by heart. Sometimes, after a single reading from *Tierra y Libertad* or *El Productor*, a laborer would feel illuminated by the new faith. The scales would fall from his eyes and everything seem clear to him. He then became an *obrero consciente*. He gave up smoking, drinking and gambling. He no longer frequented brothels. He took care never to pronounce the word God. He did not marry but lived with his *compañera*, to whom he was strictly faithful, and refused to baptise his children. He subscribed to at least one Anarchist paper, read the little books on history, geography and botany brought out by Ferrer's press and held forth on these subjects whenever possible. Like other uneducated people who have suddenly had their eyes opened to the possibilities of knowledge, he spoke in an inflated style, using long incomprehensible words. [105]

The outbreak of war intensified an already existing predilection for literature. The anarchists, like other pro-republican groups, set up schools in order to encourage their followers to read and write. Reinhold Görling reproduces in his book an anarchist poster with the words: "Read anarchist books and you will be a man." [106] The anarchist press flourished, giving thousands of unknown poets the opportunity to express themselves. Indeed, poetry was the preferred literary genre of the anarchists; 66 percent of anarchist journals, more than those of any other group, published verse. [107]

The most comprehensive study of this "poetic explosion" [108] has been carried out by Serge Salaün, who has estimated that between 15 and 20,000 poems were published in republican Spain by some 5,000 poets, most of them unknown. [109] He stresses the importance of some 500 newspapers produced at the front by individual divisions and brigades, most of which (75 percent) published poetry, and of some 800 newspapers published on the home-front, of which just under 50 percent published poetry. [110] As mentioned in the Introduction, Salaün sees this enormous production of poetry in republican Spain, with all its metrical and ideological diversity, as constituting a single *Romancero de la Guerra Civil* (*Romancero* of the Civil War). [111]

Although he views this mass of poetic production as a coherent work, Salaün also distinguishes between the poetry of the already known "professional" poets and the unknown non-professional poets. [112] The distinction is an important one. Most literary scholarship has concentrated almost exclusively on the contribution of such well-known poets and intellectuals as Rafael Alberti, Miguel Hernández, José Bergamín and Antonio Machado, all of whom wrote prolifically during the war and produced work which is widely regarded as being of high quality. The reasons for concentrating on these figures are not difficult to find. As Salaün has observed, it was these poets who "monopolised the most important communication media: the radio and the greater part of the press known as the literary press." [113] They were enormously influential as poets, but also as reviewers and editors. Perhaps even more importantly, these were the poets who were organised in the Republic's Alianza de Intelectuales Antifascistas (Alliance of Anti-Fascist Intellectuals); many were either members of the Communist Party or could be regarded as "fellow travellers." In their publications, such as the anthologies mentioned in Chapter 4, and in such journals as *El Mono Azul* and *Hora de España*, they preferred to publish their own poetry rather than that of the mass of unknown poets, despite the numerical superiority of the latter. [114]

In dealing with the anarchist poetry of the war, we are not dealing with this category. Most of the anarchist poets had no literary reputation to speak of. They were largely obscure or entirely anonymous poets who may have published only one or two poems each. Only three names, none of whom was associated with the Alianza de Intelectuales Antifascistas, are outstanding amongst the anarchist poets: Félix Paredes, José García Pradas, and Antonio Agraz. Paredes was an editor of several anarchist publications. Much of his wartime poetry (amounting to over 600 poems) appeared in the anarchist daily *Fragua Social* (Social Forge). García Pradas also worked as an editor, eventually becoming director of the newspaper *CNT*, where he published much of his own work. He also edited an anthology of anarchist verse.[115] The most famous of the trio, though, was Agraz, who as early as 1931 had begun publishing poems in the anarchist newspaper *La Tierra* under the pseudonym Gerineldo. He became an editor of *CNT*, for which he published over 200 poems in the period 1936 to 1938. Sixty-three of these poems, as well as over a hundred poems by Paredes, García Pradas and other lesser known or unknown anarchist poets were republished by Salaün in 1971.[116]

Although it is not necessary to abandon Salaün's concept of a collective anti-fascist *romancero*, it is nonetheless essential to recognise that the attitude to cultural activity held by the intellectuals or the "professionals" during the war was different from that of the anarchists. The former professed a strong commitment to the republican cause and to the idea that literature could serve that cause. They sought to establish a close bond with the Spanish people and to write poetry which people would find readily accessible. In committing themselves and their work to the popular cause, they spoke not of a *cultura popular* but of a *cultura al servicio de la causa popular*, a culture in the service of the popular cause. (This, for example, was the motto of *Hora de España*.[117]) The culture they produced and promoted was a culture *for* the people and the popular cause, but for the most part it did not stem *from* the people. The anarchists, in contrast, believed in a popular culture which stemmed from the people and served the needs of the people. Thus they frequently published their work anonymously, arguing that if poetry stemmed from the people, then the identity of the individual poet was irrelevant.

The distance that existed between the intellectuals or the "professionals" and the people for whom they wrote became more apparent as the war progressed. Although in the first months of the war there existed an immaculate image of the solidarity of the intellectuals with the people, that image had become tarnished by the second year of the war. Salaün even speaks of a "rupture" and points especially to the evidence of the journal *Hora de España*, which abandoned the popular form of the *romance* in favour of free verse.[118] The poet had, in his estimation, "returned to being, owing to the pages of this review – the most elevated platform of the select minds –, a privileged individual wearing the halo of his almost divine status and therefore marginalised in relation to the rest of the country which continued to be the victims of the everyday realities of war."[119] By mid-1937 at the latest the notion that the war demanded aesthetic criteria to be subordinated to political criteria was losing credence with the "professionals." At the Writers' Congress, as has been indicated, the signatories of the *Ponencia Colectiva* proclaimed the aesthetic compatibility of the artist's private world with objective reality. In the same month Antonio Sánchez Barbudo wrote in *Hora de España*:

We shall never believe that this propaganda art, if it can be called art, was the only, the exclusive and the proper art of the revolution and of the revolutionaries. . . and let us all await that marvellous moment of a new Golden Age which without doubt is to occur, in which art and literature will have a grandness and a splendour never imagined. . . . Surely you, like Julien Benda, would not wish that artistic and literary expression would be reduced to mere propaganda? Nor would we! 120

The anarchists were very much aware of this "rupture" in the cultural attitudes of the intellectuals, of a tendency to distance themselves from the people and to revise an initially unconditional commitment to producing poetry which unashamedly fulfilled a political function. For the anarchists the close contact with the people, indeed the inseparability of poet and readership, remained constant throughout the war. By 1937 they had become fully conscious of the difference between their own position and that of the intellectuals. The distinction is illustrated well by an article on Agraz which appeared in *CNT* in January 1937:

Antonio Agraz is an anti-fascist of the front-line; but please do not classify him as an "intellectual." The Spanish intellectuals have almost always lived at a distance from the people, and whenever one of them approached the people, whilst others dared to denigrate it, he always went without the airs which his culturally privileged position gave him. Even today when one reads certain works by many intellectuals associated with the defence of our revolutionary cause, one does not know the reasons behind such writings: whether it is the revolution itself, or rather simply the literary itch.

With the poems of Antonio Agraz this does not occur. His verses are so simple and transparent, so spontaneous and frank, that one hardly notices them; one only sees, through them, a popular sentiment, a certain social yearning, something which is present in the deepest depths of any revolutionary desire; they are verses which were born for the present struggle and not for literature. Precisely for this reason the people understands them as something quite wonderful, seeks them daily with the greatest interest, reads them again and again in the rare moments of leisure it has nowadays, and recites them at the work place or at the front. 121

This distinction between the anarchist position and the essentially communist position, which was being expressed in journals like *Hora de España*, had by 1937 even led to a certain antagonism in the pro-republican camp. The anarchists polemicised against the intellectuals, accusing them of being out of contact with the people and of disregarding the revolution. Salaün speaks even of a "campaign," waged in the pages of *CNT* in 1938 and 1939, against a number of the well-known poets or intellectuals. It was aimed at people associated with *Hora de España* or with the Communist Party, including Hernández, Bergamín, César Vallejo and of course Alberti.122 As early as 1937 Agraz had written a satirical poem which played heavily on Alberti's visit to the Soviet Union and openly accused him of cowardice:

A Rusia se fué el poeta.
¡Quién la lucha cantará!
Maldita Guerra, maldita,
todo nos lo alejarás!
Los políticos se fueron
con su misión especial;
los "intelectuales" vuelan,
no sé con qué volarán. . . .

No se acercó a una trinchera,
sino cien leguas atrás.
Cuando andabas por Toledo,
él andaba por acá.

Cuando llegaste a Madrid,
él se retiró hacia el mar.
Cuando por las costas andas,
a la U.R.S.S. lejana va,
porque si nó se conserva,
¿quién la lucha cantará?

Ya no comerá lentejas,
ni claras sopas de pan;
tendrá que sacrificarse
y comer pardo caviar.

Ya no beberá montilla;
soló vodka beberá.

(To Russia the poet went. / Who will sing of the war? / Cursed war, cursed, / you'll take everything from us! / The politicians went away / on their special mission; / the "intellectuals" fly away, / I do not know what on. // He did not go close to a trench, / but stayed a hundred leagues behind. / When you were in Toledo, / he was somewhere this way. // When you arrived in Madrid, / he retreated toward the sea. / When you walk along the coast / he goes to the distant USSR., / because if he does not look after himself, / who will sing of the struggle? // He is no longer eating lentils / nor clear bread soup; / he will have to make a sacrifice / and eat drab caviar. // He will no longer drink montilla; / but only vodka.)123

Although the anarchist position distinguished itself from that of the intellectuals to the point of outright antagonism, in practice the differences between anarchist and communist poetry are not so clear-cut. To begin with, it must be said that the above example is an exception, and that for the most part anarchist poetry did not explicitly thematicise republican internecine feuding. Anarchist poetry is remarkably undogmatic, strictly avoiding discussions of ideological abstractions. The issues debated so vehemently in the prose writings mentioned above are not to be found in the poetry; there is nothing explicitly on the question of collectivisation or redistribution of land, on the creation of a Popular Army, on the persecution of anarchists by communists, and so on. At best there are allusions to these problems. What the anarchist poets preferred to do in their work was to seek ideological common ground.

Like the communists, they found that ideological common ground in the war itself. Almost all of the anarchist *romances* of the war deal explicitly with the war. To read the poetry of Agraz, who as a citizen of Madrid was intensely aware of military developments, is to follow the progress of the war, battle by battle, from beginning to end. Published on an almost daily basis in *CNT*, the poetry of Agraz offers a detailed military chronology. Consequently it assumes an almost journalistic quality. Just as there was a convergence of fictional and nonfictional prose forms in the Spanish Civil War, so there occurred in anarchist poetry a convergence of the lyric and reportage. Poetry and history become almost inseparable. In his prologue to Agraz's *Romances de CNT*, García Pradas gives an insight into the working method of Agraz which promoted such journalistic topicality:

I have seen him writing his *romances*. Ten minutes of silence, after some wittiness from him and some shouting from me, and he had in mind the poem he would write. Each one of them has been a revelation, and its theme, frequently, was transformed into the "theme" of *CNT*. . . . To what extent can we say whether Agraz listens to Madrid or Madrid listens to Agraz every evening? . . . But whatever may be the reason for the coincidence of man and city, he moulding himself to it or it receiving from him the expression of his gratitude, Madrid and Agraz have the same sentiments and the same voice.

As a journalist, the author of this book belongs to the *CNT*, but also because of his moral background, his temperament and because of his ideology.[124]

In dealing with the war the anarchist *romances*, like the communist *romances*, devote much attention to acts of heroism and self-sacrifice performed in the service of the anti-fascist cause. The anarchists had their own heroes, people like Francisco Ascaso, who fell at the very beginning of the war, and of course Ascaso's more famous colleague Buenaventura Durruti, whose praise Carl Einstein was to sing. In February 1937 Lucía Sánchez Saornil published a poem in *CNT* which praised the anarchist hero and, three months after it had occurred, mourned his death:

El aire agitó tu nombre
entre banderas de gloria
– tu nombre, grito de guerra
y dura canción de forja –.
Y una tarde de noviembre,
mojada de sangre heroica,
en cenizas de crepúsculo
caía tu vida rota.
Sólo hablaste estas palabras,
al filo ya de tu hora:
"¡Unidad y firmeza amigos;
para vencer hay de sobra!"

Durruti, hermano Durruti,

jamás se vio otra congoja
más amarga que tu muerte
sobre la tierra española.

(The air stirred with your name / amongst banners of glory / – your name, war-cry / and tough song of the forge –. / And one evening in November, / moist with heroic blood, / in the grey of twilight / your shattered life fell. / You only spoke these words, / in your final hour: / "Unity and firmness, friends; / to achieve all that remains!" // Durruti, brother Durruti, / never was there seen a grief / more bitter than your death / on the Spanish soil.)125

The heroism celebrated here is substantially different from that exalted by such nationalist poets as Pemán. Durruti is regarded as a "brother"; the virtues he personifies are recommended for all people. In anarchist poetry, as Salaün has observed, the "solitary and romantic hero does not exist. The life of every person crystallises the destiny of the community."126 The anarchist hero is never a psychologically complex character, but is endowed with the basic virtues of the community from which he came. This inseparability of hero and community is reinforced by making heroes even of old people or of children. There exists no hierarchy of heroism; it is the community as a whole which is awarded hero status.

The inevitable concomitant of the depiction of heroism in the war *romance* is the presentation of the enemy. In anarchist poetry, as in the poetry from other points of the political spectrum, both Left and Right, a manichaean scheme is established. Just as the hero is the embodiment of virtue, so the enemy personifies evil. In demonising the enemy, anarchist poetry, just like the nationalist poetry of Pemán, for example, tends strongly toward mythification, toward attributing superhuman qualities to the enemy. One of the poems by Antonio Agraz, in fact, almost exactly parallels the central scene from Pemán's *El Poema de la Bestia y el Angel*. Agraz's poem dramatises an episode from the siege of Madrid in November 1936, in which five tanks (depicted metaphorically as monsters) menacingly approach republican lines. For Agraz, as for Pemán (in whose case it is less justifiable historically), it is the enemy who has the latest military technology at his disposal:

Rumor de acero que rueda
por el camino adelante,
pone espanto en los arbustos
que miran al Manzanares.
Cinco monstruos se aproximan
arrastrando sus blindajes,
tras el huracán de balas
que de sus troneras sale.
Fusiles que le ametrallan,
con furia, de nada valen.
Contra sus planchas de acero
se estrella cualquier ataque.
La grava de los caminos
a su paso se deshace;